Living on the Streets in Japan

JAPANESE SOCIETY SERIES
General Editor: Yoshio Sugimoto

A Social History of Science and Technology in Contemporary Japan, Volume 4
Shigeru Nakayama and Hitoshi Yoshioka

Scams and Sweeteners: A Sociology of Fraud
Masahiro Ogino

Toyota's Assembly Line: A View from the Factory Floor
Ryoji Ihara

Village Life in Modern Japan: An Environmental Perspective
Akira Furukawa

Social Welfare in Japan: Principles and Applications
Kojun Furukawa

Escape from Work: Freelancing Youth and the Challenge to Corporate Japan
Reiko Kosugi

Japan's Whaling: The Politics of Culture in Historical Perspective
Hiroyuki Watanabe

Gender Gymnastics: Performing and Consuming Japan's Takarazuka Revue
Leonie R. Stickland

Poverty and Social Welfare in Japan
Masami Iwata and Akihiko Nishizawa

The Modern Japanese Family: Its Rise and Fall
Chizuko Ueno

Widows of Japan: An Anthropological Perspective
Deborah McDowell Aoki

In Pursuit of the Seikatsusha:
A Genealogy of the Autonomous Citizen in Japan
Masako Amano

Demographic Change and Inequality in Japan
Sawako Shirahase

The Origins of Japanese Credentialism
Ikuo Amano

Pop Culture and the Everyday in Japan: Sociological Perspectives
Katsuya Minamida and Izumi Tsuji

Japanese Perceptions of Foreigners
Shunsuke Tanabe

Migrant Workers in Contemporary Japan:
An Institutional Perspective on Transnational Employment
Kiyoto Tanno

The Boundaries of 'the Japanese', Volume 1:
Okinawa 1868–1972 – Inclusion and Exclusion
Eiji Oguma

International Migrants in Japan: Contributions in an Era of Population Decline
Yoshitaka Ishikawa

Globalizing Japan: Striving to Engage the World
Ross Mouer

Beyond Fukushima: Toward a Post-Nuclear Society
Koichi Hasegawa

Japan's Ultra Right
Naoto Higuchi

The Boundaries of 'the Japanese', volume 2:
Korea, Taiwan and the Ainu 1868–1945
Eiji Oguma

Creating Subaltern Counterpublics: Korean Women
In Japan and Their Struggles for Night School
Akwi Seo

Aftermath: Fukushima and 3.11 Earthquake
Yutaka Tsujinaka and Hiroaki Inatsugu

Learning English in Japan
Takunori Terasawa

Others in Japanese Agriculture
Kenichi Yasuoka

Social Stratification and Inequality Series

Inequality amid Affluence: Social Stratification in Japan
Junsuke Hara and Kazuo Seiyama

Intentional Social Change: A Rational Choice Theory
Yoshimichi Sato

Constructing Civil Society in Japan: Voices of Environmental Movements
Koichi Hasegawa

Deciphering Stratification and Inequality: Japan and beyond
Yoshimichi Sato

Social Justice in Japan: Concepts, Theories and Paradigms
Ken-ichi Ohbuchi

Gender and Career in Japan
Atsuko Suzuki

Status and Stratification: Cultural Forms in East and Southeast Asia
Mutsuhiko Shima

Globalization, Minorities and Civil Society:
Perspectives from Asian and Western Cities
Koichi Hasegawa and Naoki Yoshihara

Fluidity of Place: Globalization and the Transformation of Urban Space
Naoki Yoshihara

Japan's New Inequality:
Intersection of Employment Reforms and Welfare Arrangements
Yoshimichi Sato and Jun Imai

Minorities and Diversity
Kunihiro Kimura

Inequality, Discrimination and Conflict in Japan:
Ways to Social Justice and Cooperation
Ken-ichi Ohbuchi and Junko Asai

Social Exclusion: Perspectives from France and Japan
Marc Humbert and Yoshimichi Sato

Global Migration and Ethnic Communities:
Studies of Asia and South America
Naoki Yoshihara

Stratification in Cultural Contexts: Cases from East and Southeast Asia
Toshiaki Kimura

Advanced Social Research Series

A Sociology of Happiness
Kenji Kosaka

Frontiers of Social Research: Japan and Beyond
Akira Furukawa

A Quest for Alternative Sociology
Kenji Kosaka and Masahiro Ogino

Modernity and Identity in Asia Series

Globalization, Culture and Inequality in Asia
Timothy S. Scrase, Todd Miles, Joseph Holden and Scott Baum

Looking for Money:
Capitalism and Modernity in an Orang Asli Village
Alberto Gomes

Governance and Democracy in Asia
Takashi Inoguchi and Matthew Carlson

Liberalism: Its Achievements and Failures
Kazuo Seiyama

Health Inequalities in Japan: An Empirical Study of Older People
Katsunori Kondo

Living on the Streets in Japan

Homeless Women Break their Silence

By

Satomi Maruyama

Translated by

Stephen Filler

Trans Pacific Press

Melbourne

First published in Japanese by SEKAISHISOSHA as *Josei Hōmuresu to shite ikiru: hinkon to haijo no shakaigaku.*
© 2013 by MARUYAMA Satomi.
English translation rights arranged with SEKAISHISOSHA, Kyoto, Japan.

This English edition published in 2019 by:

Trans Pacific Press
PO Box 164, Balwyn North
Victoria 3104, Australia
Telephone: +61-(0)3-9859-1112
Fax: +61-(0)3-8611-7989
Email: tpp.mail@gmail.com
Web: http://www.transpacificpress.com

© Trans Pacific Press 2019.

Designed and set by Sarah Tuke, Melbourne, Australia.

Distributors

Australia and New Zealand
James Bennett Pty Ltd
Locked Bag 537
Frenchs Forest NSW 2086
Australia
Telephone: +61-(0)2-8988-5000
Fax: +61-(0)2-8988-5031
Email: info@bennett.com.au
Web: www.bennett.com.au

USA and Canada
Independent Publishers Group (IPG)
814 N. Franklin Street
Chicago, IL 60610
USA
Telephone inquiries: +1-312-337-0747
Order placement: 800-888-4741
  (domestic only)
Fax: +1-312-337-5985
Email: frontdesk@ipgbook.com
Web: http://www.ipgbook.com

Asia and the Pacific (except Japan)
Kinokuniya Company Ltd.
Head office:
3-7-10 Shimomeguro
Meguro-ku
Tokyo 153-8504
Japan
Telephone: +81-(0)3-6910-0531
Fax: +81-(0)3-6420-1362
Email: bkimp@kinokuniya.co.jp
Web: www.kinokuniya.co.jp
Asia-Pacific office:
Kinokuniya Book Stores of Singapore Pte., Ltd.
391B Orchard Road #13-06/07/08
Ngee Ann City Tower B
Singapore 238874
Telephone: +65-6276-5558
Fax: +65-6276-5570
Email: SSO@kinokuniya.co.jp

ISSN   1443–9670 (Japanese Society Series)

ISBN   978-1-920901-74-5

Contents

Figures

Tables

Photos

Foreword to the English-Language Edition

This book is an English version of a book first published in 2013 in Japanese.[1] I am delighted to see it become available to a wider audience, and hope that it will make a significant contribution to the international discourse on homelessness. It is an expanded and revised version of a doctoral dissertation submitted to Kyoto University in 2010 based on research carried out between 2002 and 2008. As of 2018, there have been many changes in the conditions faced by homeless women in Japan and many new developments in the research about them. I would like to take this opportunity to discuss the changes that have taken place since the original publication in 2013, and to reconsider its meaning and purpose in that context.

Since the late 2000s, there has been wide recognition of poverty as a serious social problem in Japan, and poverty is the subject of daily reports in the media. And yet there has been little or no improvement in the situation since my book was published. The number of public assistance recipients, having reached record levels in the period since World War II, has remained high. The poverty rate rose to over 16% in the late 2000s and has hardly budged since then (Abe 2015).

On the other hand, the situation regarding homeless people who sleep in the rough has changed dramatically. The number of homeless people began to grow in the early 1990s after the collapse of the bubble economy and reached a peak in about 1999. The first *National Survey on the Conditions of the Homeless*, in 2003, counted 25,296 rough sleepers. Since then, the number has dropped steadily each year, with the result that in the latest available national survey, in 2017 it had dropped to 5,534 – one-fifth of the peak number (Ministry of Health, Labour and Welfare [MHLW] 2017a). This clearly indicates the relative success of homeless policies and the greater ease with which homeless people can now obtain public assistance. The profile of the typical homeless person has also changed. The average age of homeless people has risen steadily to the point that 59.6% are sixty years old and above; and the proportion who live on the streets long-term has also grown, with 34.6% doing so for ten years or more. This is probably because those who wish to avoid homelessness are utilizing support programs just before or soon after moving onto the streets. Moreover, the mode of homelessness that was most common at the time of the study for this book – living in parks and riverbeds in semi-permanent shelters such as tents and huts – has grown less and less common, applying to only 34.3% of homeless people in the most recent survey (MHLW 2017b). This shows the growth in efforts to discourage individuals from setting up tents in public spaces. Consequently, the creation by homeless people of a certain form of community while living in a park, as depicted in this book, has become uncommon today; there are now more programs and choices available to help those who wish to stop sleeping rough. This situation has led, however, to a greater tendency to explain the problem of those who continue to sleep rough for long periods as being the result of their personal choice or desire. In this sense, the concerns that originally motivated this study seem even more relevant today. Solutions to the problem of homelessness, which at first, it seemed, might be found fairly quickly, turned out to be elusive. The Self-Help Act for Homeless People, passed in 2002 as a temporary, ten-year law, was extended for another five years in 2012 and for another ten years in 2017. Homelessness is expected to persist as a problem for the foreseeable future.

Since the publication of this book, there has been a considerable growth in research on homelessness that is particularly concerned with the situation for women. The Women's Homelessness in Europe Network (WHEN), a network of researchers studying homeless women in Europe, was formed in 2012. Important publications since then include a 2015 comparative study of women rough sleepers in four European countries (Moss and Singh 2015) and a 2016 collection of comparative studies involving twelve European countries published by WHEN (Mayock & Bretherton eds, 2016). These studies show women to make up a minority of the homeless population, putting their share at between 14% and 41%, depending on the country (Mayock & Bretherton eds., 2016: 51-54). They also indicate that homeless women tend to use programs intended for victims of domestic violence and single mothers more than programs for homeless people as such, and therefore, if only facilities for homeless people are considered when calculating the homeless population, the number of men is magnified and the number of women diminished. In other words, homeless women, by being categorized as single mothers or domestic violence victims, have been excluded from consideration of the problem of homelessness, and this has been the historical tendency in many countries. As this shows, what we categorize under "homelessness" is very much a function of culture, even though homelessness also has properties that are common regardless of cultural or historical background.

Having summarized these recent developments, I would like next to discuss the features of homelessness in Japan that distinguish Japan from other developed countries. (This study considers Japan mainly in comparison with the societies of western Europe and North America.) The term "homeless," in Japan, is generally understood to refer strictly to rough sleepers – those who live in the streets. By contrast, in many other countries, people staying short-term in facilities are also counted as homeless, and this is the practice I advocate in this book. Women are calculated to make up 3% of the homeless population of Japan, a considerably smaller share than that in most other developed countries. But this is because in Japan, many women who become homeless – in the wider sense – are often not counted as such because they are staying in such places as the homes of friends rather than on the streets. Thus, defining homelessness narrowly as the condition of living on the streets leads to an underestimation of the proportion of women among the homeless. By the same token, in most developed countries a large portion of homeless women are single mothers, but in Japan it is almost unheard of for mothers to live on the streets with their children; there are essentially no homeless single mothers. In addition, in comparison with Europe and North America, Japanese society has only a small number of visible ethnic minorities and immigrants. Therefore, certain problems commonly observed in other developed countries, where such persons make up a large share of the homeless population, are almost non-existent in Japan. Homeless people with a history of drug addictions and homeless military veterans, who are the subject of much concern elsewhere, are largely absent in Japan. It should also be noted that research on homelessness in Japan has a close relationship to radical homeless movements. Although the situation has recently become more diverse, traditionally, support for the homeless in Japan has belonged not so much to the realm of charity as to the radical social movements that sprang up all over the world in the late 1960s. As a result, research on homelessness, which is necessarily impacted by homelessness support activities, tends to go beyond a "social-work" agenda of re-integrating homeless people into society. It shows a strong inclination to ask what is wrong with the society itself that has produced homeless people.

Related to this questioning of society is the issue of the subjectivity of homeless people, one of the main themes of this book. I would like to make some clarifying remarks here. This study owes a great deal to the discourse based on Judith Butler's arguments concerning the subject and subjectivity (Butler 1992). Butler understands the subject to be something that comes into being as the result of being invoked by the law. For Butler, the discursive practice of law, a category that includes not only juridical law but other rules and norms, has the power to compel people to make the "choice" to follow or refuse to follow it. No subject exists prior to law; rather, the subject comes into being in response to being invoked by the law. In developing her argument, Butler replaces the concept of *subject* with that of *agency*. Agency is a medium for discursive practice that is formed by, and uses, language. Neither completely active nor completely passive, agency is both determined by structure and, at the same time, capable of actively creating and transforming structure. Butler's argument is not meant to deny that a subject exists. Rather, she means to bring attention to the fact that subjects are constructed so as to appear to be pre-existing, "natural" entities, and that this construction is a precondition for their existence.

Butler's arguments are highly pertinent to a major concern of my study. By no means do I deny the subjectivity of homeless people, but I also believe that it is necessary to ask what has been left out of the picture as a result of treating subjects, incorrectly, as pre-existing entities. Historically, research on homelessness in Japan has been done in resistance to stereotypical views of homeless people as lazy or as social deviants. Researchers have thus emphasized the ways in which homeless people confirm to the dominating values of society by working to support themselves. Homeless people have also – whether intentionally or unconsciously – been portrayed as resisting those social norms, and aspects of the social order, that exclude them. This romantic view of the homeless, linked to the radical homelessness movement, sees them as a force that challenges the values of the society in which we live. It seemed to me, however, that such a view presupposed the existence of an autonomous subject, and picked out those aspects of the lives of homeless people that appeared to involve "subjectivity." Such a view, I would argue, actually served to push homeless women outside the domain of research. This is the claim I make in this book. The lives of the homeless women I portray in this book were a process, a series of responses to various circumstances under a variety of constraints and specific situations. Some of these actions and responses showed what might be thought of as subjectivity and some did not; some brought about apparently rational results, while some brought results that seemed anything but rational. By thinking of human practices in terms of *agency*, we become able to account for the full range of activities and processes involved. As for the subjectivity of homeless people, this will emerge as one aspect of the larger process of agency.

In English, too, the agency of homeless people has been the focus of a few recent studies. These studies have been concerned with the same problem described above: previous studies of homelessness, in their determination to oppose the portrayal of homelessness as a deviant activity, have focused their concern on the social structure that produces homelessness. As a result, they fell into the trap of treating homeless people as passive agents. Thus, newer studies have focused on behaviors that, because they were thought of as deviant, had previously been overlooked by the research. These include research on individuals who use drugs, leave the facility where they are staying, and become homeless (MacNaughton 2009), and research focusing on how individuals who have "chosen" to sleep rough view their own situation (Persell & Persell 2012). All of these studies represent attempts to portray the agency of homeless people, and this book can be said to belong to the same school of thought.

Since the publication of the Japanese version of this book in 2013, it has reached a wider readership than I could have imagined. In the academic world, it was awarded the Yamakawa Kikue Prize, the most prestigious academic award in women's studies in Japan. It was also honored with Academic Awards from the Japan Welfare Sociology Association and the Japan Association for Urban Sociology. This recognition no doubt stemmed from the book's focus on homeless women, a group that had been previously over looked due to its very low numbers. I would like to express once again how grateful I am for being able to meet all the women who told me their stories.

I would particularly like to thank the following individuals who helped make possible the publication of this book in English. My deepest gratitude goes out to: Stephen Filler, for putting the text into such beautiful English; Karl Smith, for carefully proofreading the manuscript and giving feedback based on his own field of expertise; Yoshio Sugimoto of Trans Pacific Press for agreeing to take on this project despite the difficulties caused by my lack of experience; and Okano Yayo for her many valuable comments. I am particularly thankful to the Japan Society for the Promotion of Science for providing financial support for the translation and publication of this book.

All Japanese names are given in Japanese order, family name before personal name, with the exception of writers who publish primarily in English, and the name of the author, Satomi Maruyama, on the title page of this book and in connection with its publication.

Maruyama Satomi
June 2018

Foreword to the Original Edition

"I was waiting for you to finally tell me what you wanted to talk about!"

She spoke to me in a reproving tone, crouched among the throngs of people bustling around the train station late at night. At last I had told her that I was writing my master's thesis on homeless women and wanted to interview her. "I came this far with you because I thought you wanted to ask me something. If that's what you wanted, wouldn't the normal thing be to tell me from the beginning? You aren't ready to become a professor if you act like that! If you're gathering information why aren't you taking notes?" I could only apologize for my diffidence and lack of resolve.

She was a woman in her sixties who had been a rough sleeper for two years and now lived in an apartment on public assistance. I had first met her two days before at the tent of a woman rough sleeper whom I was visiting. Here, at the park where she used to live, she was chatting with this woman, who was her friend, while mending some clothing. When, a little while later, a student with a camera came to visit the friend – they seemed to know each other – she intervened. "No reporting!" she said bluntly. Having been unable to bring myself to say that I was doing a study, I was flustered, and had to content myself with casual conversation. In the course of this came her invitation: "Come see me if you have the chance." She handed me her home address. This only deepened my feeling of guilt at not telling them about my study.

After that, the two of us decided to go out to pick wild onions, a topic that had come up in our conversation. The park was rich in nature despite its location in a major city, and edible plants could be found growing freely. To me, it was a glimpse of an unexpectedly luxurious aspect of life in the park. The fun of gathering wild herbs helped me forget for the moment the oppressive sense of anxiety I was feeling over my lack of progress with my study. The next day, this woman – who said that she used to cook professionally – cooked up the wild onions that we had picked and served them at a meeting of women rough sleepers being held at the park. The day after that, I paid her a visit at the address she had given me, and on the way home, finally brought up the subject of my study.

It had been a year or so since I first conceived of the desire to listen to the stories of homeless women. However, with the great majority of rough sleepers being men, it was quite difficult to meet the women, who made up only 3% of the total. For the past three years I had volunteered at a soup kitchen at Kamagasaki[1] in Osaka, and while I occasionally met female rough sleepers, I could not imagine what their lives were like. To learn more, I began volunteering for support activities where I might meet women who slept rough, such as evening patrols to check on their wellbeing. In the process, I met a number of such women, but seeing their caution in interacting with strangers, probably for good reasons, I could not bring myself to ask them to talk to me. I could not dispel my feelings of guilt: although it was partly the desire to help women in trouble that motivated me to volunteer, as long as I also had a research agenda, I was really just using them as tools for my study. And, so, while getting to know a number of women who had been rough sleepers in the past, and exchanging contact information with them, I still couldn't summon up the courage to ask them to let me interview them for my research. All the light conversation we had did not help me understand the critical questions. I was making no progress in understanding how women rough sleepers live.

Reading surveys and studies on homeless people did not help me to understand the situation of homeless women. Making no mention of such women, they had almost nothing to say about the questions that interested me at the time. How do women become homeless? How do they live in an overwhelmingly male environment? What are their gender identities? Above and beyond that, the framework of the surveys done at the time did not seem appropriate for giving women a voice. Survey forms used for large-scale studies of rough sleepers were not designed to capture the experiences of women, while research on homelessness and the language of advocacy movements seemed to presuppose men as their subjects. To counter the popular view of homeless people as lazy, researchers and activists had emphasized the fact that homeless people do work, but this was based on a monolithic image of the homeless person as a working male. Left out were other people who did not work or who were female. It appeared that the existing research offered no framework for understanding and situating the phenomenon of homeless women.

It seems to me that at that point I had completely lost confidence in my project. Too much time was passing without successful interviews. At the time, I was working at a welfare facility while continuing my research, and staying at a simple workers' hostel known as a *doya* in the San'ya district in Tokyo, which has a large population of day laborers. However, I did not want to tell potential informants where I was working, as many rough sleepers detest such facilities. I also anticipated that rough sleepers would be suspicious of someone staying in a *doya*, so when I met them in the park I would tell them that I was staying with my sister who lived nearby.

Finally, facing this woman crouched in the middle of the crowd milling about the station, I realized that I could not go on being dishonest. I confessed to her every lie I had told. Despite my concern about missing the last train back to the *doya* where I stayed during my field work, I repeated my request. "Please let me interview you. I promise to write a good thesis." "No, you've got it wrong. Don't say you'll write a good thesis. When you ask for help, you should say you don't know whether you can write something good, but you'll give it everything you've got. That's the right way to ask people for help." My eyes teared up. She continued: "You can stay with me starting tomorrow. Tonight, go back and get a good night's sleep. Tomorrow, bring all your things to my place. You don't need to bring me anything. Just a gas canister. My gas has been shut off and I don't have any money. Honestly, I would rather not have you see me like this." From that day on, I would spend much time together with her.

However, no matter how many times we talked, I could never figure out how she ended up homeless. She would repeat the same stories of her memories, and speak of what rough sleeping was like and how hard it was. Over time I got a clear sense of her life history. But no matter how many times I asked, I could not get a satisfactory answer as to why she ultimately ended up on the streets. Perhaps that part of her past, in particular, was something she wanted to keep secret. "My money was stolen. I had about a million yen at the time, and ended up penniless. And so I ended up living like that. They asked me what time it was, by the station. I heard them ask the time, and my mind went blank, as if something was pressing down on me. There was a young man, and a woman wearing glasses."

It was the same with many others: the most important facts seemed elusive. Since getting to know her, over time, I was able to hear the stories of other homeless women; but no matter how much I asked, something was always missing. One woman spoke in contradictions: right after declaring that she wished to stop sleeping rough, she would say that she preferred to remain homeless. Another, speaking of her experience exchanging sex for money with a male passerby who had approached her while she was sleeping in the rough, said "I just thought I'd have some fun with him," as if it were a pleasant memory. Apart from this, she would relate anecdote after anecdote with no rhyme or reason, including memories of sexual abuse in her childhood and relationships with men that had often gone awry. But even after I had known her for years and heard her stories multiple times, these scattered stories remained fragmentary, contradictory, and inconsistent. It was impossible to find a connecting thread that would link these stories all together as manifestations of the life course of an individual woman. The feeling that I had at the beginning my investigation, that I was far from understanding their situation, remained unchanged even after I had begun to talk with them about their lives. It appeared to be impossible to construct an easy-to-understand story of how women became rough sleepers, or to identify the common qualities of homeless women as a group, or to determine whether they were victims of social structures or self-directed subjects.

Over time, I began to think that the problem was in my determination to understand things in these terms. It gradually dawned on me, that these women's lives could not be fit into a research framework that would be logical and comprehensible from my point of view. What needed to be interrogated was the limited conception of human beings that could only see them in such terms. Indeed, this limited conception was arguably the reason that lives of homeless women had been ignored in prior research. After all, this way of living would seem to be very difficult to understand logically. If so, it was imperative to look at what had been excluded and consider different ways to understand human nature. Otherwise, my original ambition for this research would only lead to further exclusion of persons, just as prior research had excluded those who did not fit its preconceptions. This, it seemed to me, was the ultimate question that this book on homeless women needed to address.

This book, then, is about homeless women in Japan, who until now have been hardly studied at all. My first aim has been to understand and depict their mode of existence and the world in which they live. The book will focus on women rough sleepers as well as those who are homeless in a wider sense, in order to describe the mechanisms by which women become homeless and depict their unique experience. This will help serve my second aim: to make a new appraisal of homeless studies as a whole, which has assumed men as their subject, by bringing a gender perspective to the analytic framework. In this way I hope to upgrade and expand the framework of homeless studies so that it can account for women as well as men. Finally, the third aim of the book is, through a close look at the daily practices of homeless women, to consider the possibility of new and different ways of understanding human subjectivity, which hitherto has been generally assumed to be male.

1 Toward an ethnography of homeless women

Theories of Homelessness Today

These days, rough sleepers – people who live and sleep on the streets – have become a ubiquitous presence in major cities. The sight of people sleeping in cardboard boxes by the roadside or in train stations, and of blue tarp tents in parks and riverbeds, is common throughout Japan, including in smaller, regional cities. Much of the initial attention paid to rough sleepers, who first appeared in large numbers with the 1991 collapse of the bubble economy, was no doubt due to their significance as a symbol of poverty in an affluent society. Despite the attention they attracted, the number of rough sleepers grew steadily throughout the recession of the 1990s, eventually swelling to over 30,000 people.

In response to this situation, the Japanese government made a serious commitment to effectively address the needs of rough sleepers. Activities by service providers grew substantially, and support organizations cranked up their activities. As a result, the number of rough sleepers began to drop. However, the global economic downturn precipitated by the Lehman Brothers bankruptcy of 2008 caused these numbers to rise once again. More recently, the media have begun to report on people who are just a step away from rough sleeping, such as non-regular workers evicted from their dormitory after losing their jobs, and young people who spend the night in Internet cafés. Such reports make the poverty accompanied by the loss of a place to live feel more familiar and ordinary.

The subject of this book is homelessness – the condition of poverty accompanied by the loss of a home. In Japan, the word "homeless" is usually used to refer to persons sleeping rough on the streets. The 2002 Self-Help Act for Homeless People (hereafter referred to as the Self-Help Act) defines homeless persons as rough sleepers, namely, "persons living permanently and without good reason in locations

or facilities such as city parks, riverbeds, roadsides, and stations."
However, the condition of homelessness – of not having a home – can
be manifested in many ways other than rough sleeping. "Internet
refugees" staying in Internet cafés, non-regular workers evicted
from dormitories, and women taking refuge in domestic-violence
shelters are all homeless in the sense of lacking a fixed place to live.
This book will consider not only the condition of rough sleeping,
but a wide variety of forms of poverty accompanied by the loss of
a place to live, such as those just described. I will distinguish the
two by using "homelessness" to describe the general condition of
poverty accompanied by the loss of a home, and "rough sleeping"
when referring specifically to persons living on the streets.

Research on homelessness has been carried out in a wide variety
of fields, ranging from sociology, to social welfare studies, law,
architecture, and medicine. However, as suggested by the common
tendency to limit the definition of homelessness to the condition
of rough sleeping, little research has yet been done that covers the
entire spectrum of poverty accompanied by the lack of a residence,
or "homelessness" as it is considered in this book. Iwata Masami
(1995) conducted groundbreaking research with her historical
analysis of government policies to combat poverty accompanied
by the lack of a residence. Iwata's historical examination of social
welfare policy demonstrated how the homeless, including rough
sleepers, were left out of general anti-poverty measures – which
should have addressed the needs of all citizens equally – adopted
after World War II. As a result, homeless people came to constitute
a special class of the poor. Recently, as awareness has grown
that homelessness can take forms other than rough sleeping,
investigative research using a broad definition of homelessness
has gradually emerged, such as the 2004 *White Paper* of the
Japan Housing Council, and large-scale studies that extend to the
lives of former street dwellers who successfully transitioned to
living in permanent housing (Rainbow Coalition 2007; National
Homeless Support Network 2011). Other studies dealing with one
form of homelessness in the wider sense – namely, young people
spending the night in Internet cafés – can be considered as efforts
to reveal the hidden extent of homelessness (Ministry of Health,
Labour and Welfare, Employment Security Bureau, 2007; Osaka
City, Graduate School for Creative Cities, Kamagasaki Homeless
Support Organization 2008).

Far more work has been conducted focusing solely on rough sleepers, partly because people living on the streets are more highly visible. In particular, sociological studies on *yoseba*, districts inhabited by large numbers of day laborers, have long included discussions of rough sleepers. *Yoseba* are sites where day laborers gather to seek jobs. Well-known *yoseba* include Kamagasaki in Osaka, San'ya in Tokyo, Kotobuki in Yokohama, and Sasajima in Nagoya. Around the larger *yoseba* are numerous *doya*, simple workers' hostels. Day laborers will often stay in these facilities after the day's work is done. However, during periods when there is less work available, many day laborers are unable to pay the bed fee, and are forced into rough sleeping. It is said that for this reason rough sleepers could be found at the *yoseba* even during the 1980s when the bubble economy was at its peak.

Aoki Hideo's *The Lives and Deaths of Yoseba Workers* (1989), which focused on *yoseba* of that period, was a groundbreaking study that helped pave the way for later research. Aoki criticizes previous studies of *yoseba* in fields like social pathology and labor economics. In their zeal to comprehend the problem of *yoseba* with the aim of solving it, Aoki argues, such studies treat workers as persons in need of "improvement," and emphasize the inferiority of their status (Aoki 1989). Aoki argues that in addition to comprehending and analyzing the problems of the *yoseba*, it is also necessary to recognize the agency of the workers themselves, and their personal efforts to change their situation. Aoki's approach is a radical departure from previous research that had attempted to objectively assess social problems and prescribe solutions. He opposes the view that *yoseba* are a form of social pathology, on the grounds that this assumption is itself an implicit endorsement, and reproduction, of discriminatory attitudes. He argues instead for paying attention to the intentions of those living in the margins of society, and engaging with the ways in which the marginalized resist society at large. Although Aoki's major research interest at the time was day laborers in *yoseba*, his research also covered rough sleeping as a condition suffered by day laborers who had grown old or become sick.

With the 1991 collapse of the bubble economy, however, the number of day-laborer jobs plummeted. Rough sleeping ceased to be a temporary condition or a final stage for *yoseba* laborers. Rather, it increasingly became the regular condition even for workers still in prime working condition. Subsequently, as economic conditions grew increasingly dire, even former regular workers began to be seen sleeping rough, and rough sleepers became more visible across the urban landscape, no longer limited to *yoseba* areas. Under these conditions, local governing bodies with large numbers of rough sleepers, such as Osaka and Tokyo prefectures, began around the mid-1990s to create their own policies and conduct studies on rough sleepers (Urban Life Institute 2000; Osaka City University Institute on Urban Environmental Problems 2001 and others).

In 2002, the Self-Help Act was passed as the first nation-wide measure to address the problem of rough sleeping. The Self-Help Act, a temporary law with a term of ten years, mandated, among other things, the creation of employment opportunities, job training, and lodging.[1] At around this time, the construction commenced on residential facilities for rough sleepers in larger cities, including "Self-Help Centers" where rough sleepers capable of working could stay for several months while looking for work. However, with fewer jobs available, many who received assistance with their job search were unable to find work within the allotted time-frame, while others found only unstable jobs; thus, some ended up going back to rough sleeping. Support measures continue to be limited by, for example, restrictions on the repeated use of support centers. Additionally, the Self-Help Act states explicitly that when the presence of rough sleepers impedes the intended use of facilities such as parks, "necessary measures" are to be taken. There have been fears that this may be used as grounds for forcible evictions. In particular, the law divides rough sleepers into three categories: "those who desire employment but are unemployed due to a lack of jobs," "those who require services such as medical care and welfare," and "those who are avoiding normal life in society." Some have noted the danger that, by categorizing those who fail to follow the prescribed path to "self-sufficiency" as "avoiding normal life in society," the law could be used to justify evictions. Despite these problems, activity by non-government service organizations has increased dramatically since the enactment of the law, and opportunities for rough sleepers to receive public assistance have grown. As a result, it has become easier for rough sleepers who wish to escape their situation to do so.

In 2003 the Ministry of Health, Labour and Welfare (MHLW) conducted the first national field survey of rough sleepers (*National Survey on the Conditions of the Homeless*, MHLW 2003). The survey found there to be 25,296 rough sleepers throughout the country, and made it possible for the first time to appraise, on a national level, the number and living condition of rough sleepers; it significantly influenced subsequent support policies. Although the number of rough sleepers remained steady for some time after, it finally began to decline as policies began to show concrete results around 2005. The second MHLW survey, conducted in 2007, found that the number of rough sleepers had decreased by about 30% since the first survey, to 18,564 (MHLW 2007a); and by 2012, when the third survey was conducted, the decrease since the 2003 survey was about 60%. This survey also revealed that the average age of rough sleepers was 59.3 and that over 40% of them had had regular jobs before falling into rough sleeping (MHLW 2012).

The presence of women in homeless theory

The discourse on homelessness described above, however, generally takes it for granted that homeless individuals are male. And indeed, according to the estimates given in the 2012 MHLW survey, only 307 females were found among the 9,576 rough sleepers whose presence was physically confirmed – a mere 3.2% (MHLW 2012).[2] This overwhelming gender disparity clearly indicates that the mechanisms leading to poverty differ for men and women and cannot be considered separately from the gender structure of society. Yet the existing research on homelessness takes very little account of gender. The problem here is rather circular: since the research largely overlooks the presence of women sleeping rough, there is no perceived need to discuss gender differences.

For example, large-scale studies by local governing bodies and the MHLW all include questions about changes in an individual's work history to ascertain the changes in social status that preceded rough sleeping. The nature of the first job taken after finishing school; the longest job held; and the last job held before becoming a rough sleeper are supposed to reveal the process of downward social mobility. However, these questions assume working men as the norm, and are inadequate to understanding the experience of women, for whom social mobility is greatly influenced by factors such as the presence of a partner or spouse, and his employment status. In addition, the data in these studies are not broken down by gender, so only a few specific facts about women are known, such as their number or the presence or absence of a partner. In the analysis of the second MHLW survey, gender-specific figures are given for the first time in certain categories only (*Deliberative Committee on the National Survey on the Conditions of the Homeless* 2007). However, information on female rough sleepers is limited to average age, age distribution, and whether an individual stayed anywhere under a roof after commencing rough sleeping.

The estimated figures from the 2012 MHLW study (MHLW 2012) also show regional disparities in the proportion of rough sleepers who are women. The figures show that in major urban regions with high numbers of rough sleepers, the proportion of female rough sleepers is low: 1.9% in Osaka prefecture, 2.9% in Tokyo prefecture, and 2.9% in Kanagawa prefecture. In contrast, the proportion of women in less urban regions tends to be high: 32.0% in Gifu prefecture, 28.6% in Nagano prefecture, and 25.0% in Tokushima prefecture (Table 1.1). Although the number of rough sleepers is itself low in the regional areas, which makes the accuracy of these figures for women uncertain, one likely reason for the low proportion of women in major urban areas like Tokyo and Osaka is the presence of *yoseba*, which for a long time have attracted large numbers of men from around the region, searching for work as day laborers.

Regardless of the nuances in the data produced by these large-scale quantitative surveys, they do not capture the voices of homeless women, who most likely live in harsher conditions than the vast majority of homeless, who are men. The process by which women become homeless seems to differ from that for men, and it appears to involve mechanisms that make it harder for women to fall into rough sleeping. These studies, however, give no clue to the nature of that mechanism. By assuming their subjects to be male, such studies have no gender perspective, rendering it almost impossible to develop a genuine understanding of female homelessness.

Hence, an understanding of homeless women will not be found in studies of the homeless in general. We must instead look to the few studies that focus specifically on women. In Japan, Kawahara Keiko, taking a social welfare studies perspective, has investigated how welfare policies have responded to women who are homeless in the broad sense (Kawahara 2005; 2008; 2011 and others). Moon Jeong Sil has examined the process by which women become rough sleepers and the social position that they occupy (Moon 2003; 2006). Mugikura Tetsu has written a clear and detailed account of the challenges involved for a female rough sleeper whom he helped and supported over an extended period of time to transition into sustainable home living. Apart from academic studies, Miyashita Tadako has written a very worthwhile nonfiction account of her interactions with female rough sleepers during a long period working as a social worker at a social service agency in Tokyo's San'ya district (Miyashita 2008). Ichimura Misako, an artist who has lived for many years in Yoyogi Park, has written an insider account of life for a female rough sleeper and how she developed a community of friends. She uses these experiences to raise important questions about the meaning of work and beliefs about the nature of women (Ichimura 2006; 2008a; 2008b; 2009 and others). Although works such as these have begun to appear in Japan,[3] neither the quality nor the quantity is adequate for a broad understanding of the living conditions of homeless women or the mechanisms by which they are produced.

In the developed countries of North America and Europe, too, partly because the majority of the homeless are male, most research concentrates on men. However, as will be discussed later, because a wider concept of homelessness is used than in Japan, a larger proportion of people fall under the category, and with a history of research on homelessness going back to the 1960s, much more research has been carried out on women than in Japan. Most of this research has been directed at women staying in shelters, though (Russell 1991; Waterston 1999; Bridgeman 2003; Williams 2003 and others). There are several reasons for this focus: the definition of homelessness in the West typically includes residents of shelters; women have a greater tendency to use shelters than men; and the presence of significant numbers of women in shelters makes research easier. Elliot Liebow's ethnographic portrait of the daily life of women in homeless shelters, which has been translated into Japanese (Liebow 1993 [1999]), is one example. The scarcity of female rough sleepers has meant an almost total absence of studies on them; however, there has been some research into their use of space, mainly by geographers (Rowe and Wolch 1990; May, Cloke and Johnsen 2007; Huey and Berndt 2008).

Other studies have produced interesting findings that are relevant to this book. For instance, research on the differences between male and female homelessness[4] has found that compared with men, more women typically are or have been married, and a higher proportion suffer from mental illness (Burt and Cohen 1989). Other studies have

Table 1.1: Share of women rough sleepers by prefecture

	Male	Female	Unidentified	Total	Female (%)
Hokkaidō	52	9	10	71	12.7
Aomori	3	0	0	3	0.0
Iwate	4	1	0	5	20.0
Miyazaki	82	9	1	92	9.8
Akita	11	0	0	11	0.0
Yamagata	4	0	0	4	0.0
Fukushima	17	1	1	19	5.3
Ibaraki	31	4	9	44	9.1
Tochigi	47	0	1	48	0.0
Gunma	58	2	2	62	3.2
Saitama	374	11	42	427	2.6
Chiba	325	17	13	355	4.8
Tokyo	2,299	69	0	2,368	2.9
Kanagawa	1,431	44	34	1,509	2.9
Niigata	5	1	0	6	16.7
Toyama	14	0	0	14	0.0
Ishikawa	11	0	0	11	0.0
Fukui	1	0	0	1	0.0
Yamanashi	18	0	4	22	0.0
Nagano	5	2	0	7	28.6
Gifu	16	8	1	25	32.0
Shizuoka	149	9	24	182	4.9
Aichi	401	17	100	518	3.3
Mie	35	2	2	39	5.1
Shiga	9	0	2	11	0.0
Kyoto	134	8	34	176	4.5
Osaka	2,366	47	4	2,417	1.9
Hyōgo	245	9	19	273	3.3
Nara	3	0	0	3	0.0
Wakayama	20	1	0	21	4.8
Tottori	3	0	0	3	0.0
Shimane	0	0	0	0	0.0
Okayama	21	0	3	24	0.0
Hiroshima	81	9	0	90	10.0
Yamaguchi	6	0	0	6	0.0
Tokushima	3	1	0	4	25.0
Kagawa	16	0	0	16	0.0
Ehime	22	0	2	24	0.0
Kōchi	4	0	1	5	0.0
Fukuoka	395	16	12	423	3.8

Table 1.1: continued

	Male	Female	Unidentified	Total	Female (%)
Saga	10	0	1	11	0.0
Nagasaki	7	0	0	7	0.0
Kumamoto	44	3	2	49	6.1
Ōita	18	1	1	20	5.0
Miyazaki	6	0	0	6	0.0
Kagoshima	39	2	0	41	4.9
Okinawa	88	1	14	103	1.0
Total	8,933	304	339	9,576	3.2

Source: Ministry of Health, Labour, and Welfare (2012)

shown that images of the ideal family and woman in the housing market and welfare policies greatly influence the mechanisms by which women are excluded and fall into homelessness (Watson and Austerberry 1986; Watson 1999; Edgar and Doherty 2001). The trends identified in these and other studies likely apply to Japan as well. The U.S. anthropologist Joan Passaro, seeking to explain the reason why few homeless women live in the streets, conducted interviews and analyzed policies, and drew comparisons between homeless men and homeless women as well as between those women living on the streets and those living in shelters. This book owes much to Passaro's understanding of the issues.

However, except for the very few studies like Passaro's, which examine why there were so few female rough sleepers, research on homeless women generally lacks the important perspective provided by feminism. As the feminist scholar Joan Scott has said, "The study of women would not only add new subject matter but would also force a critical reexamination of the premises and standards of existing scholarly work" (Scott 1999: 29). Conducting research on homeless women does not mean making the same sort of findings concerning women that have previously been made concerning homeless men. Because the methodology and analysis of the research to date has been based on the unstated assumption that the research subjects are male, they cannot be directly applied to women, who, unlike many men, are often not wage laborers and utilize the social security system differently. The definition of homelessness, too, must be modified. While the concept in Japan has conventionally been limited to rough sleepers, women tend to be "hidden" homeless, as revealed in Western studies. Taking women fully into account requires adopting a broader definition. This broader understanding of homeless women requires not only making women the subject of the research, but also critically reappraising the entire body of extant research. There is a particular need for a fundamental reappraisal in the case of Japan; in the West, the existence of homeless women was at least somewhat recognized early on, which created an environment conducive to research focusing exclusively on women. This was not the case in Japan.

In reassessing what the study of homeless women might add to the overall field of homeless studies, we must look beyond procedural matters like reconsidering the definition of homelessness or the questions to be investigated in large-scale surveys. Above and beyond such matters, we must consider epistemological issues in the prior research. To put it differently, the neglect of women in research up until now cannot be explained merely by the small number of homeless women. There seems to be a more basic, deep structural problem in the conceptual foundation on which the research has been based. Namely, the positions and assumptions taken in research that treats homeless persons as independent and autonomous agents that engage in "resistance" has been based on the model of homeless males, a model that inevitably excludes women.

Subjects of resistance and the exclusion of women

When the number of rough sleepers first began to spike in Japan, the majority were individuals with a history of working at *yoseba*. Hence, when *yoseba* researchers shifted their focus from day laborers to rough sleepers, they continued to work with Aoki's assumptions, critically re-examining contemporary society from the perspective of marginalized day laborers.

This remained the primary orientation of sociological research on rough sleepers thereafter. For instance, Nakane Mitsutoshi argues that focusing on the "status as subjects" and "individual resistance" of rough sleepers has the potential to transform a social ideology that marginalizes rough sleepers and thus promote social change (Nakane 2001:16–17). Nakane claims that the cardboard box houses decorated with bright pictures that once could be found at Tokyo's Shinjuku Station demonstrate "a lifestyle that, to its participants, is preferable to a life of government-directed segregation and institutionalization" (Nakane 1999:92) To Nakane, then, resistance to society based on the volition of rough sleepers is promising as a force for social change. Other researchers, somewhat differently, seek to understand the subjectivity of individuals who are powerless, yet not entirely defined by the prescriptions of society – even when there is no clear consciousness of resistance. To this end, they study the strategies used by the weak to survive in daily life. Yamaguchi Keiko focuses on "survival strategies" employed by rough sleepers in the face of daily hardship, bringing out their autonomous subjectivity and creativity in redefining the constraints imposed on them. To Yamaguchi, this autonomy and creativity demonstrate the potential of urban resistance to the nation-state (Yamaguchi 1998).

Other researchers argue that habitual modes of living repeated over a period of years can form the grounds for resistance, even if not intended by the individual subjects. Tsumaki Shingo, however, argues that this is not necessarily the case, noting the difficulty in categorizing those who fail to follow the government-prescribed path to self-reliance as "avoiding life in ordinary society." Based on quantitative surveys, Tsumaki found that the opposite was sometimes true. Because the civic value of self-help through work is woven into life practices that have followed an established pattern, the failure of some individuals to leave rough sleeping can come from "life structure-based resistance" that results from the very wish "to live independently without depending on others" (Tsumaki 2003). This is an important finding: rough sleepers are not necessarily "outsiders" who deviate from ordinary civic values.

However, when Tsumaki speaks of the ideal of self-help through work being structurally embedded in a way of life, the pre-rough-sleeping life that he assumes is that of a *yoseba* worker. This image of rough sleepers supporting themselves by work has developed specifically under the assumption that they are male. There is a minority, however, who do not work or who are women. In the face of this, pointing out that some rough sleepers have in fact become self-reliant through work, although intended to counter an exclusionary attitude towards rough sleepers, serves to further exclude those who have been doubly marginalized.

The problem with Tsumaki's approach can also be found in the approach of researchers like Nakane and Yamaguchi, who focus on resistance of rough sleepers. Their approach assumes a subject with a consistent, independent will who acts on the basis of rational choices. However, presupposing an independent subject and trying to identify its will for resistance and social change, fails to recognize that the subject is a relation-bound entity. In some cases, it also leads to an exclusive focus on a single aspect – the rough sleeping – of what is actually a complex process of life practices that are sometimes accidental, involving repeated periods of sleeping rough alternated with living homeless in welfare facilities.

This view of rough sleepers as independent agents who resist society was developed as a critical response to previous research that treated them as passive objects of reform; as such its value must be reaffirmed. However, the real situation is not adequately understood through either of these binarily opposed views: We must seek a perspective that does not reduce rough sleepers to either passive objects determined by social structures, or, independent and autonomous social agents. Such a perspective must be applied not only to homeless studies, but also to research dealing with other categories of women who are contiguous with homeless women in the lower strata of society.

The position of homeless women in feminist studies

As noted above, very little research on homelessness has focused on women. However, when homelessness is defined more broadly to include all who lack a fixed residence, persons staying in welfare facilities can be included in the category. There is a body of research known as women's welfare studies which considers women who utilize such facilities.

Hayashi Chiyo, the leading force in women's welfare studies, describes the field as devoted to understanding discrimination against woman and the multiple ways it threatens them. It seeks "to secure human rights while examining public support policies" (Hayashi 2008: 190). She expresses frustration with a welfare system that divides its clientele horizontally into categories like children, the elderly, and the handicapped, but does not recognize that the problems of women arise from a sexist social structure. Taking prostitution as the starting point for her own research, and centering this research on protection services that have been implemented for women in response to prostitution, Hayashi has argued that a new "women's welfare law" is needed to provide a comprehensive response to women's issues. Since more than a small share of the population of homeless women have some connection to the sex industry, and since homeless women with no place to go, when they use welfare services, often use these Women's Protection Services, we can conclude that the subjects of women's welfare studies include homeless women.

Of the starting point for her own research, prostitution, Hayashi writes:

> Prostitution, by introducing money into sexual exchange, is a denial of the most human of qualities, sex and sexual relationships, which bring together two individuals, including their spiritual elements, and test the humanity of both partners... This creates a situation devoid of humanity... Although prostitution produces exchange value, it cannot be considered work, or a profession. (Hayashi 1990: 9)

Hayashi continues:

> Women are driven into prostitution by a social structure that leaves them with "no job, no money, and no place to live"... I suggest that to accept such individuals' own statements [that they choose to be prostitutes] at face value is too facile, and misses the larger picture. The will of an individual is the consequence of coercion of some sort or other. (Hayashi 1990: 10)

In short, for Hayashi, prostitution is the product of the structures of a sexist society, and is always "the result of some form of coercion." She thus denies that individual will or agency is involved in acts of prostitution. Hayashi's view of prostitution as sexual slavery, the product of social structures that subjugate women, represents a "human rights" approach to the discourse on prostitution.

However, while women's welfare aims to identify sexual discrimination as human rights abuse, there is a problem in its definition of the "women" whom it seeks to liberate. Hayashi writes: "in biological terms...the female sex is the life that experiences pregnancy and gives birth" (Hayashi 2008: 191). However, as feminist studies have revealed, this "biologically female sex [*sei*]" is itself a social construction. In other words, the idea that "male" and "female" are biologically distinct categories, or that normative sexuality is centered on reproductive activity between a man and a woman within a household, are cultural and social products. The appearance of feminist theory taking this perspective has been driven by the flourishing of research by and about sexual minorities, and it is no longer plausible to simplistically treat the "biological female sex" as a monolithic reality. Women's welfare, purportedly founded to redress sex-based discrimination, is thus in danger of undermining its core purpose by treating all women as entities in need of protection and creating new categories of excluded persons.

This problem is most sharply evident in the following account given by Hayashi of women's welfare, her central field of interest, which mentions rough sleepers.

> This spring, my friends invited me to walk among the village of blue tents at the edge of the Sumida River. And something one of my friends had said struck me as saying a lot about my questions about why there are so few women homeless and whether the process of becoming homeless differs for men and for women. "Homeless women cannot live by themselves. They have to live with men." That seemed to say all there is to say. It is surely not that women are dependent or lacking self-sufficiency; rather, as women, they have an instinct for avoiding sexual danger. The women's welfare that I am working for starts with this fact. (Hayashi, Hori 2000: 269)

Hayashi accepts the current hegemonic sexuality and describes women in essentialist terms as having "an instinct for avoiding sexual danger." Consequently, she views the cases of female rough sleepers living with men as saying "all there is to say." She fails to consider, for instance, the 30–40% of female rough sleepers who live alone,[5] or sexual minorities,[6] seemingly not realizing that she is treating them as if they lack an instinct for sexual danger. Women's welfare that takes Hayashi's point of view, focusing on prostitution and reducing it to coercion, treats women as uniformly in need of protection. Reducing everything to coercion based on gender and locking women into a subordinate position, it also leaves men, and women who do not receive welfare protection, out of the picture.

In opposition to such reductionist views of prostitution, sex work theory arose as the product of a movement by sex workers. Proponents of this "civil rights" approach argue that for those lacking any other way to make a living, prostitution is a viable means of survival. Given that the social structures that drive people into prostitution are not likely to change anytime soon, it is misguided to focus simply on liberating individuals from prostitution. Further, some sex workers claim that they freely chose to be sex workers even when other choices were available (Minami et al 2000 etc.). For these individuals, the problem is not prostitution per se, but its criminalization. Because prostitution is a crime, when they experience violence at work, the fear of punishment prevents them from reporting it. Civil-rights advocates therefore consider prostitutes to be workers entitled to a safe workplace, and call for improving working conditions through decriminalization.

Civil-rights advocates also reject the influence and interference of those who think that prostitution is intrinsically wrong, arguing that: "Ultimately, these people are rejecting it based on their personal preferences. If so, they have no right to interfere with people who say that they like prostitution" (Matsuzawa et al 2000: 344). This argument originated in opposition to those who would deny the agency of sex workers. Advocacy for the rights of sex workers has an undeniable urgency and importance: the reality is that prostitution has always existed, and many people continue to engage in it. Hence, rather than trying to stop it, the aim should be to eliminate the violence, failure to pay, and exploitation that are rife within the industry. While there is strong merit in this position, however, overemphasizing the individual "self" in isolation from others can conceal the fact that the "individual will" is difficult to identify, contradictory, and dependent on others. All these issues can be end up being reduced to choices made by free-willed individuals.[7]

The debate between the "human rights" and "civil rights" approaches to prostitution is analogous to the ways that individuals are viewed in homeless studies. On the one hand, the view of homeless persons as socially determined objects fails to account for the individual will of the actors and their potential to change circumstances. On the other hand, the opposing idea of the individual as a wholly autonomous subject excludes certain people and ignores relationships with others. This book examines the lives of homeless women in order to address what has been overlooked – as well as how and why it has been overlooked – in previous homelessness research characterized by these opposing views. My theoretical approach in this book is informed by the work of Judith Butler, who has conducted a profound theoretical investigation of the socially constructed nature of biological sex, and her interrogation of the conventional ideas of human subjectivity.

Gender and subjectivity in post-structuralism

Butler's work is well known for the challenges it poses to the concept of gender. The prevailing concept of gender was based on social conceptions of "masculinity" and "femininity" that reflected a binary opposition of the biological sexes "male" and "female." Post-structural research on gender by Butler and others challenged these concepts, arguing that gender was not defined by biological sex; rather, it is gender that defines sex. In short, they argued that the concept of biological sex, understood as the binary division of a variety of physical differences into the categories "male" and "female," is itself socially constructed. Sex, in this view, is not an actually-existing feature of bodies or persons, but instead a function of discourses that convey meaning to bodies and persons.

Butler applied the post-structural focus on the discursive function to gender studies, using it as the foundation for a theoretical framework for that field. Butler calls into question the very existence of "woman/female" as a concrete, fixed subject. To Butler, gender is a practice of assigning meaning that continually and repeatedly drives rules that are culturally understandable to all people. Subjects have no existence prior to this practice of conferring meaning; to the contrary, they come into being through that conferral. For if the subject existed prior to discursive practice, it would follow that the subject must have chosen to accept or reject the discourse that assigns to it a gender; but gender is not, in fact, chosen.

Butler replaced the concept of *subject* with that of *agency*. An agent can be defined as a medium for action, something that acts or carries out. The agent is a medium that is formed by, and uses, language. It is not that the subject performs language; rather, the culturally intelligible result of the discursive practice of agency is identified, retroactively, as the subject. The linguistic resources available to agency (the agent) for discursive practice are the discourses that prevail widely in the social world. And when a linguistic act is carried out, Butler argues, although it is impossible not to "quote" someone's language out of a pre-determined set of content, it is possible to misuse and abuse language. In this way, Butler considers the possibility that, in addition to things being determined by language, linguistic practice can be transformed. In short, by introducing the concept of agency as a medium of discursive practice that is neither completely active nor completely passive, it becomes possible to conceive of a process of practice that is both structurally defined and able to act on the structure.

Some empirical studies in the field of educational sociology have been conducted in Japan that are of interest for having incorporated this post-structural perspective on gender early on. These studies examined the processes by which children are "en-gendered" (Nishitai 1998; Nakanishi 2004; Katada 2006; and others). Katada Son Asahi, for examples, argues as follows. Previous research has assumed that children internalize gender roles. However, this approach, by essentializing gender in advance as a binary category, and treating children as passive entities that undergo socialization, runs the risk of enforcing gender stereotypes. By contrast, a post-structural approach treats gender as a perpetual process of construction of the gendered subject and power relations. In other words, gender is an endless process that is not defined by either the knowledge possessed or the state of the personality at any given time. Katada sees this approach as well suited for providing an account of a fluid, context-based practice at a particular time, and for grasping the diverse construction of subject and power (Katada 2006).

This book will take the same approach. In Chapter 4 and the subsequent chapters, which consider the lives of individual homeless women, I will on principle avoid treating gender as given. That is, I will not assign in advance the binary sexual categories of "male" and "female." Instead, by treating gender as a discursive practice that evolves at each situation in which gender categories are used, I will look at the ways in which gender categories are brought in and used in the context of reciprocal activity. I will consider homeless women as *agents* who use sexual/gender categories to negotiate with such ideals as "femininity" that are employed with them. In this way I will be able to highlight the process of practices by which homeless women utilize their identity as women and redefine what it means to be "feminine."

What perspective might we gain by taking this approach? Some suggestions may be found in the work of Joanne Passaro, an American anthropologist who has conducted fascinating research on homelessness and gender. Although Passaro has praised Butler's approach to gender as offering a "powerful analytic stance" (Passaro 1996: 11), she has arguably been unable to fully incorporate it into her own arguments.

Passaro focuses on the fact that many of the homeless in the United Sates are black males. In her view, the tendency for persons of a particular race and gender to remain homeless is due to the influence of gender and racial stereotypes on "social welfare legislation, the evaluative practices of social service personnel, and the evaluative practices of the rest of us, who daily decide which homeless people deserve our money and our sympathy" (Passaro 1996: 29). As a result, says Passaro, for the homeless, who depend on public support and sympathy from others, turning away from hegemonic gender roles is dangerous.

Passaro interviewed nearly 400 homeless people to investigate the differences between men and women. She concluded that because there are welfare options available to homeless women that men do not have access to, it is possible for homeless women to survive as long as they display the desirable qualities of a woman, in contrast with men, who are forced to stay on the streets. Further, those women who remain homeless in spite of this system, she says, are "the renegades of gender, the women who are wary of protection, wary of recreating toxic homes, and wary of bureaucratic condescension and paternalism" (Passaro 1996: 63). In short, Passaro attributes the difference between women who persist in rough sleeping and those who are cared for under the welfare system to whether they conform to predominant female gender roles or not.

Her understanding of gender differs from post-structuralism in that she sees it both as a latent norm of the welfare system, and, essentially, as a permanent quality that attaches to a person. Consequently, to Passaro, whether women utilize the welfare system or not depends on whether they are equipped with an identity that enables them to act in accordance with the dominant gender norms or not. As a result, by overemphasizing the difference between male and female homeless people, her analysis fails to account for the differences among homeless women and the particular hardships faced by female rough sleepers. Overlooking the major individual differences in gender identity among homeless women, and the unfixed nature of that identity, her analysis categorizes women living on the streets as deviants from the gender norm. Passaro's study is invaluable as one of the few that deals with homeless women, whose numbers are small. However, this treatment of female rough sleepers, who do not utilize the welfare system and remain on the streets, as exceptions to the rule, further excludes them from categories by which they might be understood.

It is true, as Passaro says, that the welfare system, being constituted to prioritize the modern family with its sexual division of labor, takes the form of a normative system that pressures women to conform to dominant/hegemonic female roles. Women cannot escape this fact in using the welfare system. However, in situations where a particular system is being implemented, independent governing bodies, caseworkers, and other actors apply considerable discretion in their actions; it is not the case that such normative systems constantly influence the lives of women at the individual level. The encouraged behaviors also differ from place to place, with gender only one norm out of many that shape expectations; and the other norms that are presented alongside gender are not fixed, varying according to the person, historical period, and region under which they are implemented. Sudō Yachiyo has tried to identify the expected standards for women embodied in the social welfare system. Sudō distinguishes between the characteristics of a welfare system and the situations in which it is implemented, and argues that we should focus on the mutual activity that takes place at the scene of implementation, that is, the consultation with clients at a welfare office (Sudō 2003: 97). As Sudō's approach suggests, to see what is expected of individual homeless women by the welfare system, one must consider not only the norms formally instituted in the system, but also the concrete scenarios through which the system is implemented.

The post-structural gender studies approach is to focus on this sort of concrete scenario, treating gender as an unfolding process of discursive practice. In short, from this perspective, it is mistaken to consider the welfare system's ideal for women as monolithic. Rather, the point is to look at how gender categories are used in each case in which such ideals are invoked. This approach also makes it possible to perceive the more fluid aspects of gender – the gender identity of a particular person is not always constant, but may change from time to time. Further, women are considered not as a uniform group with homogenous characteristics, but in terms of their individual differences. This perspective suits the ethnographic approach of this book, which seeks to capture the various forms of gender and unique lives of homeless women. Furthermore, taking a gender perspective that accounts for individual variation is fundamentally linked to the core content of this study, whose original motivating problem is the exclusion of women from prior research on homelessness.

Rather than the researcher, an outsider, dichotomizing the behavior of homeless women, either as structurally determined or as subjective resistance to that structure, this approach emphasizes that behavior can be both structurally determined and have the potential to change that structure. This enables us to closely observe the unique logics of the social structure that force women into homelessness, as well as those behind the choices that women make when confronted by these constraints. In this way, by observing the process of women's lives over time, this study will examine in concrete terms what has been overlooked in prior research that assumed an autonomous subject, and why that led to the exclusion of homeless women as subjects of research.

Methodology

Two principal methods were used in this research: interviews and participant observation.

The interviews were targeted at professionals working with homeless women in the welfare system. Caseworkers and staff at women's facilities in Tokyo and Osaka prefectures were asked about matters such as how the system was implemented and how it was being utilized.

Participant observation was conducted at three sites. The first site was one of the welfare facilities where homeless women stay, Residence Facility A in Tokyo prefecture.

Facility A is a welfare facility in the category of free or low-rent housing facilities.[8] It was opened to provide lodging for poor and needy persons by a non-profit organization that originally provided support for rough sleepers. When I began the research in 2002, Facility A was one of a handful of facilities explicitly dedicated to supporting homeless women. I asked permission from the non-profit running the facility to serve as a volunteer and spent two weeks there as a live-in volunteer between the end of December 2002 and the beginning of January 2003. My status at the facility at that time was neither user nor staff member, but rather "live-in guest." However, since I was given access to the offices that were open only to staff members, users of the facility probably considered me to be a staff-like figure. Subsequently, for nine months beginning in January 2003, I was employed there part-time, conducting participant observation several times a month while working there. Thus, my research in Facility A took place over a total of 10 months including my volunteer stay. In July 2003 I conducted interviews of 15 clients of the facility that lasted between one and three hours each. Unlike my usual participant observation done while working, during the interviews I took notes, and made recordings when given permission.

My second site for participant observation was Park B in Tokyo prefecture, done in parallel to my research of Facility A. Park B was home to a support organization for female rough sleepers. I participated in their activities a number of times and subsequently visited the park intermittently for 10 months, beginning in January 2003, to meet the women I had gotten to know there. When my relationships with these women had grown close enough to personally visit them, I explained that I was doing a research project, and then conducted interviews with those women who had expressed their understanding and acceptance. Rough sleepers I had become acquainted with at Park B sometimes introduced me to other female rough sleepers. For one week in September 2003 I lived with a woman sleeping in Park B in her tent.

My methodology has meant that even among the female rough sleepers in Park B, my relationships have been limited to those who live in tents in a fixed location and have relationships with support organizations and other rough sleepers.

Broadly speaking, rough sleepers can be divided into those who live in a fixed location in tents and huts that they put up in parks, riverbeds, and similar locations; and those who live as vagabonds, setting up a place to sleep at night at stations, roadsides, and the like and removing it in the morning.[9] These two groups differ greatly in lifestyle and in how they form relationships with other people. When I conducted the study in 2003, in addition to about 250 rough sleepers in Park B who lived in a fixed place in tents, there were others living vagabond style and visiting Park B only for soup kitchen meals or at night; I was unable to make contact with this group of rough sleepers.

Since my 2003 research, the number of tents in Park B has dropped dramatically due to the Tokyo prefectural government's Housing First Project,[10] and the rough sleeping situation is now much different. Today, in Park B and elsewhere, there is much less urban

Photo 1.1: Rows of tents in Park B.

space in which it is possible to set up a tent or shack and settle down. The lives of rough sleepers have thus come to be strongly influenced by external conditions, and the accounts given in this book, naturally, do not represent the full picture of lives of female rough sleepers. Most of the interviews were conducted amidst casual conversation, but for personal histories, for instance, I set aside specific times and interviewed each person between two and more than a dozen times. Most narratives were recorded with permission of the interviewee, but some parts are based on notes I made afterward of conversations as I remembered them.

Third, I collected information while volunteering, as a founding and central member, for a support group for women rough sleepers. This group was formed in Osaka in 2003 by female rough sleepers themselves along with other women already volunteering to assist rough sleepers. It had been founded with the specific aim of reducing the tendency for women to be excluded from programs to aid rough sleepers. The group held monthly meetings for sharing personal news and discussing problems, while also conducting outreach, lending small amounts of money, and, when requested, assisting in the procurement of public assistance. For women who had transitioned from rough sleeping to living in a public facility or ordinary home, the group helped with daily activities and created opportunities for meeting other people. I made notes on what I observed and heard while volunteering in these activities.

I consider my role in this group to be mainly that of a supporter rather than a researcher. Accordingly, there were times when I intervened in the lives of women and went beyond my role as observer to significantly affect their lives. By contrast, at Park B, I took the role of a researcher and did not intervene. In both cases, I was investigating women rough sleepers, but because my role was different in the two contexts, my relationships with the women were also different. However, I made a point of emphasizing to this group at every opportunity that I was doing research on homeless women, and conducted individual interviews only after repeating my explanation of the study's purpose and obtaining consent. When permission was given the interviews were recorded. The names of persons cited in the study have been withheld. Portions of the interview data marked with "[ ]" indicate my own words or explanatory text, while "..." indicates omitted material.

The structure of this book

The book is organized as follows. Chapter 2 gives an overview of the state of homelessness in Japan to provide a basis for discussing and analyzing the homelessness of women. After establishing a definition of homelessness as used in this book, with reference to Western studies, I will explain why the labor market and social welfare system were set up in a way that rendered women prone to "hidden homelessness" instead of rough sleeping. Additionally, based on the life histories of 33 women, I will examine the process of exclusion that precedes homelessness for women. By comparing this with the conditions of male homelessness, I will identify the essential qualities of female homelessness.

In Chapter 3, I provide a historical overview of the treatment of women in government anti-poverty policies from the establishment of social programs in the early 20th century to the present, based on the case of Osaka prefecture. This overview reveals that the choices for women seeking protection and support were traditionally limited to prostitution or becoming a single mother, and that this system persists today.

Chapter 4 investigates what norms women are expected to conform to when using the welfare system, based on observations at Facility A. As Chapter 3 reveals, the welfare system for poor women is a system based on the norm of the modern family. However, women do not accept these norms uncritically, but rather negotiate them on a case-by-case basis. Here I investigate this negotiation process in concrete terms as it is played out in specific cases.

From Chapter 5 onward, I focus on the living conditions of women who sleep in the rough. This chapter describes the life of female rough sleepers in Park B in Tokyo, focusing on how they secure food, clothing, and shelter; what restrictions they face living in a park inhabited by a large number of men; and what sort of relationships they form with other people.

In Chapter 6, using the women in Park B as an example, I outline the practices of rough sleepers that have been overlooked in prior research due to the failure to consider women. After looking at what meaning women rough sleepers assign to their way of life, I focus on how they decide either to continue rough sleeping or transition out of it.

Chapter 7 looks at the case of a support group for women rough sleepers in Osaka. Amidst relationships and support activities extending over a period of time, the circumstances of the women's lives changed, and with this, their desires as to whether to continue rough sleeping or not also changed. In this chapter, by observing this process of change, I consider what practices have been concealed by the assumption of a subject endowed with free will.

In Chapter 8, I critically examine the reasons why a research perspective based on the ideas of resistance and subjectivity has led to the exclusion of women, and discuss what has been overlooked as a result. I use Carol Gilligan's concept of "the ethics of care" to provide a framework for this discussion. I conclude by summarizing my arguments and offering some comments on the current situation of increasing poverty of women and the policy challenges it raises.

2 Who are the homeless women?

The hidden homeless women

The term "homeless" usually conjures an image of a middle-aged or older man, and indeed, the majority of homeless individuals in Japan are single, older males. However, while they may be few in number, there are also homeless women. These women reportedly make up a mere 3.2% of the total homeless population (Ministry of Health, Labour and Welfare 2012), and because they tend to stay in the shadows in order to avoid danger, they usually go unnoticed. Therefore, estimates of their population might be even lower than their actual numbers.

Why is the female homeless population so tiny in comparison with that of males? Because existing research has taken it as given that homeless people are male, almost no one has asked this question. Even the existence of homeless women has been virtually ignored, and there is little awareness of whether homeless women have unique characteristics.

This chapter will focus on homeless women, comparing their qualities to those of homeless men, and consider the reasons why, even though women are at great risk of falling into poverty, the majority of homeless people seen on the streets are men. Next, I will use specific cases to examine the distinctive qualities of homeless women and the process of exclusion that leads to homelessness, and consider the unique features of the social exclusion to which women are subjected.

Homelessness in developed countries

Although there was a substantial homeless population in the chaotic early postwar period, within a few years visible homelessness had largely subsided. It was not until the collapse of the "bubble economy" in the early 1990s that homeless people again became a common sight in Japan. However, in most other developed countries, such as those of North America and Europe, rising homelessness had become a problem earlier on. In the United States in the 1950s and 1960s, for example, the majority of homeless were single, older white males. These men typically lived in areas sometimes known as "skid row," comparable in some ways to Japanese *yoseba*, which were gathering places for day laborers. The average homeless person at the time was nearly fifty years old, with white males making up over 90% of the population and women only 3% (Bogue 1963). In terms of gender, this image matches closely with homelessness in Japan through the mid-1990s. However, beginning in the mid-1970s, the homeless population in the U.S. began to skyrocket, and the presence of homeless people came to be felt across large portions of the urban landscape. This period also saw the growth of the "new homeless" (Rossi 1989), people whose characteristics differed from the until-then typical homeless person. These included younger people in their twenties and thirties, African-Americans and other ethnic minorities, and women; the characteristics of the homeless population underwent a qualitative as well as a quantitative change as these individuals came to make up a substantial portion of that population. Subsequently, the number of homeless women grew, reportedly comprising 30% of all homeless (Urban Institute et al., 1999). In recent years the numbers of young and female homeless in Japan are reported to have grown as well (Ikuta 2007: 81), suggesting the advent of changes similar to those experienced in the West.

However, the greater portion of female homelessness in Western countries in comparison with Japan is likely due, not so much to there being so many female rough sleepers in the West, as to different definitions of homelessness. In Japan, the word "homeless" generally refers to people living in the streets. Even the Homeless Self-Help Act defines the term as referring exclusively to rough sleepers: " 'Homeless' refers to persons living permanently and without good reason in locations or facilities such as city parks, riverbeds, roadsides, and stations." And yet, if "homeless" is taken literally to mean "without a home," it can apply to a great variety of situations. A classic case of this would be people who spend the night in Internet cafés or fast food restaurants. Indeed, in the West the term "homeless" is generally understood to include people in such situations. Simply put, the definition is broader than that used in Japan.

A central contention of this book is that expanding the range of criteria for homelessness brings many more women into the category. As some researchers of homelessness have noted, women regularly experience "hidden homelessness," and the true scale of the problem is missed if one only looks on the streets and in shelters (Edgar and Doherty 2001: 4). In short, women are prone to suffer homelessness, a condition of lacking a stable, fixed residence, in forms other than rough sleeping. It is therefore necessary to consider the presence of these "hidden homeless" in order to understand the homelessness of women.

Defining homelessness

Research in Western countries has developed nuanced frameworks with a variety of categories of homelessness that account for these "hidden homeless." Typically, homelessness is classified into the following major categories:
   1. roofless
   2. houseless
   3. insecure
   4. inadequate.

As the name suggests, (1) "roofless" describes the condition of a rough sleeper living on the streets. (2) A "houseless" person does not sleep in the rough but lacks a fixed residence, living temporarily in public facilities and the like. (3) "Insecure" applies to someone who has a home to live in but whose living conditions cannot be considered safe or stable, because, for instance, the home belongs to someone else or the individual is a victim of domestic violence. (4) A person living in an "inadequate" environment has his or her own home, but it is so crowded or otherwise unsuitable that it would not normally be considered a "home." Between categories 1 and 4 the definition of homelessness becomes increasingly broad. Theoretical discussions of homelessness should specify which of the categories 1 through 4 are included. Based on this framework, category 1 is the one primarily used in Japan.[1] However, as this book is concerned with women, who are prone to "hidden homelessness," I define homeless more broadly, to include category 2.

Figure 2.1 depicts the main varieties of homelessness, defined more broadly to include category 2, as it applies under Japanese conditions. In the center is rough sleeping, the most extreme form

Homes of Acquaintances

↑
↓

Commercial Facilities ←——→ Rough Sleeping ←——→ Workers' Housing
Simple hostels   Dormitories
Guest houses   ↑   Live-in (at inn, etc.)
Saunas   │   Workers' lodgings (*hanba*)
Internet cafés   ↓
Fast-food restaurants, etc.   Welfare Facilities
                               Hospitals
                               Offenders' Rehabilitation Facilities

Figure 2.1: The concept of homelessness, defined broadly

Source: Iwata (2009: 96), revised.

of homelessness. The surrounding areas illustrate that there are four other general types of homelessness: staying in the home of an acquaintance; staying in commercial establishments such as cheap hotels and late-night businesses; and staying in workers' lodgings such as dormitories and lodgings provided by public institutions (including hospitals, jails, and welfare facilities) as well as those attached to a work site.[2] These different forms of homelessness cannot be clearly separated; even among rough sleepers there are quite a few who sleep in a number of different places, staying in Internet cafés or friends' homes depending on their physical condition, the amount of money at hand, or the state of personal relationships on any given day.[3] Furthermore, this diagram should not be taken to mean that the people who stay in these places are all homeless in the sense of lacking a home to return to.

What, then, is the scale of this sort of homelessness, and what proportion are women? According to a 2012 national survey, 9,576 people were visually confirmed to be rough sleepers, falling in the most extreme category of homelessness. Most of these were men, with only 307 women, or 3.2% (MHLW 2012). However, the number of homeless in the wider sense – although, as previously stated, there are difficulties with defining it – is much larger: it has been estimated that every year about 100,000 people suffer the loss of a place to live.

Of those broadly defined as homeless as per Figure 2.1, it is difficult to determine the number who stay with acquaintances or in commercial establishments. However, in terms of welfare facility

Table 2.1: Social welfare facilities offering housing: national totals

Social welfare facilities offering housing	Types	Capacity
Type 1 social welfare project		
Public Assistance Facilities	4	19,818
Welfare Facilities for the Elderly	5	146,152
Support Facilities for the Disabled	2	71,750
Rehabilitation and Support Facilities for the Physically Disabled	6	16,182
Support Facilities for the Intellectually Disabled	3	55,833
Social Re-integration Facilities for the Mentally Disabled	3	6,240
Women's Protection Facilities	1	1,363
Children's Welfare Facilities	12	65,100
Other social welfare facilities	2	203,565
Total		**586,003**
Type 2 social welfare project/other[a]	—	—
Free or low-rent housing	—	—
Unregistered facilities	—	—
Homeless Self-Help Centers / temporary protective facilities	—	—

Source: Ministry of Health, Labour, and Welfare 2011d.

Note: [a] Figures relating to Type 2 facilities are unknown.

use, according to data on residential facilities in the MHLW's annual national survey of social welfare facilities, the total capacity (bed count) is about 590,000 (Table 2.1). These facilities are known as Type 1 social welfare projects and are highly public in nature. However, there has recently been a rapid growth in Type 2 social welfare project facilities. These include free or low-rent housing facilities, which are a category of welfare facility aimed at low-income people. They have been called "poverty businesses" and are subject to much attention. Type 2 facilities also include facilities that have gone into business without even registering with the government. Many rough sleepers and other homeless people use them.[4]

In 2011, the MHLW conducted a survey to get a better understanding of free or low-rent housing and unregistered facilities. This survey found that the national total capacity of free or low-rent housing facilities was 14,964 people. Among the residents of unregistered facilities, 16,614 were receiving public assistance – a significant number when compared with the facilities run by Type 1 social welfare Projects. Moreover, the target residents of the 1,314

*Table 2.2: Types of users of unregistered facilities serving public
assistance recipients*

Target users of unregistered facilities	%
Elderly	48.9
Homeless	16.3
Alcohol dependent	2.8
Drug dependent	1.8
Other	30.2

Source: Ministry of Health, Labour and Welfare 2011a.

unregistered facilities that took in public assistance recipients were
diverse in nature (Table 2.2), but most housed elderly persons, former
rough sleepers, and others. Table 2.3 shows the main types of social
welfare facilities that house homeless persons, particularly those
as defined broadly in this book. As the table shows, these projects
vary in their goals and target users. For example, the Airin policy
provides temporary housing for day laborers, public assistance
provides for physically and mentally disabled or those made homeless
by external conditions, women's assistance services victims of
domestic violence and poverty, single mother family assistance is
for mothers and children, and elderly welfare assistance services
the elderly. All, however, provide shelter to people who lack homes
due to low incomes.

Studies that have sought to identify those lacking a home according
to the various patterns just described have compiled the results of
surveys of people in the following situations to appraise the situation:
1. Transitioners: persons who have moved on from a state of
   homelessness to regular or institutional housing with the support
   of homeless support organizations throughout the country.
2. Residents: residents of lodgings run by homeless support
   organizations.
3. Welfare offices: surveys of the cases in welfare offices throughout
   Japan for which the provision of public assistance has been
   approved for homeless people.

The results of these surveys indicate that the proportion of women is:
(1) 7.6%; (2) 6.5%; (3) 11.9% (National Homeless Support Network
2011). It is therefore clear that in all cases where homelessness is
more broadly defined, the proportion of women is higher than the

3.2% found among rough sleepers. In other words, in homelessness broadly defined, women are more prevalent than among rough sleepers alone. Thus, when a broader range of people who lack a place to live are taken into consideration, homelessness affects a considerable number of women.[5]

Why are there so few women rough sleepers?

Structural bondage to the home

Why, then, are there so few women rough sleepers compared to men? And why do women who are destitute of housing tend to become "hidden homeless" rather than rough sleepers? These phenomena are closely linked to the adoption of the modern family as the fundamental living unit of Japanese society. The "modern family" is a family founded on a sexual division of labor, in which the man performs wage labor outside the home while the woman does domestic labor inside the home. Public policy on labor, welfare, and other matters has been created with this type of family as its model.

The influence of this model in labor practices is most evident in the concept of a "family wage." The fundamental idea is that the husband's performance of long, paid labor outside the home is made possible by the wife's performance of reproductive labor, such as housework and childrearing. Hence, the man, the family representative, is paid wages sufficient to support his wife and children as compensation for the total labor of the couple including the wife's unpaid work. Based on this concept, the wages of regular male laborers were set to a standard that was sufficient to support an entire family, and conversely, when women performed wage labor, these wages were kept low on the assumption that they were merely supplemental income for the family. Indeed, 55.0% of working women are part-time or otherwise irregular employees, but only 20% of working men are (MHLW 2011a). Further, when male wages are scaled to 100, the wages of women workers are a mere 69.3, and even for women who are regular workers, the number is still a very low 72.1. In short, by taking on the responsibility of reproductive labor, not only have women been forced into unstable working situations, but their wages have also been structurally held down.

Table 2.3: Main residential facilities used by homeless persons (Osaka prefecture)

Type of project	Facility name	Activities	Legal basis	Users
Airin policy	Airin temporary emergency evening shelter	Provides temporary emergency lodging to day laborers who have been forced into rough sleeping		Single persons
Homelessness policy	Living Care Center	Admit persons without a home within the city of Osaka who, due to age or illness require short-term support, and help them return to independent living through lifestyle guidance, etc.		Single persons
	Self-Help Center	Provide food and lodging to homeless persons with the desire and ability to work, assist with job hunting, and support self-reliance through employment	Special Measures Act to Assist Self-Support of Homeless Persons	Single men
Public assistance	Rehabilitation Facility	Care for persons who have difficulty living by themselves due to a significant physical or mental disability	Public Assistance Act	Single persons
	Relief Facility	Care for persons who need help and guidance due to their physical or mental condition and who have good prospects for re-integrating into society in the near future	Public Assistance Act	Single persons
	Accommodation Facility	Admit low-income clients with no place to stay due to fire, eviction, high rent, etc., or unable to secure a place to live for economic or other reasons	Public Assistance Act	Single persons

	Facility	Description	Relevant Act	Target population
Mother-child welfare	Mother-Child Living Support Facility	For single mothers unable to give their children adequate care, these facilities take in mothers and children together and offer living support	Child Welfare Act	Mothers and children
Women's Protection Services	Women's Consultation Center	Serve women taking refuge from violent partners; women who are poor, have a transient lifestyle, or lack a home; or women needing help to become self-reliant; also serve the children accompanying such women	Anti-Prostitution Act; Domestic Violence Act	Single women; mothers and children
	Women's Protection Facility	Admit women in need of protective care have been approved for admission by the director of a Women's Consultation Center	Anti-Prostitution Act; Domestic Violence Act	Single women; mothers and children
Elderly welfare	Nursing home	Admit and provide care for individuals 65 or older for whom receiving care at home is difficult due to physical, mental, environmental, or economic factorss	Act on Social Welfare for the Elderly	Single persons
Rehabilitation and protection	Offenders' Rehabilitation Facility	Take custody of individuals who have committed crimes or offenses for a set period of time, and help them to rehabilitate and become self-supporting	Offenders Rehabilitation Act	Single men
Other	Free or low-rent housing facility	Project that provides free or low-fee housing in simple hostels for impoverished persons, or provide access to housing or other facilities		
	Unregistered facility			

This system modeled on the modern family has affected taxation and social benefits (insurance payments) as well as wages. A married woman whose husband is the main income provider can receive a spousal income tax exemption for up to 1.03 million yen (~USD 9,000) of annual income, and can be included as a dependent on her husband's social insurance policy with an income of up to 1.3 million yen (~USD 11,500). This means that working women have an incentive to limit their income by choosing part-time work. As for the social pension system, while it is currently being revised, under present policy, the wife of an employee is eligible for Type 3 insurance status without any contribution; clearly, preference is being given to families in which the man works for wages while the woman handles the reproductive labor. In short, the modern family is the basis of the tax, social insurance, and other systems, which are set up to give maximum benefits to this sort of family.

Hence, if women have a male partner as the main wage earner, their economic situation may be comparatively stable under such a system. However, if they deviate from the model of the modern family by remaining single or losing the male earner due to death or divorce, the potential for poverty suddenly becomes much greater. In a labor market based on the sexual division of labor, most jobs for women are low-pay and unstable, making it difficult to earn enough to live on. This is seen most clearly in the case of women who are heads of single-parent families; many of them are impoverished as a result of being responsible for raising children and working part-time or for low pay at the same time. They provide the clearest example of the poverty that women experience in a society based on the sexual division of labor.

Moreover, these types of poverty tend to manifest more clearly in old age. Because pension payments are determined by how much and what type of work was done, women, who are often kept from paid work by housework, childrearing, and elderly care, or have unstable jobs, can easily fail to meet the requirement of twenty-five years of contribution that is a prerequisite to receiving a social pension; and if they do qualify for the pension on the basis of years of underpaid employment, it may be insufficient to support a minimal standard of living. This can be clearly seen in the average monthly payments from the Employer's Pension Fund, which were 187,545 yen (~USD 972) for men and 106,912 yen (~USD 972) for women, while average National Pension Fund payments were 58,490 yen (~USD 532) for men and 47,252 yen (~USD 429) for women – lower for women in both cases (Social Insurance Agency 2007).

Another obstacle to women forming an independent household is their own sense of being bound to the home. For mothers with small children, there is considerable resistance to the idea of divorce. Further, it has been found that women who are victims of violence from their partner can be dominated by that partner, lose their normal ability to judge and act, and descend into an apathetic, despondent state (Kawakita 1999 and others). This can make it extremely difficult to escape. The belief that a life of rough sleeping is particularly difficult for women may also put the brakes on leaving home. As a result, the economic obstacles to becoming independent combine with women's own psychological sense of constraints to prevent many women from initiating divorce. Indeed, Japan's annual divorce rate of 2.0 per 1,000 people is the lowest among developed countries (Ministry of General Affairs, Statistics Bureau, 2012).[6]

The United States, with its high divorce rate, has experienced what has been called a "feminization of poverty" since the late 1970s. This refers to a situation in which half or more of poor families have a woman as head of household; the majority of these are single-mother families. As an explanation for the cause of this phenomenon, researchers have cited the fact that even as higher divorce rates and lower marriage rates lead to more female-headed households, women continue to be driven into low-paying jobs, and that social welfare and social security policies provide inadequate compensation for this social disadvantage (Goldberg and Kremen 1990). This feminization of poverty can be found in most advanced countries, but Japan has been thought to be a special case in which it has failed to materialize clearly. Reasons given for this include Japan's low divorce rate, the small number of female-headed households in the first place, and the somewhat successful effect of the child allowance, which offers economic support to single-mother families (Axinn 1990; Sugimoto 1993). However, as June Axinn, the first researcher to discuss the feminization of poverty in Japan, has put it, "Ironically, Japanese women at this moment are not independent enough to achieve feminization of poverty; they cannot afford divorce and economic independence" (Axinn 1990: 104). In order to leave home and run an independent household, women need to achieve economic independence, and Japanese women are not yet in this position. In other words, the formation of a female-headed household itself is very difficult under contemporary social conditions.[7]

With a labor market and social security policies based on the normative model of the male bread-winner family, it is very difficult for women to make an independent living. This pressures women who are tempted to leave home to decide against it, making it nearly impossible for women even in the worst domestic conditions to escape. As a result, the number of female-headed households, which are highly susceptible to poverty, is kept low. This is one reason for the low number of female rough sleepers.

The inferior status of welfare and public aid recipients

Another reason for the small number of female rough sleepers is the social welfare system. With the base assumptions of the male-breadwinner model of the modern family, women's cases tend to be treated as social welfare or public aid rather, than as social insurance.

The systems by which a welfare state protects the livelihood of its citizens can be divided into two distinct types: insurance and welfare/aid (allowance). The fundamental expectation is that people will work; this system provides welfare and public aid when circumstances make this impossible. Social insurance, such as unemployment insurance, health insurance, and retirement pensions, is based on contributions deducted from workers' wages. Then, when welfare or public aid are needed, due to unemployment, illness, or old age, for example, payments are made as an entitlement earned by these contributions. Hence, no means test is required to receive them. In contrast, a living allowance, of which public assistance is the most common type, is intended to support a minimum standard of living even where no contributions have been made, for those who for whatever reason have been excluded from social insurance. Because a living allowance is provided as a charitable, unearned benefit rather than as a right, it carries a stigma. Not only is a means test required for eligibility, but the standard of living provided is intentionally kept to a bare minimum.

It follows that there is a hierarchical relationship between insurance and aid, one which mirrors the gap between men and women. Because men are expected to work for wages, when circumstances make them unable to work they are likely to be entitled to social insurance. Women, however, are more likely to have not been employed long enough or to have worked only for low pay. Thus, when women require income assistance, they tend to receive it in the form of social welfare or public aid. In short, insurance and aid make up a two-tiered system that distributes benefits to men and women unequally.

Hence, when men fall through the social security net and seek social welfare or public aid, they are subject to a strict test of their working ability. If they are found able to work – even if there is no actual work available – they will be denied welfare and public aid, leaving them prone to becoming rough sleepers.[8]

Conversely, since the majority of women have been disqualified from social insurance by working at low-paying jobs, they are not candidates for unemployment insurance or the Employer's Pension Fund. They are thus more likely than men to be eligible for welfare and public aid. However, women who use these services are stigmatized and must undergo a means test to receive benefits. This test extends not only to the property and income of the woman herself but to her relationships with males who could potentially provide her with income, subjecting her life to detailed surveillance and control.

Women, then, are at a disadvantage when it comes to employment and social security; the institutions of society make it difficult for them to leave home and earn an independent living. But if they are willing to undergo a humiliating means test extending to their relationships with men and a minimal standard of living, then amenities like the welfare system and public assistance are readily available. One reason, then, for the scarcity of women rough sleepers is that these systems come into play right when women are on the verge of going out on the streets.

The way poor women live

We will now look at what prior research has found about how poor women actually live under these conditions. As stated before, the most typical case of female poverty is that of women who lack a breadwinning male partner. Studies on such women have been insufficient to give a clear picture of their living conditions. I will begin by considering single-mother households and elderly women living alone, two categories of poverty-susceptible women on whom a comparatively large body of research has accumulated.

According to the *National Survey of Single-Mother Households* (MHLW 2007b), in 2003 there were an estimated 1,230,000 such households. This number is in an upward trend due to the increasing number of divorces; 89.6% of single-mother households are the result of divorce. For single-mother families that resulted from the death of the father, a survivor's pension provides some guaranteed income, but for families with divorced mothers, for whom this is not available, the economic situation is harder. Since a full 59.1% of divorced-mother households have never received child support payments from the father, economic assistance is available, in the form of a childrearing allowance, for single mothers with incomes below a certain level. However, even with these forms of assistance, many families are unable to maintain a minimal standard of living. In these cases, public assistance is supposed to provide sufficient support to maintain this standard. While the proportion of all households receiving public assistance is 18.9 per 1,000, for single-mother households it is 129.6 per 1,000 (National Institute of Population and Social Security Research 2009). This is a clear indication of the high rate of poverty among single-mother families.

Even including all the aid provided to single-mother families, the average annual income for such families stands at 2.13 million yen (~USD 18,000), a mere 38% of the 5.64 million yen (~USD 48,000) for two-parent families. This is despite the fact that 84.5% of single mothers work. With pay for women's jobs low to begin with, when work is combined with parenting there are limits to what can be earned, forcing women into poverty. This situation vividly illustrates the problem of a society that is set up to make it difficult for families that do not conform to the hegemonic sexual division of labor to successfully combine childrearing and work.

The effect of this disadvantaged economic position of single-mother families extends to the procurement of housing as well. Kuzunishi Lisa et al. (2004), in their study of the living situations of single-mother families, have shown that such families have low home ownership rates in comparison to regular families, and often live in private rental property. A high share of single-mother families also live in public housing, taking advantage of policies that prioritize single-mother families.[9] Furthermore, many single-mother families, unable to function as independent households, resort to living with the mother's parents, siblings, or friends; 32.5% of single-mother families are in this category. The availability of help with childcare and housework no doubt influences the decision to live with relatives or friends, but in other cases the decision to cohabit is likely made unwillingly, for instance, when insurmountable economic pressure or violence from the male partner force women to live elsewhere. This situation can be considered to be a type of hidden homelessness. Kuzunishi et al. found that 73.8% of single-mother families had moved in the process of becoming such a family. Out of these, 20.9% of those households that moved to private housing, and 30.3% of those who moved in with parents or siblings, moved again within one year. Kuzunishi et al. cite this as evidence that these women were forced into unstable housing situations.

As for elderly women, the *Comprehensive Survey of Living Conditions* (MHLW 2009) reports 3,070,000 households made up of single women age sixty-five or older. Because women, on average, live longer than men, many women spend their later years alone. There are about three times more single-elderly-women households than single-elderly-male households. Many such women are in economically troubled situations; the average yearly income of households including a person of sixty-five or older is 5,101,000 yen (~USD 43,000), but for single-person female households it is 1,807,000 (~USD 15,000), making this type of household the poorest type of household with an elderly member (Figure 2.2). That poverty is something that elderly women are especially susceptible to is shown in the fact that elderly women make up the largest share of public assistance recipients (Figure 2.3). The pension system plays a significant role in this poverty of elderly females. As noted before, twenty-five years or more of contributions are required to receive pension payments, but due to periods of not being employed because of housework, childrearing, or elderly care duties, or working at low-pay part-time jobs, many women fail to satisfy the minimum contribution period. Nor does the National Pension Fund solve the problem: if one makes insurance payments for forty years between ages twenty and sixty, the weekly stipend is less than 70,000 yen per month (~USD 593), which by itself is insufficient to support a minimal standard of living. It is hardly surprising that women, who more often participate in the National Pension Fund than in the Employer's Pension Fund, are at greater risk of poverty.

Izuhara Misa (2005) studied the living situations of older women and found that women who do not marry, or who lose their husbands at a young age through divorce or death, lack the opportunity to inherit property or take advantage of company employee benefits. Hence, as it is difficult for them to live in their own home or in rental property, in many cases they live in low-income facilities such as public housing or nursing homes.

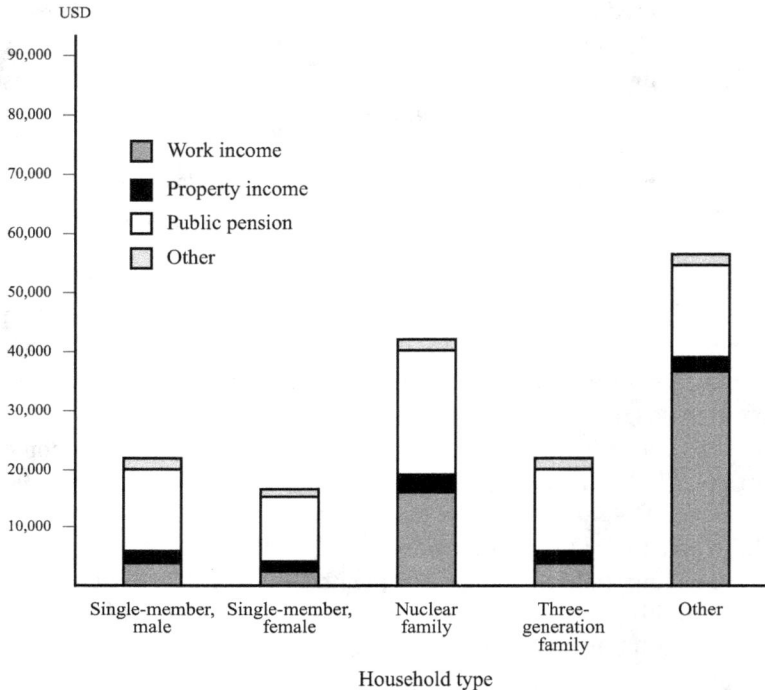

Figure 2.2: Sources of yearly income for households with elderly persons 65 and over

Source: *Comprehensive Survey of Living Conditions* (MHLW 2010).

As all of this illustrates, female-headed households, particularly single-mother households and elderly single female households, because they lack a male breadwinner, tend to be poor. Thus, a significant number of such families that have trouble finding independent housing are forced into homelessness, living with parents or other relatives or in public facilities.

The process of exclusion

We will now look at the specific process by which women lose their homes, based on their life histories prior to becoming homeless. The histories used will be those of the thirty-three women I interviewed

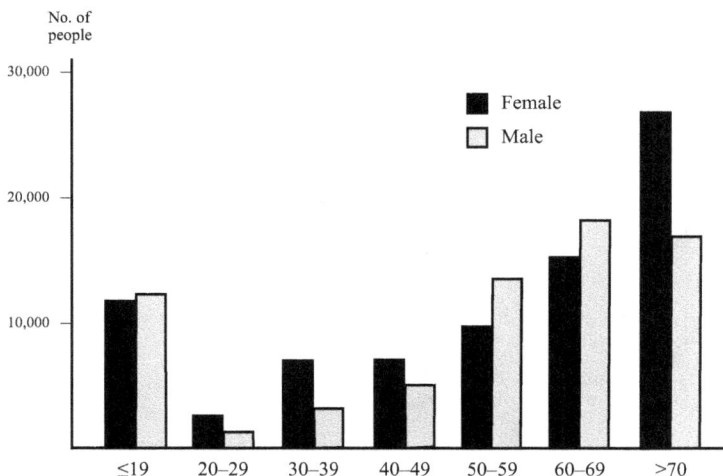

Figure 2.3: Number of public assistance recipients by age
Source: National Institute of Population and Social Security Research 2009.

who provided detailed life stories (Table 2.4).[10] Nineteen of these are women I met on the streets and in parks in Tokyo and Osaka between 2003 and 2009. I got to know the other fourteen at a facility in Tokyo, described in Chapter 4.

Regarding the numerical figures derived from the data, to clarify the distinguishing characteristics of women, I will compare these figures with the findings of prior research that focused primarily on men. My source for this comparison is the *Discussion of the National Survey on the Conditions of the Homeless* (2007) conducted by the MHLW. I will use figures derived from the cross-tabulated statistics for men only from the contingency tables.[11]

Since the sample size for my study is small and the format and time-frame for the interviews were not uniform, its statistical value is small. Further, whereas the MHLW survey whose data were used for comparison was limited to rough sleepers, my study included homeless persons staying in facilities, so that they cannot be directly compared without qualification. Despite these limitations, given that almost no previous studies have focused specifically on homeless women, this comparison has definite value for understanding certain characteristics of homeless women.

Table 2.4: Life histories of thirty-three homeless women

① Homeless due to husband's or partner's unemployment

1. (Sumiko, 70 years) Graduated from elementary school

Housing	Family of birth	Home of relative	Live-in employment	Apartment	Live-in employment	Family of birth	Live-in employment	Apartment	Workers' barracks	Apartment
Relationship		Single	Single	Husband, Husband's children	Single (divorced)		Single	Common-law husband (Carpenter)	Common-law husband	Common-law husband
Work	—	Helping with relative's family-operated business	Various jobs	Part-time work at factory	Inn (ryokan)		Inn (ryokan)	Part-time: factories, cleaning, etc.	Food preparation	Part-time: factories, cleaning, etc.
Age	—	12	13	? (2 years)				42	? (5 years)	

2. (29 years) Graduated from middle school

Housing	Rough sleeping	Hospital	Free or low-rent housing facility
Relationship	Common-law husband	Single	Single
Work	Public assistance	Public assistance	Public assistance
Age	69	69	69

Housing	Household members	Employment	Income	Age
Family of birth	Single	Various part-time jobs		15
Apartment	Single	Full-time company employee		
Women's Consultation Center	Single		Public assistance	29
Inn (ryokan)				9
Free or low-rent housing facility	Single	Full-time company employee	Public assistance	29
Offenders' Rehabilitation facility	Single		Public assistance	29
Apartment	Husband (employed full-time), Child	Full-time company employee		20
Apartment	Husband (III), Child		Public assistance	25
Mother-Child Living Support Facility	Child (Husband in facility)			
Apartment	Husband (Child in facility)		Public assistance	
Apartment	Single (Husband in facility)		Public assistance	29
Jail	Single		Public assistance	29
Father's home	Father			29

3 (Fujiko, 48 years) Graduated from high school

Housing	Household members	Employment	Age
Family of birth		Hospital office work, Hospital office work	During 20s
Apartment	Husband (driver)	Full-time housewife (some part-time work)	
Apartment	Husband		
Rough sleeping	Husband		46

Continued overleaf

Table 2.4: continued

4. (53 years) Educational history unknown

Apartment	Rough sleeping	Shelter	Apartment
Husband (Carpenter)	Husband	Husband	Husband
Part-time office work			Public assistance
Life insurance sales			
During 20s	50	52	53

5. (66 years) Graduated from high school

	Privately-owned house	Older sister's home	Live-in employment	Apartment	Rough sleeping	Relief Facility	Apartment
Family of birth	Husband, Child, Mother-in-law	Single (divorced)	Single	Common-law husband (self-employed)	Common-law husband	Single	Single
			Inn (ryokan)	Inn (ryokan)		Public assistance	Public assistance
	28	33	33		59	65	65

6. (Yūko, 65 years) Graduated from high school

Apartment	Apartment	Apartment	Rough sleeping	Private women's shelter	Rough sleeping	Women's Protection Facility	Rough sleeping

7. (71 years) Graduated from middle school

Dwelling	Household	Occupation	Age
Family of birth		Full-time company employee	During 20s
Apartment	Husband	Full-time company employee	During 20s
	Single (divorced)	Full-time company employee	During 20s
	Single	Family-operated business	40
	Common-law husband (Carpenter)	Family-operated business	52
	Common-law husband	Some part-time work as cleaner, etc.	55
	Single (taking refuge from partner)	Public assistance	
	Common-law husband		
	Single (taking refuge from partner)		
	Husband		
Public housing	Husband	Public assistance	61
Apartment	Husband	Public assistance	63

8. (31 years) Graduated from middle school

Dwelling	Household	Occupation	Age
Privately-owned house	Family of birth	Full-time company employee	17
Apartment	Husband, Child		19
Apartment	Single	Bar or nightclub hostess, etc.	21
Prison	Single		22
Privately-owned house	Family of birth	Bar or nightclub hostess	22
Apartment	Female acquaintance	Bar or nightclub hostess	During 30s
Apartment	Female acquaintance	Bar or nightclub hostess	During 30s
Apartment	Common-law husband (Carpenter)	Part-time cleaner	51
Rough sleeping	Common-law husband		62
Apartment	Common-law husband	Public assistance	69

Continued overleaf

Table 2.4: continued

Person 8 (continued)

Lived with	Family of birth	Husband	Husband	Husband	Common-law husband	Doya	Apartment	Apartment
Residence						Doya	Apartment	Apartment
With	Family of birth	Husband	Husband	Husband	Common-law husband	Husband	Husband	Husband
Occupation	Hairstylist	Hairstylist	Part-time supermarket worker			Cleaner at doya	Public assistance	
Age	15	26	30	30	31	47	53	55

9 (Itsuko, 69 years) Graduated from elementary school

Residence	Privately-owned house	Rough sleeping (shaded)	Apartment	Hospital	Live-in employment	Prison (shaded)	Live-in employment	Workers' barracks	Rough sleeping (shaded)	Apartment
With	Family of birth	Husband, Child	Husband, Child	Husband, Child	Single (divorced)	Single	Single	Husband	Husband	Single
Occupation	Match factory, farming	Match factory	Cannery		Geisha		Pachinko parlor	Food preparation		Public assistance
Age	13	15	18	22	22		46	55		69

10. (72 years) Graduated from middle school

Residence	Dormitory	Privately-owned house	Privately-owned house	Apartment	Rough sleeping (shaded)	Hospital (shaded)	Apartment

(Continuation — previous life course)

Residence			Apartment					Apartment
Household / marital status		Husband, Child	Single (divorced)	Husband	Husband	Husband	Single	Husband
Occupation	Nurse	Nurse		Fortune teller				
Age	15	18		46	65	70	71	72

11. (62 years) Graduated from middle school

Residence		Apartment	Workers' barracks			Rough sleeping	Apartment
Household / marital status		Husband, Child / Child (Husband deceased)	Single	Husband	Husband	Husband	Husband
Occupation / income	Full-time company employee	Public assistance		Food preparation at dormitory	Cleaner at doya		Public assistance
Age	15	40	During 50s	During 50s		61	62

② Homeless due to own unemployment

12. (50 years) Graduated from high school

Residence	Privately-owned house	Dormitory	Apartment	Apartment	Hospital	Apartment	Apartment	Apartment	Rough sleeping
Household / marital status	Family of birth / Husband (farmer)	Single (divorced)	Single	Single	Single	Single	Single	Single	Single
Occupation / income		Staff at daycare center	Staff at Sauna	Part-time cleaner at hotel	Public assistance (III)	Part-time cleaner along with public assistance	Part-time cleaner at hotel	Left job due to illness	
Age	25		30	32	34	34	36	49	50

Continued overleaf

Table 2.4: continued

Hospital	Free or low-rent housing facility
Single	Single
Public assistance	Public assistance
50	50

13. (Kazuko, 68 years) Graduated from middle school

Family of birth	Live-in employment	Apartment	Apartment	Home of friend	Rough sleeping	Hospital	Free or low-rent housing facility	Hospital	Free or low-rent housing facility
	Single	Single	Single	Single	Single	Single	Single	Single	Single
	Full-time company employee	Full-time employee (paid by day)	Part-time cleaner, more than one employer			Public assistance	Public assistance	Public assistance	Public assistance
	15	22	48	50	66	66	67	68	68

14. (80 years) Graduated from middle school

Apartment	Home of relative	Apartment	Rough sleeping	Hospital	Private nursing home

Family of birth	Hospital	Free or low-rent housing facility	Family of birth	Single	Husband (Government employee)	Single (divorced)	Single	Single	Single	Single	Single
Single	Single	Single	Helping family-operated business	Full-time employee at publishing company	Part-time employee at publishing company	Part-time employee at publishing company	Part-time employee at publishing company			Public assistance	Public assistance
Public assistance	Public assistance	Public assistance			During 30s						
78	79	79	15	15						78	78

15. (69 years) Graduated from elementary school

Family of birth	Live-in employment	Home of friend	Rough sleeping	Inn (ryokan)	Free or low-rent housing facility
Husband	Single (Husband deceased)	Single	Common-law husband (Carpenter)	Single (taking refuge from partner)	Single
Family-operated business	Various restaurants, etc.	Restaurant		Public assistance	Public assistance
20	27		59	69	69

Continued overleaf

Table 2.4: continued

16. (71 years) Graduated from middle school

Residence	Family status	Occupation / Income	Age
Family of birth			
Apartment	Husband (bank employee)	Full-time housewife (some part-time work)	26
Apartment	Single (Husband deceased)	Various restaurants	During 40s
Apartment	Single	Living on savings	66
Hospital	Single	Public assistance	71
Public nursing home	Single	Public assistance	71
Free or low-rent housing facility	Single	Public assistance	71

17. (65 years) Graduated from elementary school

Residence	Family status	Occupation / Income	Age
Privately-owned house	Family of birth		
Live-in employment	Single	Cook	12
Parents' home	Family of birth	Restaurant, makeup sales, etc.	17
Privately-owned house	Husband, Child, Mother-in-law	Full-time housewife	21
Dormitory	Single (divorced)	Cook	28
Apartment	Husband	Full-time housewife	30
Live-in employment	Single	Cook	30
Apartment	Husband (company employee)	Cook	31
Live-in employment	Single (divorced)	Waitress at inn (ryokan)	46
Privately-owned house			
Rough sleeping			
Hospital			
Apartment			

18 (Midori, 53 years) Graduated from middle school

Housing	Household	Occupation	Age
Privately-owned house	Family of birth		
Live-in employment	Single	Assistant nurse	17
Apartment	Single	Bar or nightclub hostess	18
Apartment	Husband, Child	Bar or nightclub hostess	25
Live-in employment	Single (taking refuge from partner)	Waitress at inn (ryokan)	41
Rough sleeping	Single		50
Apartment	Single	Public assistance	52
	Single	Patient care at hospital	59
	Single		62
	Single	Public assistance	63
	Single	Public assistance	63

19. (63 years) Graduated from middle school

Housing	Household	Occupation	Age
Privately-owned house	Family of birth		
Live-in employment	Single	Bar or nightclub hostess	18
Live-in employment	Husband		20
Live-in employment	Single (taking refuge from partner)	Bar or nightclub hostess	
Live-in employment	Husband (same profession)	Staff at pachinko parlor	43
Live-in employment	Single (taking refuge from partner)	Food preparation at various workers' barracks	49
Rough sleeping	Single		53
Live-in employment	Single	Food preparation at workers' barracks	53
Rough sleeping	Husband		54
Rough sleeping	Single (Husband deceased)		60

Continued overleaf

Table 2.4: continued

Temporary emergency facility	Relief Facility
Single	Single
	Public assistance
61	61

20 (Keiko, 49 years) Graduated from middle school

Privately-owned house	Dormitory	Live-in employment	Privately-owned house	Privately-owned house	Live-in employment	Rough sleeping	Rough sleeping	Rough sleeping	Hospital
Family of birth	Single	Single	Husband, Husband's family	Parents (divorced)	Single	Single	With male acquaintance	Single (taking refuge from partner)	Single
	Full-time company employee at factory	Various restaurants	Full-time housewife		Food preparation at various workers' barracks				
	14	15	23	24	29	37			46

Apartment
Single
Public assistance
46

21. (55 years) Graduated from high school

Privately-owned house	Privately-owned house	Privately-owned house	Live-in employment	Dormitory	Privately-owned house	Live-in employment	Rough sleeping	Rough sleeping
Family of birth	Husband, Child	Mother, older brother (divorced)	Single	Single	Mother, older brother	Single	Single	Husband
	Full-time housewife	Elderly home helper	Staff at pachinko parlor	Elderly home helper	Elderly home helper	Housekeeper		
	26	40		46		54	54	55

22. (30 years) Graduated from middle school

Foster home	Live-in employment	Rehabilitation Facility	Rough sleeping	Free or low-rent housing facility	Psychiatric hospital	Free or low-rent housing facility
Family of birth	Single	Single	Single	Single	Single	Single
Single	Various restaurants, etc.	Public assistance	Single	Public assistance	Public assistance	Public assistance
3	15			27	29	29

23. (36 years) Graduated from high school

Apartment	Apartment	Rough sleeping	Free or low-rent housing facility
Family of birth	Single	Child	Single (child in facility)
Single	Temp agency	Public	Public
Assistant			

Continued overleaf

Table 2.4: continued

(continued from previous case)

Occupation	Age
nurse	20
worker	21
assistance	34

24. (78 years) Graduated from elementary school

Residence	Lived with	Occupation / Income	Age
Rented home	Family of birth	Helping family-operated business	17
Older sister's home	Single	Helping family-operated business	30
Older brother's home	Mother	Various restaurants	34
Public housing	Mother	Various cleaning jobs	34
Live-in employment	Single	Waitress at inn (ryokan)	37
Prison	Single	Restaurant	48
Temporary emergency facility for elderly	Single		75
Women's consultation center	Single		75
Private nursing home	Single	Public assistance	75
Inn (ryokan)	Single	Public assistance	77
Free or low-rent housing facility	Single	Public assistance	77
Rough sleeping			
Rough sleeping			
Apartment			

25. (61 years) Graduated from middle school.

Residence	Lived with	Occupation	Age
Rented home	Family of birth	Printing factory	17
		Electrical equipment manufacturer	20
Rehabilitation Facility	Mother	Traveling sales	24
Prison	Single		
Rehabilitation Facility	Single	Food preparation	61
Privately-owned house	Mother	Cleaning	52
Public housing	Single	Food preparation	
Privately-owned house			
Apartment			
Rough sleeping			
Apartment			

Table (continued)

Housing	Family of birth	Family of birth	Family of birth	Inn (ryokan)	Apartment		Apartment	Public assistance
Relationship				Single	Husband	Single (divorced)	Husband	Single
Employment	Food manufacturing plant	Spinning plant	Bar or nightclub hostess		Part-time at inn (ryokan)	Part-time at inn (ryokan)		
Age			20	34	41	49	60	61

56. (70 years) Graduated from elementary school.

Housing	Live-in employment	Live-in employment	Apartment	Apartment		Live-in employment	Rough sleeping	Rough sleeping	Apartment
Relationship	Single	Single	Husband, Child	Child (Husband deceased)	Child	Single (Child deceased)	Single	Husband	Husband
Employment	Charcoal maker	Restaurant		Various construction businesses	Cook	Various construction and other jobs			Public assistance
Age	12	16	17	24		48	56	60	68

③ Homeless due to loss of relationships

27 (Aki) Graduated from high school.

Housing	Apartment	Apartment	Home of friend	Women's consultation center	Free or low-rent housing facility
Relationship	Family of birth	Husband (Full-time company employee)	Single (taking refuge from partner)	Single	Single
Employment	Full-time company	Full-time company		Single	Public assistance

Table 2.4: continued

(continued from previous page)

Occupation	employee	employee	employee, then left job due to illness		Single
Age	18	25	28	39	39
					39

28. (82 years) Graduated from elementary school

Age	Housing	Household	Occupation / income
19	Family of birth	Older sister's family	Babysitting
23	Privately-owned house	Husband (self-employed), Child	Full-time housewife
	Privately-owned house	Husband, Child	Housekeeper
39	Apartment	Husband	Housekeeper
75	Home owned by daughter	Husband, daughter's family	
80	Apartment	Son (Husband deceased)	Public assistance
81	Temporary emergency facility for elderly	Single (taking refuge from son)	
81	Free or low-rent housing facility	Single	Public assistance

29 (Eiko, 66 years) Graduated from elementary school

Age	Housing	Household	Occupation / income
Teens	Family of birth		Babysitting
Teens	Live-in employment	Single	Spinning plant
23	Live-in employment	Single	
Late 20s	Apartment	Husband (Carpenter)	Part-time work at factory
50	Apartment	Single	Part-time work, public assistance
53	Apartment	Older sister, older sister's child	Part-time work
53	Rough sleeping	Single	
63	Apartment	Single	Public assistance

30. (Tamako, 41 years) Graduated from middle school

Housing	Household	Work	Age
Privately-owned house	Family of birth	Full-time company employee (Hired under disability employment quota)	15
Privately-owned house	Family of birth	Part-time work at sewing factory	28
Privately-owned house	Family of birth	Part-time work at hospital cafeteria	35
Apartment	Husband	Part-time work at factory	29
Public housing	Husband	Part-time work as cleaner	
Inn (ryokan)	Single (taking refuge from partner)		32
Home of friend	Common-law husband		32
Rough sleeping	Common-law husband		35
Home of friend	Common-law husband		36
Rough sleeping	Common-law husband		36
Apartment	Common-law husband	Public assistance	38

31. (57 years) Educational history unknown

Housing	Household	Work	Age
Family of birth	Husband, Child	Full-time housewife	18
	Child (divorced)	Bar or nightclub hostess	35
Apartment	Husband, Child	Bar or nightclub hostess	42
Apartment	Husband, Child	Full-time housewife	54
Rough sleeping	Single		55
Apartment	Husband		56
Rough sleeping	Single		56
Apartment	Single	Public assistance	57

Continued overleaf

Table 2.4: continued

32. (80 years) Graduated from middle school

Family of birth	Dormitory			Dormitory	Apartment	Free or low-rent housing facility
Single	Single	Husband, Child	Mother, Father (Husband deceased)	Child (Husband deceased)	Older sister	Single
	Nurse			Nurse		Public assistance
		23				79

33. (45 years) Graduated from middle school

Privately-owned house	Privately-owned house	Live-in employment	Older sister's home	Women's consultation center	Free or low-rent housing facility	Apartment
Adoptive parents	Adoptive parents, husband	Single (divorced)	Older sister's family	Single	Single	Single
Bar or nightclub hostess	Part-time work	Restaurant			Public assistance	Restaurant
20	30	40	41	41	41	41

Note: For each subject the age at the time of interview is provided. Additionally the highest level of education completed is provided in brackets. Four rows of cells are used to show the life history of each woman. Row 1 shows the place or mode of residence; Row 2 shows any cohabitants; Row 3 shows any jobs held; and Row 4 shows the age when the person began this phase of life. Shaded areas indicate a condition of homelessness. Areas framed in bold lines indicate the presence of a male partner.

%

100
90
80 — ■ Married
70 — ■ Divorced or bereaved
60 — □ Never married
50
40
30
20
10

Women   Men
(*n* = 33)   (*n* =1,920)

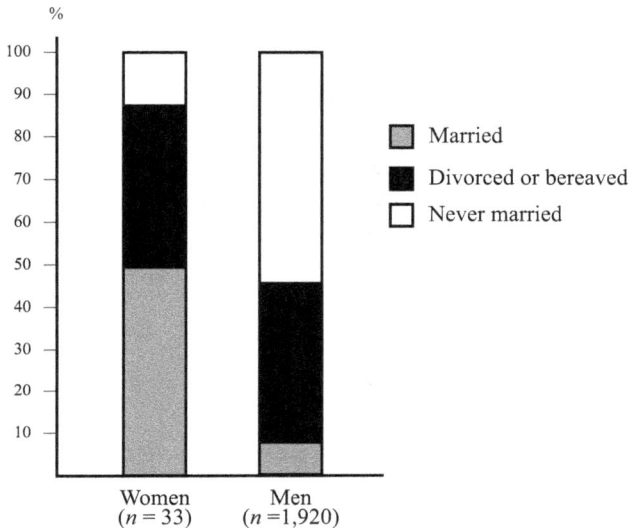

Figure 2.4: Marriage history of homeless men and women

Source of data for men: *Discussion of the National Survey on the Conditions of the Homeless,* (2007).

What is different about homeless women?

The average age of the thirty-three homeless women I spoke with was 59.0 years. Compared with the MHLW study, whose subjects averaged 57.5 years of age, my research subjects were slightly older, partly because it include women living in facilities.

A distinguishing feature of the female subjects of my study was that most of them (90%) had been married (including common-law marriage); while over half of the male subjects of the MHLW study had never been married. Of my subjects who had been married, more than half had been married more than once (Figure 2.4). This large number of marriages suggests that for women, having a male partner is one tactic for supporting one's livelihood. Also distinctive was that nineteen women, more than half the total, had been married but had no children. Poor households are often thought to be multi-child households, but the preponderance of childlessness among homeless women is probably due to two reasons. First, women with children are likely to be reluctant to leave home even when their relationship

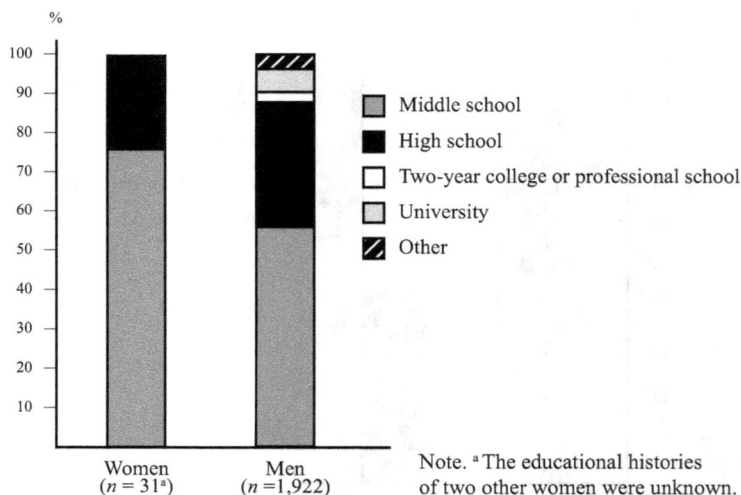

Figure 2.5: Educational history of homeless men and women

Source: Data for men is from MHLW, *National Survey on the Conditions of the Homeless*, 2007.

with their husband is poor; second, women with minor children are eligible for welfare support, and may receive support from their children once they become adults. A further distinction is that while homeless people, in general, have low levels of education, for women it is even lower than for men, with more than half having no more than a middle school education (Figure 2.5).

In terms of work history, while some women's first employment after graduation from school was as a regular company employee, the majority started in part-time or other low-paying, unstable jobs (Table 2.4). Experience working as part-time cleaning staff, as hostesses in bars or other entertainment venues, as resident workers at inns, or serving food at workers' residences, was particularly common.

Twenty-six of the thirty-three women had experienced rough sleeping, but, as women who seek welfare payments can usually obtain them, most of their rough-sleeping experiences were relatively short-lived.

Previous studies of rough sleepers have generally looked at the process of exclusion leading to rough sleeping, focusing on work as an indicator of downward social mobility. For example, Iwata, looking at changes in work and residence in tandem, divided the process of exclusion by which males become rough sleepers into three categories: rapid descent, long-term exclusion, and workers' housing (Iwata 2008). However, using work history as an indicator of social mobility is inherently geared towards working males, and is not appropriate for analyzing women's experiences.[12] Hence, to understand the specific nature of exclusion experienced by women, one must consider not only work but also family relationships when looking at the life histories of women who become homeless. By looking at the main factors directly leading to the loss of home for these thirty-three women,[13] their situations can be categorized into three types:

1. Homelessness through husband's unemployment: both members of a couple become homeless when the husband loses his job.
2. Individual unemployment: a single woman becomes homeless due to her own unemployment.
3. Loss of relationships: a woman becomes homeless after the loss of a relationship with her husband, family, or others.

Of the thirty-three women examined in this study, eleven were type 1, fifteen were type 2, and seven were type 3. I will present specific cases of each of these categories in the analysis that follows.

The exclusion of women: some cases

(1) Unemployment of husband
This pattern consists of a cohabiting couple becoming homeless when the husband loses his job. It closely matches the path of exclusion experienced by homeless men that has been portrayed in previous research. The husband often works in the construction industry, the classic type of work for men who become rough sleepers. The majority of male rough sleepers have either never married or are divorced, but the women in this category become homeless without divorcing. Because many of these women experience poverty before becoming homeless, many worked along with their husbands, but it was the unemployment of the husband, the main household provider, that led to the loss of home.

Case 1: Sumiko (Table 2.4; other cases likewise)
Sumiko is seventy years old and walks with a limp due to leg problems (she is certified as having Grade 5 disability on a 7-point scale, with 1 the most severe). At around the end of elementary school,

her father remarried, and she lived for a period with her stepmother and step-sibling(s). Shortly after that, she became a trainee at a relative's barbershop. Under pressure to marry against her will, she left home and moved around, working as a live-in nanny and at other jobs. She then married. Her husband had been married previously and brought his two children to the household. Sumiko worked part-time. Later, her husband was imprisoned. Unhappy with having to raise her husband's children in his absence, Sumiko left home on her own. She then took a live-in job at an inn. At age forty-two, she met her current husband and moved into a small apartment. Her husband was a construction worker and Sumiko worked part-time to supplement their income. For a time, they both worked at a worker's residence; he worked on-site while she worked in the kitchen. However, her husband found less and less work as he got older, and they repeatedly borrowed money to cover expenses. Falling behind in payments, they left home together to live in the streets.

Sumiko, with a low level of education and a poor relationship with her immediate family, wishing to leave home quickly, took a variety of live-in jobs during her first working period. Her second husband was a construction worker, the classic unstable job for men. The two of them, both living unstable lives, met and began living together. This is a common marriage pattern for homeless women, including some who meet their partner after becoming rough sleepers.

(2) Loss of one's own job

Whereas homelessness caused by a husband's unemployment (Pattern 1) resembles that of homeless men, this pattern is distinctly female in character; it involves a woman living alone who becomes homeless after losing her job. It includes women who remain unmarried throughout life as well as women who become single through death or divorce, with the latter more numerous. Jobs that can be filled by middle-aged or older women tend to be low-paying and unstable, but this pattern is also distinguished by many women managing, despite this, to survive on a low income for long periods. Since these jobs are not usually covered by unemployment insurance or the Employer's Pension Fund, women who become unable to work due to illness or age can suddenly find themselves homeless. Some women in this category suffer from mental illness or mild intellectual disabilities, making them susceptible to conflicts with others and unable to hold a job for long.

Case 13: Kazuko

Kazuko is sixty-eight. After finishing middle school, she worked as a regular employee at a glass factory. At twenty-two she switched to working at a photo album manufacturing company where she was paid daily, with no unemployment insurance or pension plan. She rented an apartment while working at this company for twenty-six years. However, it became difficult to get by without any pay raises, so she quit and instead combined two part-time cleaning jobs, with a friend helping to cover the rent. Her friend invited her to move in with her to save money on rent, so she stayed with this friend's family while continuing the part-time jobs. She lived this way for about ten years. Dismissed from her job due to her old age, she was no longer comfortable staying with her friend's family, from whom she had borrowed large amounts of money, so she began rough sleeping. She has never married.

Case 21: A

A is fifty-five. After graduating from high school, she stayed at her family home helping with housework. At twenty-six she married a man who worked at a general trading company and had three children. A lived very comfortably as a full-time housewife. However, her husband focused only on work and neglected his family. Problems including the bullying of her children and her husband's infidelity contributed to a nervous breakdown, and she divorced at age forty. The children stayed with her husband and she returned to her own family. Living with her mother and older brother, she started work as a home helper for the elderly. Subsequently, she left to be a residential worker at a pachinko (pinball/slot machine) parlor, then left that job to be a live-in helper at a dormitory. Interpersonal problems at the dormitory led her to return to her family. However, neighborly disapproval and other problems made staying at home uncomfortable, so she left to be a live-in maid. She became a rough sleeper after losing this job.

While Kazuko never married, A began living alone after getting divorced. Kazuko tried to change jobs when she was nearly fifty, but, unable to find work, she managed to get by combining part-time cleaning jobs. After that, she began staying at her friend's home. Because women are generally equipped with housekeeping and other life skills, many of them resort to living at their parents' home or staying with friends or relatives.

By contrast, A enjoyed a comfortable life with her husband, an elite company employee, but her divorce plunged her suddenly into an insecure existence. As a full-time housewife with little work experience, the few types of work available to A were equivalent to the work of a housewife, namely, home care, domestic help, and the like. She probably could have returned to her family home after losing her job, but she chose to sleep rough instead, suggesting that her parents' home was not a comfortable place for her to be.

(3) Loss of relationships
Along with pattern 2, loss of employment, the other classic pattern of homelessness for women involves poor relationships with family members. Many women flee physical abuse from their husbands, but some suffer violence from other family members. This pattern leads to the most sudden, dramatic life change, because the victim loses both income and residence at the same time.

Case 31: B
B is fifty-seven. After leaving high school without graduating, she got a job as a regular employee at a textile factory. At eighteen she married a man who worked at a company involved with computers, and became a housewife. She had four children. At thirty-five she divorced, left home with her children, and began working in the bar and hostess industry. After three years she opened her own, independent business. At forty-two, she remarried, to a man working for a machinery manufacturer, and commenced living with her children in an apartment. Since she continued to run her business, that income, combined with her husband's, supported a comfortable life. At fifty-four, health problems forced her to close her business. She had long endured psychological abuse from her husband, so when she stopped working and her youngest child got married, she left home. For some time she stayed in hotels and saunas, but when she ran out of money she moved to the streets.

Case 28: C
C is eighty-two years old. She walks with a cane due to leg problems. After graduating from elementary school, she helped at her older

sister's home doing babysitting, housework, and the like. Because she didn't go to school for long, to this day she is a poor reader. At twenty-three, she married a builder and had two children. C became a full-time housewife enjoying a stable life in her own home. However, at forty-five her husband was incapacitated by illness and required nursing care. From then on, she lived off her husband's disability pension. C worked as a housekeeper to support the family budget, but insufficient income forced them to sell their house and move into an apartment. At seventy-five, she and her husband moved into their daughter's home, but her husband's care and other issues placed too high a burden on their relationship with their daughter's family, so after her husband's death, C moved to her son's home. Because her son received public assistance due to mental illness, with C's pension they were able to make ends meet. However, physical abuse from her son forced C to seek emergency temporary shelter at a facility for the elderly. Having no place to go after that, she entered a facility (see Chapter 4).

B left home due to her husband's abuse, and C due to her son's abuse. Escaping from violence often means, as in B's case, the simultaneous loss of income, shelter, and friendships, and having to rebuild from scratch in a separate place; many hardships result. To make matters worse, because B had to go into hiding to avoid being tracked down by her husband, she faced persistent obstacles to rebuilding her life, such as having to go by an assumed name and being unable to obtain a residence card.

Because C had little schooling, she is functionally illiterate. Although this difficulty may not be obvious in the context of casual social interaction, the fact is that among women who had little education and grew up in poverty, the number who cannot read proficiently is amazingly high. Not only are such women limited in the types of work they can obtain, they also lack adequate access to information about welfare and other programs available to them.

Of the various ways that women fall into homelessness, patterns 2, loss of own employment by women who lack a breadwinning male partner, and 3, loss of relationships, are paths of exclusion unique to women. In pattern 2, loss of one's own job, because the labor market limits most jobs for women to low-paying and unstable ones, those women cited in this study who remained unmarried or lost their husband by death or divorce were unable to get a regular job. They lived austere lives in small apartments while working part-time. Other women took residential jobs. When they lost their job due to illness or old age, they became homeless. As noted before, because most of the jobs such women work at do not participate in the Employer's Pension Fund or unemployment insurance, illness and old age led directly to homelessness. In pattern 3, loss of relationships, women left home to escape serious conflicts in the family, including violence. Even if they had lived comfortably up to that point, the loss of the main breadwinner plunged them into sudden poverty. As can be seen, the life histories of homeless women, particularly single women, clearly reveal the structural disadvantages suffered by women in a sexist society.

Furthermore, supporting the claim that women are susceptible to hidden homelessness, many women, unable to live independently, had been forced to stay in the homes of parents and friends. Because women often are skilled in housekeeping and other tasks, it is probably easier for women than for men to find people to stay with. A wide range of living facilities for women also exist, and prominent in this study were women who moved around in various states of homelessness other than rough sleeping, by staying with acquaintances or in such facilities. This is one of the clear distinguishing features of homelessness in women.

The problem of women's homelessness

As this chapter has demonstrated, when the definition of homelessness is expanded to include not only rough sleepers but all those lacking a fixed place to live, the term applies to many women. Homelessness is not a problem for men alone. Further, the homelessness of women, particularly single women with no families, has been shown to involve a distinctive process of exclusion.

The sexual division of labor, under which men do paid labor and women do domestic labor, determines not only the division of work roles within the family, but also the structure of the labor market; for this reason, women have little choice but to take unstable, low-paying jobs. As we have seen, this makes it difficult for single women to make a living, and was a major factor leading women into homelessness.

One reason that few women are rough sleepers, despite a social structure that leaves single women susceptible to poverty, is that because of the difficulty women have making a living independently, it is hard for women to escape from home. Another reason is that there are more welfare programs available for women living in poverty without a male breadwinner than there are for men. These help to sustain women's livelihood despite the stigma they bring and the low level of support they provide.

The difference between homelessness in men and women, then, is strongly determined by the welfare system. When homelessness is understood broadly as the lack of a fixed place to live, it is the welfare system that determines what sort of person is taken up by that system and what sort of person is left out on the streets. In the next chapter, I will look at the historical development of the welfare system, and how it came to create different outcomes for men and women.

3 Establishing welfare for homeless women

Policies on homelessness

Social welfare was originally developed to defeat poverty. As society grew richer overall, however, the main object of social welfare changed: originally directed towards certain poor people, it came to encompass the welfare of all citizens, particularly groups such as the elderly. But if poverty at one time seemed on the verge of defeat in the post-World War II period, it has recently bounded back in new forms described by such terms as "working poor" and "Internet café refugees." In the context of this postwar period, this chapter will conduct a historical review of how the Japanese government has dealt with poverty and intervened in the lives of poor people, tracing the lineage of these programs through to the present day.

Welfare policies do more than provide aid to combat poverty. They also have a structural function, defining poverty by selecting from a variety of conditions and situations. The social welfare system thus determines whether a person is "poor" or not. Those people deemed worthy of aid are supported, while those deemed not worthy are excluded. This chapter will consider the axis that defines this separation, for this axis of separation is indicative of the public standards for what sort of life is considered desirable. Social welfare, as an aggregate of normative values, is directed not only at the poor, but everyone. It is a social system that, by categorizing people as meeting or failing to meet normative standards, regulates life in society as a whole.

The central welfare system for addressing poverty today is public assistance (*seikatsu hogo*). Under this system, all citizens whose standard of living is below the minimum level are equally eligible to receive benefits, and there is no screening of beneficiaries to assess their merit based on some moral standard. However, as suggested by the reported 20% capture ratio (the share of poor families living below the minimum standard of living who receive public assistance),[1] assistance is not being provided equally and indiscriminately to all who live in poverty. In particular, benefits are severely restricted for those of working age, with some potential recipients turned away before they can even apply, and others subjected to investigation of their moral character.

The classic example of this unequal awarding of benefits is in the treatment of homeless people with no fixed residence. This category of homelessness includes not only rough sleepers, but those in a broad range of insecure situations who sleep in simple hostels, workers' dormitories, and Internet cafés, or who lodge temporarily in hospitals or other facilities without having a place to which they can return. The postwar welfare system went from being a selective anti-poverty campaign exclusively for poor people, to seeking to improve the welfare of all citizens. Its implementation came to be based on the classification of persons according to their affiliations, such as nationality, registered domicile, and work unit. However, since poverty can be accompanied by the loss of a residence, job, and other such affiliations, as the welfare state continued to grow, such homeless individuals became subject to special treatment that differed from typical anti-poverty programs such as public assistance, and this put them at risk of being excluded.

Iwata Masami's 1995 study gives an excellent account of the development of government policies towards these homeless persons. Iwata conducted a survey of historical measures taken in Tokyo after World War II to address "poverty with the lack of a fixed residence." By investigating these policies in the context of their historical precedents and in relation to general welfare policies, she revealed how the hidden assumption behind the postwar welfare system – namely, that an individual has a fixed residence and a family and work affiliation – became normalized (Iwata 1995). My own work for this book owes much to Iwata's rich, provocative work. And since the normalization of a particular life pattern by social welfare has forced those who deviate from it into a long-term disadvantaged position, expanding social inequality, Iwata's focus on the exclusionary function of welfare is even more relevant today, when poverty and inequality are under the spotlight.

There is, however, one problem with Iwata's arguments: they do not engage with gender issues. This is due to Iwata's focus on understanding the type of homelessness addressed by government policies on "vagrant persons," which in practice meant focusing on policies directed towards men, who make up the majority of those living in the streets. Homeless women were therefore excluded. This in itself reflects the gendering of the welfare state. In a society based on the sexual division of labor, the status of women in the labor market remains low. As a result, various forms of welfare have developed that guarantee only a minimum standard of living for women who lack a male partner as the main wage earner. They have evolved to perform the function of taking in women suffering from poverty and the loss of a home just before they are forced into rough sleeping. From this comes the tendency for women, because they stay in facilities of some sort, to become "hidden homeless." Furthermore, in most cases, these policies have belonged to a separate framework from those directed at "vagrant persons." To understand the homelessness of women, therefore, it is necessary to investigate systems other than those concerned with "vagrant persons."

Keeping the above points in mind, in this chapter I will examine government responses to homelessness by looking at policies and facilities that are directed at women. On this basis I will seek to identify the axes that are used to classify poor women for policy purposes. Because a similar analysis of policies for postwar Tokyo prefecture has already been conducted by Kawahara Keiko (Kawahara 2005), in this chapter I will instead use data from Osaka prefecture[2]. A more detailed analysis of these cases remains to be done; here I will make a historic overview of the position in which poor women have been placed.

Prewar government policies

General policies for homelessness

Although general government policies for homeless poverty before World War II were not specifically restricted according to gender, it is safe to say that, as today, most were targeted at men. Records often fail to indicate the gender of beneficiaries, but some include entries referring to women and families.

The first universal poverty policy enacted after Japan became a modern nation-state (1868) was set in the Poor Relief Regulations (*Jikkyū kisoku*) of 1874. Because the expectation was for individuals to rely on mutual aid from families and local communities, only those who had no access to such aid were eligible for benefits, namely, the ill, elderly, children, and others who could not work. However, because aid was only given to persons registered in a household, homeless poor were not included. Such persons were given assistance only when they collapsed on the roadside, under the "fallen passerby" policy.

These limited national policies had to be supplemented by local initiatives. In Osaka prefecture a large Poorhouse was built in 1871 to house rough sleepers and other persons with no relatives to help them. Regulations on Medical Aid for the Poor were issued in Osaka prefecture in 1881 and on Aid for the Needy and Medical Aid for the Poor in Osaka city in 1889. These provided relief for persons not covered under the Poor Relief Regulations, mainly poor persons suffering from illness. At the private level, in 1881 Kobayashi Sahē established the Kobayashi Workhouse, which took in the sick, the handicapped, disaster victims, and rough sleepers, training those who were capable of working. The workhouse was large, initially housing 190 residents, and rising to nearly 400 after relocation to Komatsubara. The number of "beggars" in Osaka city reportedly decreased dramatically after the workhouse was opened. Initially more than half of the users were women, but the share of men grew over time.

At the time, the rapid swelling of slums in Osaka prefecture, such as Nagomachi, with an influx of migrants from the countryside attracted widespread attention as a social problem. Beginning in the 1910s, the prefecture opened workers' lodgings affiliated with employment agencies in the belief that public safety and a secure supply of labor required identifying those migrants who could make useful workers and placing them in "facilities free of bad influences from vagrants and persons without a home" (Osaka Prefecture, Social Affairs Section 1920: 390). The Rice Riots of 1918 led to implementing such social projects on a much larger scale.

The city government of Osaka, anticipating a national trend, established a Social Affairs Department to help contain social unrest. Among the many projects it undertook, the main one directed at homeless poverty was opening communal lodgings to supplement the workers' lodgings. These were cheap public accommodations intended as alternatives to the cheap inns known as *kichin yado*, which were considered to be of inferior quality and subversive to social order. They were used mainly by single male workers, but some also accepted families. The Imamiya Shelter was established as a communal lodging specifically for "persons without a home including vagrants found in parks and elsewhere, beggars, and unemployed persons" (Osaka City Office, Social Affairs Department 1923: 44); the number of rough sleepers in the city of Osaka dropped dramatically after it was established. Hard-working families in these communal lodgings had the option of moving to special city-run housing. Social work projects prioritized workers and families from their inception, while measures for rough sleepers belonged to a different category. This remains the case today.

In the private sector, in 1912, the Osaka Kōsaiin Hospital was established as a successor to the Osaka Jikei Hospital and the Kobayashi Workhouse, which had provided medical care to the poor. Kōsaiin Hospital conducted a variety of activities, including medical care, vocational training, and childcare. The Osaka Jikyōkan Social Welfare Corporation was opened in 1912 by Nakamura Mitsunori, a former police officer. Jikyōkan was an inexpensive lodging for workers that catered to individuals, the majority male, but including a very small number of women. It continues to provide large facilities for rough sleepers in Kamagasaki and elsewhere, In 1920, the Kōjōryō hostel was opened for families within Jikyōkan. In addition, the Osaka Poor Relief Association was founded in 1931 to take in rough sleepers from parks and other places.

The Poor Relief Law was passed in 1929 to replace the 1874 Poor Relief Regulations, creating a universal framework for aid to the poor. This law made far more people eligible for aid than the previous Regulations. However, the law maintained a strong pre-modern flavor, denying help to those who were fit to work regardless of circumstances, denying any "right" to claim benefits, and revoking the voting rights of aid recipients. Conversely, special consideration was given to certain cases of poverty, such as victims of accidents and natural disasters, which were considered to be unavoidable and hence treated with a certain generosity. Soldiers and their families were also given special treatment. The 1904 Imperial Edict on Relief for the Families of Non-Commissioned Officers and Common Soldiers was enacted during the Russo-Japanese War, and during World War I the Military Relief Law was passed. The level of benefits provided under these laws was nearly double that for other recipients of aid or for single-mother families. Soldiers were valuable to the nation-state and thus protected.

Policies for single-mother families

The poverty policies discussed above were not limited by gender, but the first measures specifically targeting women provided assistance to mothers and their children. The first of these in Osaka Prefecture was the Osaka Home of Orphans, opened in 1904, the year of the outbreak of the Russo-Japanese War, by Kashima Toshirō using his personal funds. It had a nursery (daycare center) and temporary lodgings for the families of soldiers serving on the front. Its lodgers were families who had lost their main wage earner due to the war. Many charitable institutions during the Meiji period were aimed at children, and these new facilities supported mothers as an extension of their services for children.

Nurseries or daycare centers were another type of facility that cared for mothers and children. The shelter for mothers and children that was opened in 1922 at the Futaba Nursery School is well known, but the Izuo Aijien nursery in Osaka prefecture had already begun taking in mothers and children in 1918. In providing nursery care for the children of working families, the Izuo Aijien encountered children of female-headed households in truly horrific circumstances, such as victims of parent-child murder-suicides brought on by poverty, or children suffering stunted growth due to malnutrition. For this reason, the Seppukan, a shelter for mothers and children, was added to the nursery, providing lodgings, work introductions, and other services. The facility was initially supposed to be for families who had lost the father through death or abandonment, but in reality,

> Some have been transferred here from police stations and government offices; this includes mothers and children found wandering the streets at night; vagrant children whose families were being sought in their hometowns; and families who had been taken into shelters after the father's imprisonment plunged them into sudden poverty. Ordinary widows are a minority of the cases. (Izuo Aijien 1919: 15)

In other words, a more diverse group of mothers and children used the facility. The aim in providing support was to encourage

> Remarriage for those who desire it, and chaste behavior for those who do not or who have a husband; protecting women from falling

into immorality due to despair; and improving their condition both
materially and spiritually. (Izuo Aijien 1919: 15)

In other words, the marriage system was taken as given, and chaste
behavior was called for to prevent deviation from the norm.

In Japan in the 1920s, economic recession led to widespread
poverty. Female-headed families were hit especially hard. Prompted
by an unending stream of reports of mother-child suicide-murders,
concerned individuals launched a movement to demand a Mother-
Child Protection Act (or Mother's Pension Act). The government,
too, began to consider establishing such a law, but with the passage of
the 1929 Relief and Protection Law, the idea was taken off the table
on the grounds that the Relief and Protection Law made provisions
for single mothers and their children. However, eligibility for aid was
limited strictly to pregnant women, new mothers, and women with
children less than a year old. To compensate for these inadequate
policies, private organizations in Osaka prefecture expanded their
relief services for mothers and children. The Hakuaisha Orphanage
in Osaka opened the Naruo Mother's House to lodge mothers
and their children. The next year, in 1930, the Osaka Home of
Orphans also opened a Mother-Child Protection Section to begin
accommodating mothers and children full-time. Two years later, the
Han'ai shelter was opened for mothers and children.

At the beginning of the Shōwa period (1926–1989), financial panic
led to deteriorating economic conditions. As the situation of the poor
became more and more desperate, there were widespread efforts
to pass a Mother-Child Protection Act to improve the conditions
of the proletarian class, primarily by the Social Democratic Party.
However, continued persecution by authorities forced this movement
to greatly scale back. The movement for a Mother-Child Protection
Act eventually became subsumed as an element of the women's
suffrage movement.

At the time, the high number of mother-child suicides drew the
attention of many women and convinced many of the need for a
social movement to protect "motherhood" by campaigning for
a "Motherhood Protection Act," another term for a Mother-Child
Protection Act. From the perspective of the women's suffrage
movement, this was an essential way to attract more women
supporters. In response to these efforts, the Women's Federation
for Promotion of the Motherhood Protection Act was formed as a

grand coalition of women's groups, and the Motherhood Protection Movement went into full force.

This movement was informed by an extreme ideology of "motherhood" that viewed the protection of "motherhood" or "maternity" (*bosei*) as essential to the liberation of women. A Mother-Child Protection Act was finally passed in 1937, but its provisions were not what the movement had sought. The law applied to women without a spouse caring for children thirteen and under. While this expanded the eligibility criteria of the 1929 Poor Relief Law, the financial support provided was barely changed. By contrast, payments to female-headed households under the Military Relief Law, which applied to the families of military personnel who died in service, were nearly twice as much. Further, the law contained an eligibility test, stipulating that: "no aid will be provided to mothers unsuited to raising children due to their character, actions, or other reasons." In short, the law was established purely as a poverty relief measure that was not to damage the family system; mothers who were rated as failing to meet moral standards were excluded from its purview. The Mother-Child Protection Act has been severely criticized for being founded on the idea that protecting motherhood was essential for achieving women's liberation. This idea, which united the movement to get the act passed, helped to create a normative system that imposed the mothering role on women (Imai 2004).

Following the passage of the Mother-Child Protection Act, the number of facilities for lodging mothers and children increased in Osaka prefecture and elsewhere. The first public shelter built was the Mother-Child Home that was added to the Taishō Civic Hall in 1937 to replace the Seppukan of the Izuo Aijien, mentioned earlier. As the national climate turned more warlike, the need for mother-child facilities to help the families of solders increased. To house the widows of soldiers and their families, the city-run Sumiyoshi Mother-Child Home and the Isao House Abeno were opened in 1938 and the Isao House Jōhoku in 1939. In the private sector, the Kōtoku-ji temple Zenrinkan Mother-Child Home opened the Yao (city) Zenrinkan in 1941 to house and care for mothers and children who worked at the employment project there. Facilities for the families of soldiers proliferated in the private realm as well; in 1937 the Hakuaisha Orphanage opened a new mother-child home, the Malta Home, for the families of soldiers at the front. Such mother-child facilities for the families of soldiers are described as being far superior to facilities catering to the ordinary female-headed households that were the targets of the Mother-Child Protection Act.

Policies for single women living alone

Measures targeting single women living alone originated separately from those aimed at mothers with children. The first facility built in Osaka prefecture for individual women was the Osaka Women's Home, opened in 1907. Starting with the Russo-Japanese War, Japan commenced an all-out effort to compete economically with the Western powers, which created a strong demand for factory workers, mainly for heavy industry. As a result, cities came to be full of people from the countryside seeking work. The Osaka branch of the Christian Women's Reform Society, led by Hayashi Utako, to protect such women from danger and temptation, resolved to "create facilities providing job introductions, job brokerage services, and personal advice" (Christian Women's Reform Society, Osaka Branch 1929: 4), and opened the Osaka Women's Home on Nakanoshima island. At the local station, this organization offered advice and job introductions (to work as maids and in other positions) to women who had just arrived in Osaka, as well as providing lodging.

The Osaka Women's Home was the third facility in the country aimed at individual women, having been preceded in Tokyo prefecture by the Crittenton Jiaikan, founded by the Christian Women's Reform Society, and the Kyūsaisho, founded by the Salvation Army. Christian organizations like these played a central role in the then-burgeoning anti-prostitution movement. One aim of this movement was to give support to women to get out of prostitution. Consequently, the two Tokyo facilities proclaimed their main goal to be saving women from prostitution; by contrast, the Osaka Women's Home was unique for its time in having a stated goal of promoting women's economic independence, by offering help to all women seeking work.

The Christian Women's Reform Society and the Salvation Army have been praised for their anti-prostitution movement and for supporting women to leave the trade. At the same time, anti-prostitution activists have been criticized for their condescending attitude towards their clients, as indicated in phrases like "women of an immoral profession." Further, because the movement treated monogamous marriage as the ideal, "it was conducted, not so much from the point of view of the prostitutes themselves, as from an ideology of "motherhood" that stuck to the ideal for women of "good wife, wise mother" (*ryōsai kenbo*) (Fujime 1997: 302). With hardly any public policies in place to help poor women, it was undoubtedly beneficial for women to volunteer to help prostitutes get out of the trade. However, there was also an insurmountable gap in social class between the volunteers and the women who were forced into prostitution by poverty.[3]

The Osaka Women's Home was not explicitly a facility for helping prostitutes, though. Rather, its job introduction service was intended "to work for the happiness of families and the benefit of society by helping prevent women in the prime of youth from losing their way in life" (Christian Women's Reform Society, Osaka Branch, 1937: 5). This approach was consistent with a sexual morality that aimed to support and protect the married life of chaste young women from good families. As time went on, however, it began to declare rescuing prostitutes to be its central mission. Hayashi Utako, a leader of the anti-prostitution movement, was a resident of the Women's Home, and the headquarters of the Osaka branch of the Christian Women's Reform Society was based there. Thus, the Women's Home had come to function as a base for the movement.

The anti-prostitution movement in Osaka gathered new momentum, capitalizing on the destruction by fire of the Sonezaki brothel district in 1909 and the Nanba Shinchi brothel district in 1912. However, as contemporary records of those admitted to the Osaka Women's Home show, help was provided to a wide variety of women in poverty. Those admitted included not only prostitutes seeking to leave the business but a broad range of women, including job-hunters, women who were pregnant or had recently given birth, single-mother families, rough sleepers, and apparent victims of domestic violence (see Table 3.1).

In fact, the help given to prostitutes at the Osaka Women's Home was only cursory; this activity was really the province of a different organization, the Japan Rescue Mission. The Japan Rescue Mission was founded by English missionaries to give aid to Japanese prostitutes, and first came to Osaka prefecture in 1927 after successfully establishing a relief organization for women in Sendai. The Rescue Mission began helping prostitutes from the Tobita brothel district to leave their work. They would first take refuge at the Osaka Women's Home and then be released to the

Table 3.1: Persons admitted to Osaka Women's Home in a single year

Reason for admission	Number
Came to Osaka to find work	79
Left home	
Attracted by the city	5
Had falling-out with husband	10
Had falling-out with family	11
Other reasons	11
Ran away from "shameful profession"	43
Left to avoid being sold into prostitution	3
Became pregnant accidentally	5
Arrived after wandering with no destination	6
Came to cultivate her mind	10
Came to find a place to stay	18
Lost work as a maid due to illness or other reason	3
Came because of a court trial	1
Infants or children accompanied by mother	13
Infants born this year at the Home	3
Total	221

Source: Osaka Women's Home, 1934.

Rescue Mission, where they were shielded from their employers. Originally, the Mission worked from a series of private homes, but in 1932, to prevent women from being pursued by their employers, a Jiaikan facility was opened in the remote area of Mozu and activities were significantly expanded. However, prostitutes were regarded as "fallen women" and the aim of the Rescue Mission was to preach Christianity to them, giving the project a strong flavor of proselytizing from a position of class privilege. Moreover, about this time at the Osaka Women's Home the practice became established of sending prostitutes to the Rescue Mission and mothers with children to the Hakuaisha. This cooperation between organizations led to the sorting of women based on their type of poverty and their family structure.

However, this situation was short-lived. In 1940, with the signing of the Tripartite Pact between Japan, Germany, and Italy, England became an enemy country and English missionaries returned home immediately, ending the Rescue Mission's activities. The remaining Japanese employees of the Rescue Mission built an annex to the Osaka Women's Home in Ibaraki city. They continued to care for the women who remained but, as the war intensified, were unable to take on new clients. In 1945, the main Osaka Women's Home was also relocated to Ibaraki to escape the firebombing of the city, and activities were further scaled down.

Postwar government policy

General policies for homelessness

At the war's end in 1945, all of Japan was engulfed in poverty. The air raids on the city of Osaka had left many people without homes, and the streets were full of rough sleepers, repatriates from abroad, the unemployed, and war widows. Firebombing victims, orphans, repatriates, and others camped out in the Osaka station area. With the influx of people from other regions their number reached 30,000. To cope with this problem, numerous new shelter facilities were constructed between 1946 and 1947.

According to the Osaka city government, these "shelters for vagrant persons and simple hostels could be roughly grouped into four categories" (Osaka City, 1966: 310–311): inexpensive hostel facilities for single male laborers; facilities for single male rough sleepers that provide guidance for living and employment to enable "independence and a fresh start" within three months; sick and elderly rough sleepers who were placed in the Kōsaiin or in hospitals; and families, serviced by the Family Kōseiryō shelter, a low-rent lodging facility intended to help achieve "independence and a fresh start" as quickly as possible. Facilities such as the Sekimeryō shelter were also opened for repatriate families.

As these categories show, in the chaotic postwar period, people were already being classified on the basis of ability to work and type of family. However, because these city-run facilities were inadequate for dealing with the growing numbers of poor who lacked housing, the prefectural and city governments turned some of them over to the care of private organizations that had been aiding the poor since before the war. "Vagrant mothers and children" were sent to places like the Holy Family Home, which had been providing settlement support since before the war.

The main entity providing guidance and protection services to the rough sleepers in the Osaka station area was the Citizens' Consultation Office, which had been housed within the station grounds during the war. Beginning in 1946 this office began housing people temporarily, taking in "vagrants." These persons were categorized as "children," "vagrant men," "vagrant women," "mothers with children," "suffering from (regular) illness," "suffering from tuberculosis," "elderly," and "suffering from mental illness," and sent to the appropriate facility. At the end of March 1948, there were some 19,649 such persons, over half of whom were adult males, and about 20% of whom were adult females, some with children. In 1949 the Consultation Office was renamed the Umeda Kōseikan and expanded its role to become the intake facility, not only for "vagrants," but for everyone needing protection services within the city of Osaka, providing temporary shelter and classifying them according to the above categories. This system of centralized administration later became known as the "Osaka method." From here, individuals were sent to a wide range of places, such as juvenile facilities, workers' lodgings, or hospitals. Women, if accompanied by children, would go to Mother-Child Homes like the Akagawa Home or the Yao Rinpokan. Unaccompanied women were sent to protection and Rehabilitation Facilities for prostitutes such as the Chōkōryō or the Seibiryō.

New policies on poverty were enshrined in the (former) Public Assistance Act, passed in 1946, which was replaced by a new Public Assistance Act in 1950. The latter reflected the same ideals as the new Constitution of Japan of 1947. The Public Assistance Act was highly progressive compared to previous policies in that it made all persons suffering economic hardship at or below a certain level eligible for benefits, equally and without discrimination, and entitled them to apply for these benefits with no eligibility test of ability to work or personal morality. For poor and homeless people, basic policies for applying for and receiving benefits in their current location were specified. Public Assistance Facilities were classified into five types, including Rehabilitation Facilities, Relief Facilities, and lodging facilities. In the following year, 1951, the Osaka city government determined that "the period of emergency measures to care for vagrant persons has nearly come to an end." With this, the city began to reorganize and upgrade the "varied multitude" of facilities that had been created ad hoc after the war for rounded-up "vagrants" and people in desperate need of accommodation. As of 1955, the city of Osaka had established a system of "lodging and protection facilities" (Osaka City 1966: 312) as follows: six facilities for rehabilitation, including the Umeda Kōseikan, the Kōsaiin, the Mikuni Family Home (converted from a Mother-Child Home), and the Sekime Family Home (converted from a home for repatriates); six lodging facilities, including the Kōkyō family home; and two simple hostels. These facilities, apart from the Kōseikan, the Kōsaiin, and the three family homes, accommodated single males almost exclusively.

In the 1960s, rough sleepers in Osaka prefecture increasingly concentrated in the Kamagasaki area, which was lined with numerous simple hostels and barracks. After a riot in 1961 (since then, there have been numerous riots by Kamagasaki residents in protest of unfair treatment), regional government entities sought to create labor and welfare policies that would enhance security, and began to build facilities such as the Airin Kaikan, which administered welfare programs for the entire area, and the Nishinari Workers' Welfare Center.

In 1966, due to ageing facilities and other factors, the Umeda Kōseikan, which was by then responsible for an intense program of assessment and protection of homeless poor in the city of Osaka, was restructured and renamed the Central Rehabilitation Consultation Office. In 1971, the Airin Kaikan was absorbed by this office, renamed the Osaka City Rehabilitation Office, and relocated to the Kamagasaki area where the demand for services was high. At this point, its target clientele changed, from persons in need throughout the city of Osaka, to persons living specifically in the Kamagasaki area who lacked a stable home and needed protection services. This meant that a system was now in place under which rough sleepers in Kamagasaki, and nowhere else, received very special treatment, getting public assistance from the Rehabilitation Office rather than from a welfare office. Most of the facilities that needy persons were sent to by the Rehabilitation Office, reflecting the demographics of rough sleepers, were for single males. However, in 1962 the Airinryō, and in 1965 the Imaike Seikatsukan, were opened to accommodate families in the Kamagasaki district. The aim was to move stable families out of Kamagasaki by giving them priority for public housing. The result was that women, who at the time of the first riot made up nearly half the population of Kamagasaki, gradually disappeared from the district, while the concentration of single men to create a labor base in the area was encouraged. As time went on, Kamagasaki became the overwhelmingly single male neighborhood that it is today.

Day laborers in Kamagasaki lived in workers' hostels and barracks while doing jobs for periods ranging from a single day to several months. Their lives were fundamentally unstable, but when the economy was strong, and jobs plentiful, rough sleepers were comparatively few. However, the number of day laborers who slept outside began to grow in the 1990s, and before long rough sleepers could be found not only in Kamagasaki but everywhere. The job of housing and protecting these individuals went to places such as Life Care Centers, which developed in Kamagasaki to provide extra-legal assistance by providing short-term shelter, and Public Assistance Facilities, Short-Term Hospitals for people in critical need on the streets, and other facilities common in Osaka but rare in other regions.

Beginning in 1999, more ambitious policies for rough sleepers were establishedin Osaka. Mobile advisory services for rough sleepers were introduced in 1999. In 2000, three Self-Help Centers were opened, which provided several months' lodging and job-seeking assistance. Other new facilities included temporary short-term refuges in parks and overnight shelters. The national government became involved in 2002 with the passing of the Self-Help Act for Homeless People. These activities, however, were mainly directed at single men. Although some of the temporary refuges in parks admit couples and women who make up only 3% of rough sleepers, are not covered under homelessness policies but instead under policies for single women, as will be discussed later.

Mother-Child Policies

The first Public Assistance Act of 1946 superseded the Military Relief Law and the Mother-Child Protection Act that had provided aid to mothers and children in the prewar period. Under the Act, Mother-Child Homes that had escaped destruction in the war were re-classified as lodging facilities and used to provide shelter and protection to single-mother families in need of a place to live. As an emergency measure to help people who had lost their homes in the war, Osaka prefecture also opened new facilities, such as the Akagawa Home, which housed mother-child repatriate families, in 1946, and the Mikuni Mother-Child Home for those who had lost their homes in the war. The opening of such facilities at this time was not so much a welfare measure for mothers and children as it was an attempt to manage the effects of the war, and in the postwar chaos, the users of these facilities seem not to have been only mothers and children. Notes made by an individual connected with Mother-Child Homes state that Osaka prefecture at the time had five facilities for mothers with children (Osaka Association for Research on Social Work History 1985: 303), but a considerable number of mother-child families were run under general programs for lodging and protecting those lacking a home. In addition, private organizations like the Shitennōji Hiden'in and the Holy Family House, at the same time as caring for "vagrant children" and other war victims, are recorded as taking in "vagrant mothers with children."

In 1947, Mother-Child Homes went from being governed by the Public Assistance Act to being governed by the new Child Welfare Act. The reasoning behind this change, which was stressed by female members of the national Diet and others, was that it was essential to children's interests to make sure the homes protected "the unity of mother and child with the needs of the child coming first." This, it was thought, was more important than regulating the homes provided through the Public Assistance Act. In Osaka prefecture, accordingly, fourteen facilities, including the newly established Moriguchi Mother-Child Home and the Sakai City Mother-Child Home, were certified as Mother-Child Homes under the Child Welfare Act.

However, in the 1950s, just when one might have expected postwar policies on vagrants to have outlived their purpose, soaring prices caused by the Korean War brought new hardship to many people, and the number of "vagrant mothers and children" rose sharply again. The Mother-Child Homes run under the Child Welfare Act were insufficient to accommodate these numbers, so in 1952, starting with Yao Zenrinkan, seven Mother-Child Homes were returned to the jurisdiction of the Public Assistance Act to take in and shelter "vagrant mothers and children" sent by the Umeda Kōseikan. The treatment of "vagrant" single-mother families was distinctly inferior to that of other mother-child families, such as repatriates and families impoverished by the death of the father in the war. However, two years later, these seven facilities were advised by government officials that, now that social conditions had settled down, they should end their status as Public Assistance Facilities and convert to a less costly type of facility.

In the 1950s many new Mother-Child Homes were opened. Following a 1949 directive entitled Key Policy Points for Mother-

Child Welfare, which specified the urgent need to expand the number of Mother-Child Homes, new homes appeared throughout Japan in rapid succession. In Osaka prefecture, concentrated in the Osaka suburban area, many public Mother-Child Homes were built, in places such as Izumi Ōtsu, Yao, Takaishi, Ikeda, Takatsuki, Izumisano, Suita, Kishiwada, Izumi, and Minō. To regulate this activity, in 1950 the Ministry of Health and Welfare issued its Guidelines for the Administration of Mother-Child Homes. The guidelines emphasized that the purpose of Mother-Child Homes was "to serve children," and that they must focus on "the well-being of children, who are the future of society" and on "rearing fine and healthy children." Here, the rights of mothers were considered only incidentally, in their role of accompanying children. The guidelines further stated that "to avoid becoming a refuge for self-indulgent women trying to escape the family system, or a place that fosters a weak, dependent character," clients should be selected by careful screening. Support for divorced and poor women was linked with personal moral deficiencies – i.e. "self-indulgent" behavior or a "dependent character" – and the idea that recipients should be screened based on their actions was explicitly stated.

Subsequently, from the late 1960s to the 1970s, the number of women admitted to Mother-Child Homes decreased, and the number of homes began to be cut. This was partly because a support system for single-mother families had been put in place, albeit imperfectly, with the introduction of other policies for housing mothers and children and the Mother-Child Welfare Act. The increased number of employment opportunities for women was also a contributing factor. But another major reason was that the poor environment and deterioration of facilities of the Mother-Child Homes built in haste to accommodate war victims had become an obstacle to their use. Many Mother-Child Homes in Osaka prefecture, especially in the suburban towns, were closed during this period. With the passing of time, the number of households headed by divorced mothers increased, while the earlier function of mother-child welfare, that of government-funded assistance to war widows, became less important. The trend turned towards an expectation that clients would make efforts to help themselves.

Domestic violence is first mentioned in a 1982 notice by the Ministry of Health and Welfare. This notice mandated that women escaping violent treatment from their husbands, even if a divorce has not been concluded, be given shelter in a Mother-Child Homes to protect the welfare of any children. Later, as spousal violence came to be recognized as a social problem and not simply the internal conflict of a couple, the ministry released a "Notice regarding women in need of protection from the violence of a husband or other partner." Mother-child welfare had once again become an issue in need of a government response. This notice made it possible for victims of domestic violence who needed to conceal their whereabouts to be accommodated outside their prefecture of residence. Additionally, childless, single victims of domestic violence were also entitled to protection services at Mother-Child Living Support Facilities (the term introduced in 1998 in place of "Mother-Child Homes"). Finally, with the passage in 2001 of the Act on the Prevention of Spousal Violence and the Protection of Victims (hereafter, the Domestic Violence Act), most Mother-Child Living Support Facilities began to offer temporary emergency protection to victims of domestic violence. As part of this trend, also in 2001, four such Mother-Child Living Support Facilities in the city of Osaka began offering temporary protection to mothers and children suffering from domestic violence.

Policies for single women

The first policies for poor, single women in the postwar period were directed at prostitutes. Only three days after the end of the war, on August 18, 1945, the government began to deliberate the creation of "recreation and amusement facilities" for the occupying soldiers. Under the slogan of "protecting the purity of morally upstanding Japanese women," 70,000 prostitutes were recruited to service Allied personnel. This policy divided the women of Japan into two categories: ordinary women whose chastity needed to be protected, and a "sexual breakwater" of women who were prostitutes. However, the rapid spread of sexually transmitted diseases at these facilities forced the government to close them, and in 1946, at the request of occupying powers' General Headquarters, the longstanding licensed prostitution system was abolished.

The abandonment of the system was only superficial, however. In fact, the government moved prostitution to designated areas where it was tacitly allowed to continue. At the same time, "women of darkness," streetwalking prostitutes who could not be managed systematically, were subjected to a sterner crackdown. Also in

1946, Guidelines on Protection Care for Women were released
that called for the rehabilitation and protection of streetwalking
prostitutes and for measures to prevent prostitution. In 1947,
seventeen Women's Protection Facilities were opened throughout
Japan to take in prostitutes.

In Osaka prefecture, inquiries were made into delegating this
project to the Osaka Women's Home, which had offered protection
services to women since the prewar period, but this idea was
abandoned because the death of founder Hayashi Utako that year
left no one to take charge. Instead, the Salvation Army Chōkōryō
and Seibiryō (later relocated and renamed the Ikuno Gakuen) were
opened for this purpose. Streetwalkers and single female rough
sleepers who had been picked up were also sent by the Umeda
Kōseikan to these facilities. A roundtable discussion by involved
parties revealed that there was a "panpan hospital" exclusively for
streetwalking prostitutes ("panpan" was the slang term for these
women), and that prostitutes who created problems by repeatedly
fleeing from the hospital and returning to streetwalking were
placed in mental institutions and forcibly sterilized (Igarashi 1986:
153). The Osaka Women's Home, for its part, was reopened as a
Rehabilitation Facility for women under the Public Assistance Act
five years later, in 1952.

Despite efforts to control prostitution and support women trying
to leave the trade, the number of women driven into prostitution by
poverty grew, leading to the passage of the Anti-Prostitution Act
in 1956. This law made prostitution illegal, but acts of prostitution
themselves were not subject to punishment. However, the law, showing
its inherent sexism, mandated punishment for street prostitutes who
solicited sex in a public place, for "degrading public morality," while
male customers were not prosecuted. It also mandated the creation
of Women's Protection Services to prevent prostitution by taking in
and rehabilitating women and girls who, "based on character, actions,
or surroundings, are in danger of falling into prostitution." These
Women's Protection Services were distinct from other welfare projects
in that they provided welfare but were also governed by criminal
law. In accordance with this law, Osaka prefecture set up Women's
Consultation Centers in Umeda and Tennōji in 1957, and in Nishinari
ward, Naniwa ward, and Minato ward in 1959. These offices provided
counseling and temporary protection to "at-risk women." Two new
facilities were created to provide longer-term accommodation as

Women's Protection Facilities in addition to the Chōkōryō and Ikuno Gakuen: the Tamamoryō in 1958 and the Akaneryō in 1961.

However, the number of women admitted to these Women's Protection Facilities was low from the beginning, at less than 60% of capacity. This number decreased even more as time went on and those involved in prostitution devised clever ways to stay within the law, such as conducting only non-coital sexual activities (Figure 3.1). This set one trend that would determine subsequent developments and effects of the Anti-Prostitution Act. From the inception of the law, the Women's Protection Services were not only for prostitutes. Their clients were "not limited to women actually engaging in prostitution in the so-called red-light (*akasen*) districts, but also include a wide group of women who were in danger, as runaways or vagrants, of falling into prostitution." A broad interpretation of the "danger" of "falling into immorality" resulted in a variety of types of women not involved in prostitution receiving protection services.

In 1970, an official notice by the Health and Welfare Ministry affirmed that even "girls and women determined not to be in danger of falling into prostitution" who had serious problems making a living in society and were unable to use other services could be cared for by Women's Protection Services. Taking the lead from this, the Osaka prefectural government began to officially allow facilities under the jurisdiction of the Anti-Prostitution Act to provided protection services to a variety of types of homeless and poor women to fill vacant spaces, including "women who had become unemployed, lost a place to live, or suffered failed relationships, and women who were escaping violence from a husband or other person" (Osaka Prefecture Women's Consultation Center 2001: 12). As Figure 3.1 shows, the number of users of these facilities shot up at about this time. In Osaka prefecture, which lacked sufficient facilities for people discharged from mental institutes, these Women's Protection Services supplemented the welfare system for disabled individuals by taking on the role of accommodating those with mental and intellectual disabilities. Before long, the number of women deemed "not in danger of falling into prostitution," came to greatly surpass the number of prostitutes, the original targets of the Women's Protection Services in these facilities. In 1992, following a second drop in the number of users, the Ministry of Health and Welfare issued a new notice that explicitly included women "not currently at risk of engaging in prostitution" who were suffering from "failed family relationships," "poverty," "sexual victimization," and other difficulties. This was a public declaration that Women's Protection Services had departed from their original purpose of preventing prostitution. During this period of decreased use of these Women's Protection Facilities, Osaka prefecture, citing aging facilities and other issues, combined three Women's Protection Facilities into the Osaka Prefecture Women's Self-Help Center, which since 1997 has been the sole Women's Protection Facility in the prefecture.

A new policy direction was set in 1999. In the notice entitled "Policies for women needing protection from violence of spouses or partners," the Ministry of Health and Welfare classified Women's Protection Facilities together with Mother-Child Homes (later renamed Mother-Child Living Support Facilities), as facilities for the protection of female domestic violence victims. The notice ended the original policy of distinguishing Protection Facility users with a history of prostitution from those without it, and ended the use of the term "at-risk women." The Protection Facilities founded under the Anti-Prostitution Act carried a certain stigma. These changes appear to have been intended to reduce that stigma as Protection Facilities were opened to victims of domestic violence. When the Domestic Violence Act was enacted in 2001, the only existing facilities that could be deemed appropriate for sheltering domestic violence victims were facilities under the Anti-Prostitution Act such as Women's Consultation Centers and Women's Protection Facilities. As Figure 3.1 shows, in this same year there was a surge in the number of users of Protection Facilities.

In Osaka prefecture, the Women's Consultation Center began to focus mainly on providing temporary emergency protection services,[4] while longer-term protection was conducted by the Women's Protection Facility (Prefectural Women's Self-Help Center).[5] The next year, 2002, the city of Osaka opened a city-run Living Care Center in the Osaka Women's Home (a Public Assistance Facility) to provide temporary shelter to domestic violence victims.[6] As a result, poor, homeless women in Osaka prefecture were sent for protection either to a Women's Protection Facility or to a Public Assistance Facility based on their location. The outcome was that single women without families who lived within Osaka city limits were given protection services based on the Domestic Violence Act, while those outside the city continued to rely on facilities run under

No. of
people

250 —

200 —

150 —

100 —

50 —

1960   1965   1970   1975   1980   1985   1990   1995   2000   2005   2010

Year

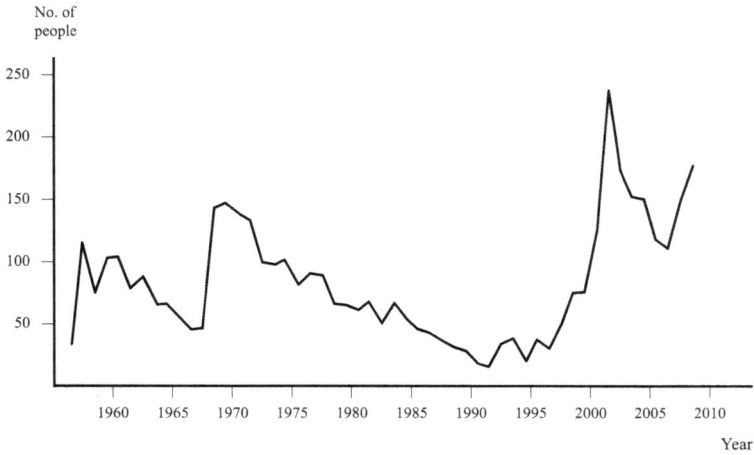

*Figure 3.1: Number of women admitted to Women's Protection
Facilities in Osaka prefecture*

Source: Osaka prefecture Women's Consultation Center, *Summary of Women's
Protection Services (1984-2009).*

the Anti-Prostitution Act. After the Domestic Violence Act enactment,
domestic violence victims began to be prioritized by such facilities,
while it became more difficult for prostitutes and other homeless
women to access them. The 2004 Action Plan on Human Trafficking
also gave Women's Protection Facilities responsibility for the care of
victims of human trafficking.

A breakdown of reasons for utilizing the Women's Protection
Facility in Osaka prefecture given by recent users (Figure 3.2) shows
that women with a connection to prostitution make up less than 10%
of users. Instead, about 70% entered to escape domestic violence and
20% "lacked a place to live."[7] However, in comparison with Public
Assistance Facilities, which were originally charged with taking in
women not "in danger of falling into prostitution," the Women's
Protection Facilities, which were created to reform and rehabilitate
prostitutes, are distinctly short of funding and personnel, as will be
discussed in Chapter 4. The Anti-Prostitution Act, then, which was
intended to correct and rehabilitate prostitutes, has come to be used
by many impoverished women with no connection to prostitution.
This suggests that the time has come to rethink this law.

No. of
people

250 —

200 —

- ■ Spousal violence
- □ No place to live
- ▨ Consumer lending debts
- ◪ Mental illness
- ■ Prostitution
- ▨ Other

150 —

100 —

50 —

1992 1993 1994 1995 1996 1997 1998 1999 2000 2001 2002 2003 2004 2005 2006 2007 2008 2009

Year

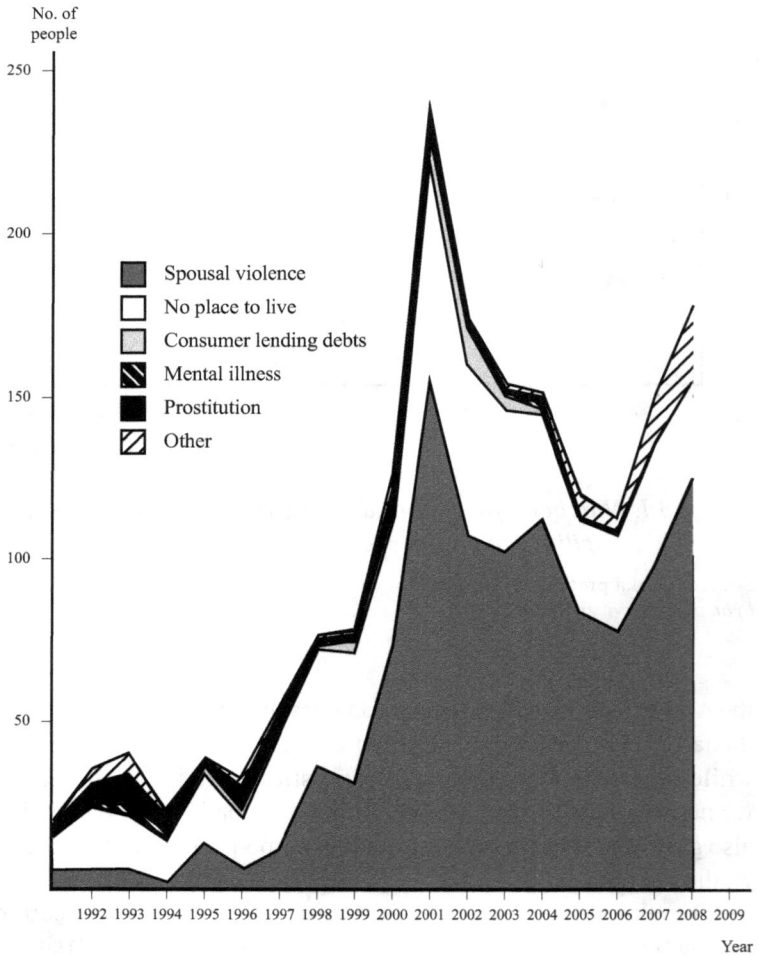

Figure 3.2: Reasons for entering Women's Protection Facilities in Osaka prefecture

Source: Osaka Prefecture Women's Consultation Center, *Summary of Services*, 1991–2009. Prior to 1997, the Osaka Prefecture Women's Consultation Center was known as the Osaka Prefecture Women's Consultation Center. The publication entitled *Summary of Services* went through several slight name changes between 1985 and 2009.

Two views of women in anti-poverty policy

As we have seen, throughout the history of welfare the first question asked of potential recipients has been whether they can work or not. The policy of denying benefits to those able to work has remained fundamentally unchanged and is a basic premise behind all anti-poverty policies, from the earliest Poor Relief Law to the public assistance of the present, when non-discrimination and equality are trumpeted as the highest values. However, in the case of women, this is not the only criterion for qualification. Even more important is whether a woman conforms to the dominant values of society. In this sense, along with her ability to work, the main factor determining whether a woman receives welfare is how well she conforms to ideals of the modern family, in which men perform paid labor and women perform household labor.

The earliest category to receive protection services was mothers who were raising children with no male breadwinner. However, programs were created with varying eligibility standards, depending on the reason that a family had come to be headed by the mother. On one end of the spectrum, military widows and their families were privileged over other single-mother families. Of these others, programs were created later, and benefits were lower, for the families women who had divorced or had never married. Recipients were assigned to higher or lower categories based on their degree of conformity to the values of the modern family and their usefulness to the nation-state. Women who deviated from the desirable lifestyle by divorcing, and unwed mothers, were seen as morally deficient and thus less deserving of public assistance.

Likewise, programs for single women without children belonged to a separate lineage from those for single mothers. They originated as relief measures for prostitutes, and were developed not so much to protect the human rights of women as to maintain public order and sexual morality. These policies implicitly degraded prostitutes, and later included punishments, while assigning no responsibility to male customers. As time went on, these anti-prostitution policies began to provide protection not only to prostitutes but to women suffering from various forms of poverty, on the grounds that these women were "at risk" of falling into prostitution.

In this way, single women, whose deviation from the standard marriage system made them a threat to the modern family, were targeted for punishment, which went hand-in-hand with protection. Today, under the Domestic Violence Act, victims of domestic violence have come to be prioritized over other single women. However, if we look back at statistics on women receiving protection services in the Meiji period, their circumstances appear to be not very different from those of such women today: women who appear to have been fleeing violent husbands, prostitutes, rough sleepers, and others. What has changed from era to era is only what type of poor woman is given precedence in receiving protection services, and what law provides the rationale. In short, the question of who is given protection and who is forcibly controlled, who is criticized and who is condemned, is a highly political one, related to the ways in which women's needs are interpreted.

At present, public policy for the protection of victims of domestic violence is also generally implemented in one of two types of facility for women: mother-child facilities and protection facilities for prostitutes. Hence, when poor women in a state of homelessness, broadly defined, are given welfare, they have historically been categorized in only one of two ways: as mothers with children to raise, who are given protection services, or as prostitutes who need to be corrected and rehabilitated. While women were directed and encouraged to participate in the marriage system, at the same time, prostitutes were mobilized to satisfy male sexual desire not satisfied within that system. By making them subject to punishment and correction, they were confined to the status of deviants. These two categories of woman, "mother" and "prostitute," were both essential to the stabilization of the marriage system. The beneficiaries of this setup were: men, who were able to satisfy their sexual desires outside of the marriage system; the nation-state, which was able to keep the marriage system stable; and the holders of capital, who, ensured of a supply of women to bear children and perform household labor, could continue to reproduce the labor force without disruption.

Nancy Fraser has noted how seemingly gender-neutral social policies are, in fact, highly gendered (Fraser 1989). Male workers who experience difficulty can receive benefits like unemployment insurance and social security. Because these are considered to be compensation for their labor, the level of benefits is comparatively high, less stigma is attached, and there is little surveillance or intervention in the recipient's life. The reality today for a woman conforming to the normative female role, namely the wife of a paid male worker whose main job has been household labor, is different. When she is in trouble, the role that her moral behavior played in bringing on her difficulties is questioned, and the stigma accompanying the receipt of welfare is inherent to the system. Moreover, many women are unable to extricate themselves from poverty even with these benefits. The welfare system inherently differs for men and women. It is set up on the assumption that women will perform their gender-prescribed roles. Moreover, the system functions to pressure women who depend on it into feminine roles, directing and channeling the lives of poor women into a course conducive to social stability. What has been distinctly lacking is any conscious desire to transform a system that is inherently sexist, or to help women to live with dignity as human beings.

Recently, workfare-type programs, which differ from conventional programs based on the sexual division of labor, have become more common in the field of welfare for women, with increasing pressure on women and men alike to seek employment. To be sure, economic independence can lead to greater freedom for women. But given that today the model of a worker is based on the idea of working men backed up by the domestic labor of women, this emphasis on seeking employment forces the double burden of housework and outside employment onto women, inevitably aggravating their poverty.

The next chapter will use case studies to look at how homeless women live under, yet keep some distance from, a welfare system designed to steer women's lives in a particular direction.

4 Gender norms and the use of welfare facilities

Embodied views of women in the welfare system

In the last chapter, we looked at the historical development of the welfare system for homeless women in order to identify the criteria that determined who was worthy to receive benefits and who was not. These criteria differed for men and women. For men, the first factor considered was ability to work, but for women it was different. Not only was ability to work considered, but also how closely they conformed to the dominant role for women within the dominant family system, which assigned paid labor to men and household labor to women.

It stands to reason that as well as leading to different welfare options for men and women, such a system functions to steer the lives of those dependent on it in specific directions. In Chapter 1 we noted Joanne Passaro's study of this phenomenon as it applied to homelessness. Passaro noted that because homeless women have welfare options available that are not available to men, they are able to survive as long as they conform to the expectations embedded in the welfare system. Under these circumstances, "the only women who remain homeless are renegades of gender, the women who are wary of protection, wary of recreating toxic homes, and wary of bureaucratic condescension and paternalism" (Passaro 1996: 63).

In fact, as Passaro says, the welfare system forces women into the hegemonic gender roles that have been set for them by prevailing family norms. For this reason, Passaro sees the difference between those women who use welfare and those who do not in terms of whether they conform to the dominant gender roles or not. This understanding of gender treats it both as a static norm or ideal embedded in the welfare system, and as a fixed, inherent personal quality. Thus, Passaro sees women rough sleepers who persist in living on the streets as women who do not conform to hegemonic gender roles. However, this understanding of gender overlooks the great individual variety in the way gender is performed by homeless women, and that such performance is not necessarily consistent over time. In short, women living on the streets are viewed as deviating from gender norms.

Passaro's approach also fails to recognize that the gender ideals embodied in the welfare system are not necessarily the ones invoked when the system is utilized. In return for welfare support, a wide range of expectations may be presented to the recipient concerning her life behaviors.

As discussed in Chapter 1, and building on previous experiential research findings informed by post-structural theory, I will therefore treat gender as a continual process in which gendered subjects and power relations are constructed by people making use of gender categories. This approach enables us to avoid Pasarro's mistake of presupposing that the normative roles for women embodied in the structure of the welfare system are static and unchanging, and treating the individual actors as either having internalized these roles or as rejecting them. Rather, we can focus on the process in which each instance of mutual activity is carried out with continual negotiation among the actors involved, with gendered concepts. This will make it possible to observe specific cases of the welfare system's normative prescriptions for women as they appear in the everyday use of welfare by homeless women. We will also be able to observe the various and not always consistent ways that gender functions for individual homeless women.

To this end, this chapter surveys the ways in which a welfare system that embraces the view of women described in Chapter 3 is instituted in particular regions. Tokyo prefecture will be used as a representative example. We will then look at what sort of homeless women end up using different types of welfare facilities based on different laws as a result of this system. Next, we will consider free or low-rent housing within Tokyo prefecture, focusing on situations that demonstrate how women live and how the welfare system is administered. This chapter aims to show what public expectations are set forth for homeless women to follow, and the relation these expectations have to gender within these facilities. Specifically, I will take an ethnographic approach, looking at daily scenes to describe the nature of the process leading to the receipt of welfare; how the recipient and those she knows and interacts with perceive and interpret the meaning of their lives; and the processes that determine the progression of the program of support and the individuals' lives after leaving the facilities. Based on that, I will investigate the standards that women are expected to follow when they use the welfare system and how these are related to gender.

Welfare policies for homeless women

Existing welfare facilities catering to homeless women

As was shown in Chapter 2, there are several types of welfare available to homeless women, including public assistance, Women's Protection Services, and mother-child welfare. We will now consider which homeless women, with what needs, use which system, and the relationships between different systems.

The Public Assistance Act, which created a system for assisting poor people, stipulated that "all aid provided for under other laws will be prioritized over any protection provided for by this law." In other words, in cases where a person could receive protection and assistance under, for instance, policies aimed at the disabled or elderly, the other provisos would be used first. Women's Protection Services also fundamentally prioritized other laws. As shown in Chapter 3, Women's Protection Facilities were originally designed for the protection and rehabilitation of women who were or were at risk of becoming prostitutes, but because of repeated government notifications and additions to the foundational law, the range of people eligible to use them expanded. A 2002 notice by the Ministry of Health, Labour and Welfare, in addition to those with a history of, or in danger of, engaging in prostitution, names the following people eligible to use Women's Protection Facilities: "victims of spousal violence (including common-law spouses)" and "persons who, because of serious problems making it impossible to live a normal life, such as failed family relationships and poverty, and because no other facilities are available to solve these problems, can be considered in genuine need of protection and assistance" ("Implementing Women's Protection Services to carry out the Domestic Violence Act"). As a result, they are used by women with a great variety of problems, such as poverty, disability, or family violence. However, for women in poverty, because public assistance and Women's Protection Services are both founded on laws that give priority to other laws, it is unclear which should be used.

Hence, when poor women apply to use welfare, they can go to one of two types of facility: welfare offices and Women's Consultation Centers. Welfare offices are facilities that deal with the programs founded on the six acts related to welfare: the Public Assistance Act, the Child Welfare Act, the Act for the Welfare of Mothers with Dependents and Widows, the Act on Social Welfare for the Elderly, the Welfare for Disabled Persons Act, and the Welfare for Intellectually Disabled Persons Act. In terms of services to homeless women, welfare offices arrange for public assistance, placement in protective facilities, and, for mothers with dependent children, arrange for admission to Mother-Child Living Support Facilities. Women's Consultation Centers were created under the Anti-Prostitution Act. As well as containing on-site temporary protection facilities, these offices place individuals in Women's Protection Facilities. Since the enactment of the Domestic Violence Act, many have also functioned as Spousal Violence Victim Support Centers providing counseling and support for victims of domestic violence.

Homeless women with no stable place to live can begin by inquiring at one of these two types of facility. Normally, they are offered two weeks of temporary shelter at a Women's Consultation Center or other facility designated by a local governing body. After that, various factors determine whether they go to stay with relatives, find a place to live and begin receiving assistance, or move into a facility. These factors include individual preference, the reason for losing one's home, one's status as a single individual or mother with dependent children, ability to work, income, personal assets, and the presence or lack of relatives to provide support. In some cases, women who are judged to need only a place to live, such as those escaping domestic violence, are assigned housing, but if a more complex administrative process is needed or if supervision or financial support is called for, they are admitted to a facility as a starting measure. Because it can be difficult to determine whether living assistance is needed for people who until that time have been rough sleepers, the regular practice is to initially admit them to a facility. Once admission to a facility has been decided, the type of facility used must be decided.

Table 4.1 shows the main facilities that homeless women endur-
ing economic hardship resort to after initially using temporary
emergency protection.[1] Of these, those that are exclusively for
women are Women's Protection Facilities and Mother-Child
Living Support Facilities; in cities, there may also be Relief and
Rehabilitation Facilities for women. Also, although there are
facilities that accept both men and women, in such cases, because
the gender of the users is not reported clearly, it is impossible to
ascertain how many women use them. What kind of facility is
used depends on factors such as household structure and whether
one is single or with children, where one sought help, and how one
lost one's home. These decisions are often determined not only by
the individual client's situation but by external factors, including
the individual assessment of caseworkers and the availability of
facilities. In particular, if a single local self-governing body has
multiple facilities with overlapping functions, local rules will
determine how these functions are distributed, leading to many
local differences.

The right column of Table 4.1 shows the national capacity
fulfillment rate (the number of users divided by the total capacity)
for these facilities. While the level of usage differs greatly from
region to region, the fulfillment rate for Women's Protection
Facilities, at 38.2%, is far below that of Public Assistance Facilities.
Furthermore, Table 4.2 shows the costs and staff numbers of these
facilities. Although the differing purposes of these facilities make
it difficult to generalize, the operating expenses and per capita cost
for Women's Protection Facilities are low in comparison with relief
and Rehabilitation Facilities, probably because their original target
was stigmatized prostitutes. In free, low-rent, and unregistered
facilities, things such as fees, quality of service, and room size
vary widely according to who is running them, but generally,
their expenses are considerably lower than those of Type 1 social
welfare facilities.[2]

Users of women's facilities in Tokyo prefecture

Next, focusing on facilities that take in female clients, and taking
Tokyo prefecture as the model, we will look at the details of how
facilities with a variety of functions based on different laws are
actually used. Table 4.3 shows the different types of facility

Table 4.1: Residential facilities used by homeless women

Project type	Name	Activities	Capacity fulfillment rate (%)
Public assistance	Relief Facility	Admit individuals who have difficulty with daily life tasks due to a significant physical or mental disability, and provide living assistance	100.5
	Rehabilitation Facility	Admit individuals who for physical or mental reasons require care or lifestyle guidance, and provide living assistance	79.5
	Accommodation Facility	Provide living assistance to families without a home, and provide housing assistance	61.6
Women's Protection Services		Take protective custody of at-risk women (women considered likely to engage in prostitution based on their sexual behavior and environment)	38.2
Mother-child welfare	Mother-Child Living Support Facility[a]	Admit women without a spouse or in equivalent situations and the children of these women in need of custody, and provide protective care along with living support to promote self-sufficiency	
Other	Free or low-rent housing facilities	Provide simple housing at no or minimal cost to needy persons, or enable them to use housing or other facilities	
	Unregistered facility		

Note: Facilities that provide only temporary emergency protection are not included. [a] Because capacity of Mother-Child Living Support Facilities is measured by number of families, and the number of residents includes children, capacity fulfillment rates could not be calculated.
Source: Tokyo Metropolitan Government Bureau of Social Welfare and Public Health (2011), Ministry of Health, Labour and Welfare (2011d)

Table 4.2: Monthly costs and standard staff allocations of residential facilities used by homeless women

	Administrative expenses per resident (yen)	Operating expenses per resident (yen)	No. of staff
Public assistance			
Relief Facilities	175,100	64,240	18
Rehabilitation Facilities	121,100	68,050	13
Accommodation Facilities	29,800	—	3
Women's Protection Facilities	87,800	54,600	9
Mother-Child Living Support Facilities	118,090	3,550	6
Free or low-rent housing/ Unregistered facilities	135,310 (Fees are paid using public assistance money)		Not prescribed

Note: Calculated per Tokyo prefectural standards, which take each facility to have a capacity of 50 residents. Mother-Child Living Support Facilities are taken to have a capacity of 20 families, and the costs are calculated for a single family. Public assistance amounts are those awarded for ages 41–59.
Source: Chūōhōki (2012).

Table 4.3: Numbers and capacities of residential facilities in Tokyo prefecture used by homeless women

Project type	Name	Number	Capacity	Share of users who are female
Public assistance	Relief Facilities	10	948	Half or less?
	Rehabilitation Facilities	10	922	3 facilities are women-only (capacity: 130)
	Accommodation Facilities	7	567	70%
Women's Protection Services	Women's Protection Facilities	5	230	All
Mother-child welfare	Mother-Child Living Support Facilities	36	746 (households)	All households are female-headed
Other	Free or low-rent housing facilities	170	5,316	Some facilities are women-only
	Unregistered facilities	—	—	Some facilities accept women (including domestic violence shelters)

Note: Facilities that provide only temporary emergency protection are not included.
Source: Ministry of Health, Labour, and Welfare 2011d.

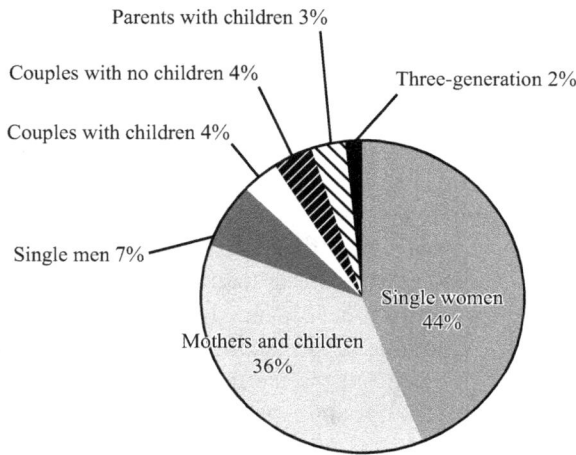

Figure 4.1: Family types of Accommodation Facility users

Source: Special Ward Association for Personnel and Welfare, Business summary of facility operations, 2010.

in Tokyo prefecture that are likely to accommodate significant numbers of people who are homeless in the wider sense. The gender of shelter users is not identified, but with all-male and mixed-gender shelters included, the total share of women is probably less than half of the total capacity. Out of 10 Rehabilitation Facilities in the prefecture, three are exclusively for women.[3] There are seven Accommodation Facilities, and since the passage of the Domestic Violence Act in 2003, these have come to specialize in providing temporary emergency shelter in anticipation of the growing number of women in need. As a result, 80% of the users are women (Figure 4.1). Most of those using free or low-rent housing facilities are male, and a lack of clear data on the gender of users makes the number of women unclear, but my research has identified about twenty facilities solely for women, as well as facilities that take both men and women. Facility A, discussed later, is an example of a free or low-rent housing facility exclusively for women. The exact conditions at unregistered facilities, too, are sometimes unclear, making the number of women users uncertain, but it is safe to say that some facilities are mixed-gender, while others, like domestic violence shelters, are exclusively for women.

Next, we will compare in more detail the situations of the users of these facilities, looking only at the four types for which statistical data from business summaries and reports are publicly available. These are: Rehabilitation Facilities, Accomodation Facilities, Women's Protection Facilities, and Mother-Child Living Support Facilities.[4]

Figure 4.2 compares occupancy rates to maximum capacity. These rates vary widely according to type: Women's Protection Facilities have the lowest rate, at less than 60%; Mother-Child Living Support Facilities are at about 80%; and Rehabilitation Facilities are at full capacity. Accommodation Facilities have an occupancy rate of about 80%, but because these facilities specialize in emergency temporary protection, occupancy rates are likely to be uneven, making it difficult to compare with other types of facility.

Figure 4.3 shows the distribution of users by age. Women's Protection Facilities have a younger clientele than Rehabilitation Facilities. Mother-Child Living Support Facilities, because they are for mothers with children, do not have any clients in their sixties or older.

The length of stay (Figure 4.4) is short for Accommodation Facilities, which specialize in providing emergency lodgings. By contrast, Women's Protection Facilities and Mother-Child Living Support Facilities have some clients who remain for more than three years.

The reasons for entering a facility are shown in Table 4.4. Although it is difficult to compare different types of facilities, because their methods for gathering statistics differ, the most common reasons are as follows, in order of frequency. Rehabilitation Facilities: lack of an address, no place to return after leaving hospital; Accommodation Facilities: escaping violence from husband, escaping rough sleeping; Women's Protection Facilities: poverty, pregnancy and childbirth; and Mother-Child Support Facilities: difficulty finding a home, violence from husband or other. As we can see, poverty and difficulty finding a home are major reasons for using every type of facility. Violence from a husband or partner is also a common factor,[5] as is difficulty functioning in society due to disability or other causes.

Figure 4.5 shows the employment status of facility users. Employment rates are high for Women's Protection Facilities and Mother-Child Living Support Facilities. This can be partly explained by the fact that in contrast to Public Assistance Facilities, which provide a monthly allowance of several thousand yen

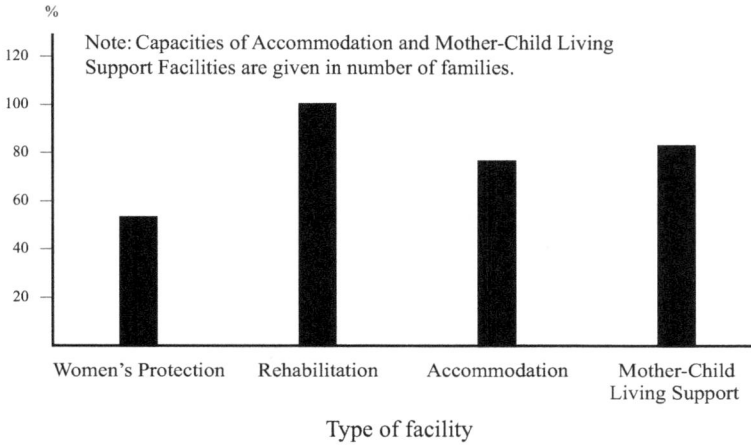

Figure 4.2: Facility occupancy rates by type

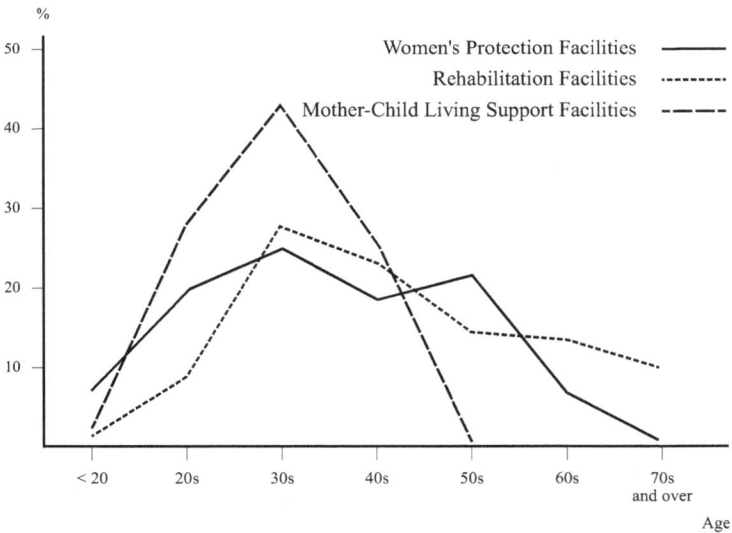

Figure 4.3: Age of facility users

Note. Because information on age of users of Accommodation Facilities is only available for the heads of household, it is omitted form the graph.
Source: see Chapter 4, Note 4 regarding this figure, Table 4.4, and Figures 4.4–4.6.

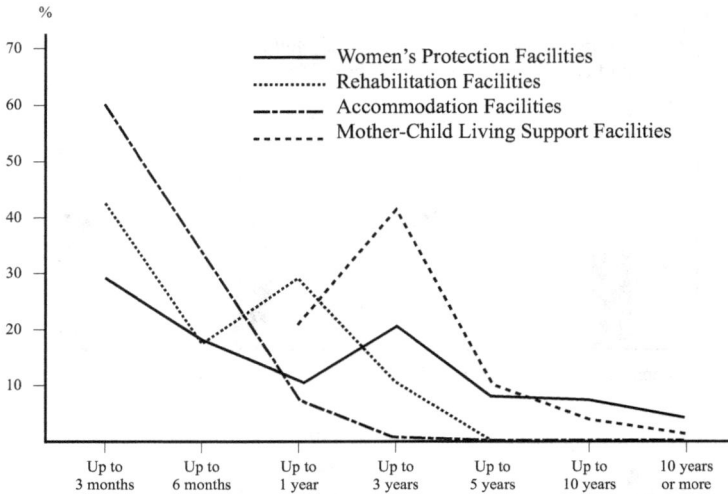

Figure 4.4: Length of stay

Note. For one Rehabilitation Facility and one Accommodation Facility, facility statistics taken were not for the length of stay of a family being discharged, but the length of stay for current residents. For Mother-Child Living Support Facilities, data was not available for stays of "up to 3 months" and "up to 6 months." All such cases are included under "up to 1 year."

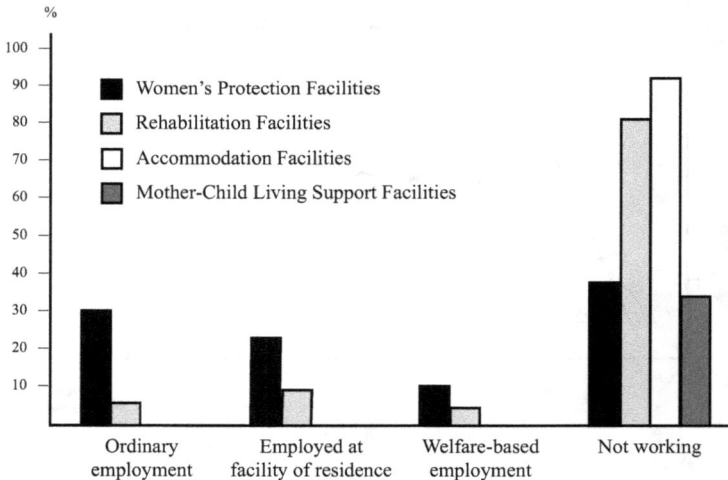

Figure 4.5: Employment status of facility residents

Note. Data was unavailable on the type of employment of those employed while staying at Accommodation and Mother-Child Living Support Facilities.

Table 4.4 Reasons for entering a facility

Women's Protection Facility	%	Rehabilitation Facility	%	Accommodation Facilities	%	Mother-Child Living Support Facility	%
1. Poverty	87.4	Lack of a home	49.8	Taking refuge from partner's abuse	23.5	Unable to obtain housing	47.3
2. Pregnancy and childbirth	28.7	Discharged from hospital with no place to return	23.3	Rough sleeping	14.7	Abuse from partner	20.8
3. Disability or illness	27.5	Difficulty living at home	17.2	Behind in rent payments	10.7	Economic difficulties	17.1
4. Learning how to raise children	24.7	Evicted from previous home	3.7	Conflict with family members	8.9	Poor living environment	7.2
5. Abuse from husband or partner	23.1			Difficulty living independently in society	7.7	Mentally and physically unstable or disabled	3.0

Note. Multiple answers collected for Women's Protection Facilities.

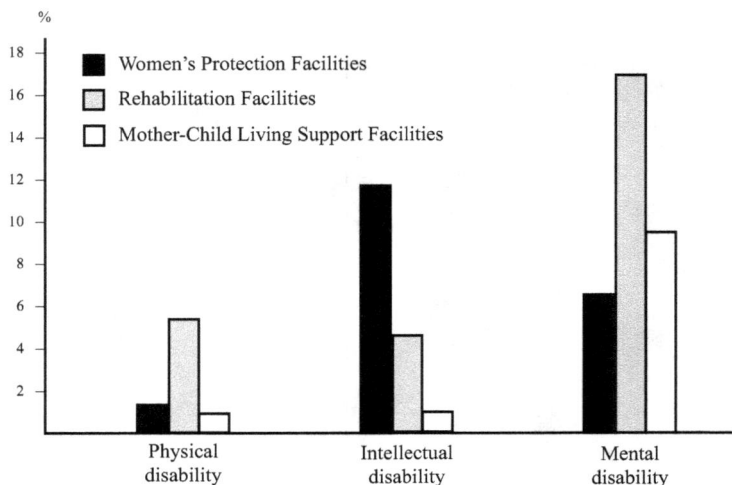

Figure 4.6: Percentage of facility residents with disabilities

Note. Includes only holders of disability certificates. No data available for Accommodation Facilities.

(~USD 50–100) regardless of employment status, no such allowance is provided by Women's Protection Facilities or Mother-Child Support Facilities, so that users must work if they wish to purchase items such as cigarettes and cosmetic products. Employment rates for Accommodation Facilities are low, probably because these provide emergency temporary protection.

Regarding the proportion of users with disabilities (Figure 4.6), Rehabilitation Facilities have a high share of users with mental disabilities, while for Women's Protection Facilities, the share of users with intellectual disabilities is high. This is probably the result of the recent efforts of some Protection Facilities to actively assist clients in obtaining a Rehabilitation Certificate (*ryōiku techō*, a disability certificate for persons with an intellectual disability).

On the reason for leaving a facility (Figure 4.7), for Accommodation Facilities, which provide temporary emergency protection, "moving into ordinary housing with public assistance" is the most common. For Women's Protection Facilities, the most common is that "the client became able to live independently,"[6] while for Mother-Child Living Support Facilities, it is "other."

%

70

60

50

40

30

20

10

Women's Protection Facilities

Rehabilitation Facilities

Accommodation Facilities

Mother-Child Living Support Facilities

Other

Return to home or hometown

Left without warning

Left at own initiative

Transfer to another facility

Hospitalization

Ordinary housing with public assistance

Independent living

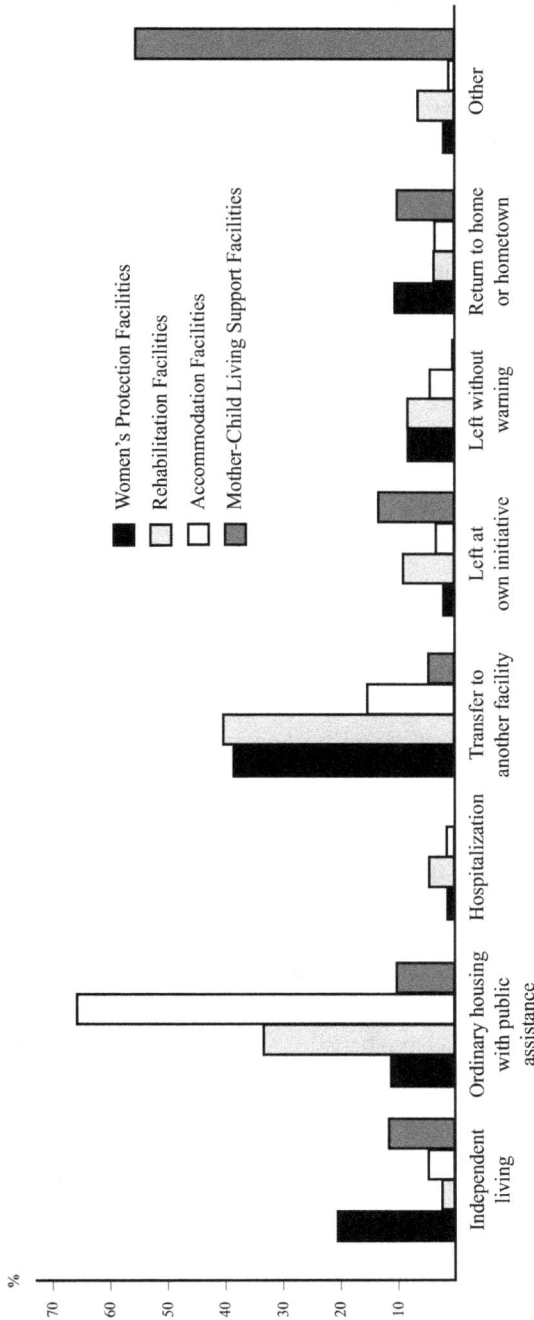

Figure 4.7: Reasons for leaving facility

Note. For Women's Protection Facilities, data on "destination after leaving" and "living situation after leaving" were used. Persons whose main income after leaving came from employment or pensions were classified under "independent living." Those receiving public assistance were classified under "ordinary housing with public assistance," or other situations, when data-gathering methods differed, situations were classified into common categories. Those that could not be categorized were classified as "other." For Mother-Child Living Support Facilities, those classified as "other" included such cases as: moving to "better housing" by being selected for public housing (34.5%) and "termination of term of residence" (10.6%).

As we have seen, despite certain differences, many of the women who are homeless in the broad sense clearly face similar issues, giving similar reasons for entering support facilities. These facilities include Rehabilitation Facilities, Accommodation Facilities, Women's Protection Facilities, and Mother-Child Living Support Facilities. Likewise, a similar situation probably holds for women's free or low-rent housing and other facilities for which statistical data were not available. However, occupancy rates differ greatly for Public Assistance Facilities and Women's Protection Facilities. Public Assistance Facilities, especially Rehabilitation Facilities, have been constantly full, and a lack of sufficient space led to the creation of women-only Rehabilitation Facilities in 2007. Free or low-rent housing facilities have also grown in number. By contrast, as we have seen, an amazing 60% of the capacity of Women's Protection Facilities goes unused. A separate investigation of this imbalance in facility use, considering administrative costs and other factors, is strongly needed.[7]

Introduction to Facility A

In this section, I will examine in more detail the way homeless women live in these facilities, and how the welfare system is employed to direct the life course of these women.

The facilities investigated for this study were free or low-rent housing facilities. As indicated in Table 2.3 in Chapter 2, free or low-rent housing facilities "provide basic housing, as well as other facilities, to financially needy persons at no cost or for a minimal fee." Most of their users are public assistance recipients. However, unlike Public Assistance Facilities, whose users are placed there by public authorities, free or low-rent housing facilities are Type 2 social welfare projects, which are considered to have a low impact on their users. Thus, their users have private, contractual relationships with the facility.

Because a free or low-rent housing facility can be opened with comparative ease once it is registered, a wide variety of organizations, mainly non-profits, have done so since about 2000, and their numbers have been growing. However, the fees for many such facilities are quite high considering the quality of the accommodations and services provided, and there have been many media reports depicting free or low-rent housing facilities as breeding grounds for the "poverty business." To better regulate free or low-rent housing facilities, many local governing bodies have created their own guidelines, and the Ministry of Health, Labour and Welfare has conducted a study to get a better idea of conditions. That study (MHLW 2011a) found there to be 488 confirmed free or low-rent housing facilities, 14,964 former rough sleepers and others using those facilities, with 13,790 of them receiving public assistance. These facilities are concentrated in urban area where there is a shortage of such housing, with about 40% of the total in Tokyo prefecture.

Facility A, where I conducted part of this study over ten months between December 2002 and October 2003, was a free or low-rent housing facility in Tokyo prefecture, exclusively for single women. It was opened in 2002 by a nonprofit corporation that had long provided support for rough sleepers. At the time, the number of free or low-rent housing facilities had already begun to grow in Tokyo, but there were few facilities catering to women. The nonprofit, having already operated several free or low-rent housing facilities for men, opened Facility A to meet the needs of women. Descriptions involving Facility A in this chapter all refer to the period from 2002 to 2003 when this study was conducted.

Written materials provided to users of Facility A explained that: "We are a space where our clients prepare themselves for a new life in the community." In other words, it was intended to be a transitional facility for people who lacked housing. Hence, with a view to its clients' lives after they were released, the facility aimed to connect them with social resources, such as medical and welfare organizations, so they would have access to adequate support later. In addition, because Facility A's users included victims of domestic violence, to ensure their safety, its address, as with many other women's facilities, was not made public. Facility A was designed to accommodate seventeen people. It was housed in a refurbished old building that was formerly a traditional *ryokan* inn. It included double-occupant bedrooms of about 5.5m², common areas such as a dining room and smoking room, and an office (see Figure 4.8). One staff member was present at all times, and during the day one cooking staff member was there to prepare the three meals that were served daily.

Usage fees included rent, which was set at 53,700 yen (~USD 455) per month, the maximum amount that could be provided by public assistance for housing, and a general service fee of about 2,300 yen

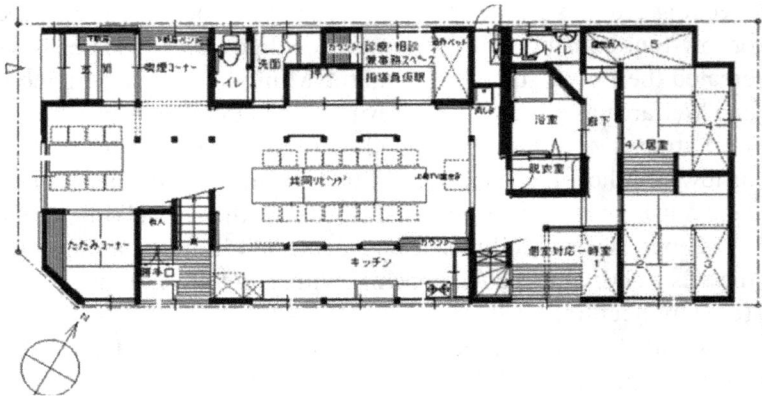

Figure 4.8: Layout of ground floor of Facility A. The entrance is on the upper left. The large central area is the living and dining room. Numbered spaces on the right are personal living areas.

(~USD 19.5) per day, meaning that the daily cost to a user was about 4,100 yen (~USD 35). Because almost all residents were on public assistance (a few paid their fees with pension money and used public assistance to make up the shortage), they paid this amount out of a monthly benefit of about 130,000 yen (~USD 1,100). According to the *Survey of the State of Housing Facilities* conducted by Tokyo prefecture (Tokyo Metropolitan Government Bureau of Social Welfare 2003), the fees for Facility A, compared to other free or low-rent housing facilities, were higher than the average of 3,235 yen (~USD 27.4)/day.[8] However, the services provided by Facility A included all eight items considered in this study: assistance in daily activities (provided by 83.9% of housing facilities), responding to complaints (91.6%), health management (88.8%), employment assistance (90.1%), housing search services (54.5%), aftercare following discharge (15.4%), assistance in using welfare services (65.0%), and leisure activities (21.0%). As this shows, for a free or low-rent housing facility, the quality of Facility A's service was relatively high.

Free or low-rent housing facilities obtain their clients in two ways: by introduction or request from a welfare office, and by their own recruiting efforts in the streets or other public places. The former

```
                    6:00    Wake up
                    7:00    Breakfast
                   11:30    Lunch
          2:00–10:00 p.m.   Bath (daily)
                    5:30    Dinner
                   10:00    Curfew, Lights Out, Bed


     Withdrawal of Cash: Monday–Friday 9:00–12:00
     *No withdrawal on weekends or holidays.

     Laundry time: 7:00 a.m.–5:00 p.m.
```

Figure 4.9: Facility Time Schedule for Users

type of client makes up 52.2% of the users of housing facilities run by nonprofit corporations, and the welfare offices apparently approve of the environment and activities of these free or low-rent housing facilities to some extent (Tokyo Metropolitan Government Bureau of Social Welfare 2003). Accordingly, all client admissions to Facility A were made through the introduction or request of a welfare office. The specific process was that a caseworker from the welfare office, after approving the provision of public assistance, would recommend Facility A to a recipient who needed a place to live. That individual would visit the facility and learn about its operations, and after concluding a contract with Facility A, would move in.

Facility A had a 10:00 p.m. curfew, but residents could otherwise go out at any time, and could spend the night elsewhere with advance permission. When staying at the facility, residents followed a set time schedule. They woke up 6:00 a.m. and lights went out at 10:00 p.m., with three mealtimes at 7:00 a.m., 11:30 a.m., and 5:30 p.m. (Figure 4.9). Tasks such as cleaning, setting the table, and washing dishes were rotated among the residents. Otherwise, although some residents had appointments for outpatient therapy or participated in community workshops, fundamentally, individuals could spend time as they chose, watching television, going for walks, conversing, and the like. Baths could be taken daily, and washing machines were available for use. The residents' money was, as a rule, managed by

Facility A aims to help prepare its residents to begin new lives in the local community. The following are the rules for living here. Please make them a part of the rhythm of your life.

1. Daily life follows the schedule you received separately. Please work to live your life in a stable, regular rhythm by following it.

2. Tasks for cleaning the facility are assigned to residents in turns. Please take care of the place assigned to you. Also, make sure to keep your clothes clean, bathe regularly, and clean your room.

3. Drinking alcohol and gambling are strictly forbidden in this facility. Borrowing and lending money are strictly forbidden.

4. Smoke only at the designated places. Smoking in bed is strictly forbidden.

5. You are responsible for your own belongings. Valuables should be given to the staff member on duty. Please use only your own toothbrush, shaver, towel, and other personal items. Do not borrow or lend these items.

6. Food at meals will be prepared and served by the people on duty. Staff members will be glad to advise and support you. We hope you will enjoy preparing meals while keeping safe. Remember to clean up afterward.

7. The funding for running this facility is provided by housing and living assistance money that is paid to each user. This money is collected by the facility when the user moves in, and cash payments are made to the user for needs such as transportation money for visiting the hospital. When the user moves out, all expenses are settled. Unused money is returned to the user.

From the Director

Figure 4.10: Rules presented to facility users

the staff, but the residents could withdraw money with permission. Also, almost all facility users were on some sort of medication, but most had their medication managed by staff members so that they would not forget to take it. The rules were reviewed for each person applying for residence, and the applicant's agreement was obtained prior to concluding the admission contract (Figure 4.10).

Facility residents

During the ten months in which this study was conducted, twenty-four women made use of Facility A. The average user age was 60.5.

According to the categories used by Facility A, the reasons for staying in the facility were: escaping rough sleeping – six people; no place to return after discharge from hospital – five; difficulty taking care of oneself when living alone – four; domestic violence[9] – three; transferred from another facility – three; other or unknown – three. However, these categories only give the immediate reason for entry; in many cases several factors overlapped. For instance, six women used the facility to escape rough sleeping, but when other women with a history of rough sleeping are included the total comes to twelve. Additionally, five women suffered from mental disorders and three from intellectual disabilities.

I will now discuss the four residents of Facility A who provided the most extensive narratives and anecdotes depicting their treatment and the processes that led to their coming to Facility A.

Sumiko, age seventy (Chapter 2, Table 2.4), who was introduced in chapter 2, came to Facility A to escape from rough sleeping. Sumiko had a mild congenital handicap that caused her to walk with a limp (Grade 5 disability). She was a caring and conscientious person. Both residents and staff trusted her. I will not repeat that life narrative here, but after accumulating debts from borrowing money to make ends meet, she ended up a rough sleeper along with her husband. Four days after they began sleeping by a train station, they learned from a volunteer they happened to meet that they might be eligible for public assistance, and after visiting a welfare office together, they began receiving benefits. However, because there were no facilities they could use as a couple, her husband went to a men's facility, and Sumiko, after checking into a hospital for an examination, parted with her husband to enter Facility A.

> It was lonely at first, being separated from each other. My husband was taken away. As for me, I went right to the hospital. "You need to be hospitalized," they said. It was hard, having no idea what would happen to me. I felt lonely and helpless. After four or five days, I figured that once I got better they'd take me somewhere else. It was frightening. Before I came here I was really nervous and worried. Even after I got here, until I figured things out, I wondered what kind of place it was. Until I understood how it worked here, I worried about it – I didn't know what kind of person they took care of here.

Sumiko, recalling that time, says that separating from her husband was very painful, even if it enabled her to receive public assistance. Also, her unfamiliarity with Facility A caused her much stress and worry until she got used to it.

Kazuko, age sixty-eight (Chapter 2, Table 2.4, 13), also introduced in chapter 2, moved into Facility A after leaving the hospital because she had no place to return to. Due to a childhood injury, she was nearly blind in one eye, and she suffered from high blood pressure and other ailments, so she visited doctors regularly for treatment. Without repeating her life history here, she became a rough sleeper after losing her job and leaving the home of a friend where she had been staying. After two months of rough sleeping, a volunteer she had met accompanied her to a welfare office, and she began to receive public assistance.

> [Q: Did you know before then that you could go to the welfare office for information about receiving public assistance?] No. I thought it was mostly men who go to that kind of place.

As Kazuko's statement shows, her understanding of who used the public system was tied to gender: her belief was that it did not apply to women. Afterward, she spent time in the hospital, and had some tests, and then moved into a different all-women's free or low-rent housing facility. Life there was "unbearable," and feeling her presence was a burden on others, "I just wanted to be left alone."

> Well, ———— [staff member] was fine, but ———— [staff member] was really two-faced – you couldn't trust her. I'd always say to my roommate, "I'm always walking on eggshells, trying not to upset people," though everyone said "you have to be grateful for being able to live here at all... You might get upset about things, but you can't leave. You have to put up with whatever happens." [Q: What was the worst thing?] I'd have to say it was the way the people in charge ran things. Their attitude. She was horrible.

Kazuko stayed there for about a year, but was hospitalized again when her physical condition deteriorated. When asked whether she had considered returning to the same housing facility, she replied, "I'd rather live on the streets than go back there." She then moved into Facility A.

[Q: How did you end up here?] You'd have to ask the caseworker.
The caseworker found it for me based on what they thought. [Q: Did
you express any wish about what kind of place you'd like to live in?]
No, because I didn't know what was there. I didn't know there were
welfare facilities like this for women only, or where they were. [Q:
And then you visited with the caseworker?] Right, the caseworker
brought me over...

When asked to explain how she ended up in Facility A, Kazuko
responded that only the caseworker knew; it was apparent that she
was brought there without being offered any choice between types of
facilities or being asked about her preferences.

Aki (Chapter 2, Table 2.4, 27) is forty years old. She moved into
Facility A to escape domestic violence from her husband. She has
paralysis on one side of her body, and walks with a walking stick.
She goes out to meet with a self-help group to cope with her addictive
behavior, and uses Facility A basically as a place to sleep. After
graduating from high school, Aki worked as a regular employee at a
supermarket and a research firm. At twenty-eight she married a man
from her workplace. That same year, she suffered a stroke, which left
her paralyzed on one side. Her husband, she says, repeatedly told her
"I didn't marry you to take care of you." After that, she spent her time
in rehabilitation and doing housework. Unfortunately, she habitually
gambled at pachinko (a pinball-type game), and gradually spent her
husband's salary, her pension, and money for living expenses, finally
accumulating debts. At about this time her husband began physically
abusing her. When she was thirty-nine, she went to stay with a friend
to get away. That friend consulted with a local health center, through
which she was introduced to a Women's Consultation Center, where
she was admitted for two weeks of temporary protection as a victim of
domestic violence. There, a doctor diagnosed her as having a gambling
addiction. The doctor advised her to join a self-help group to cope
with her disorder, and she moved into Facility A as a base for doing so.

Namie, age sixty, had transferred from another facility. (Because
her life history is unclear in many respects, it is not included in Table
2.4 of Chapter 2.) She suffered from paralysis in one hand and from a
constant, slight physical tremor. This made it difficult for her to hold
eating utensils and carry things, but she could get by in daily life on
her own. She says she was told at facilities where she has previously
stayed that her intellectual level was somewhat low, but she had never

received a Rehabilitation Certificate. After graduating from middle school, she worked delivering newspapers and milk. She married at thirty-one. Her husband became violent when he drank, and the marriage lasted only two years. They had no children. After that, her husband was imprisoned, but Namie remained in his parents' home after they divorced, continuing delivery work. She says that she began to suffer physical tremors after a traffic accident she was involved in while working. Although the details of her subsequent history were unclear, after two years of rough sleeping she was hospitalized for testing. After leaving the hospital she received temporary protection at a Women's Consultation Center, then moved into a Women's Protection Facility. Subsequently, she transferred to a Rehabilitation Facility, but after being evicted following a dispute with another resident, she came to Facility A.

As the life histories of these women show, the reasons given for moving in to Facility A were chosen out of convenience; the factors that led to admission were complex and not reducible to simple categories. Women like Kazuko and Namie were classified under "no place to go after discharge from hospital" and "transferred from another facility," but their original reason for moving in was that they were sleeping rough. Aki's immediate reason for moving in was domestic violence, but she also suffered from compulsive gambling, and the two problems were inseparable.

As with Sumiko and Kazuko, almost none of the users of Facility A had a clear consciousness of the reason they had moved into this facility rather than others. And like Sumiko, many other women reported feeling anxiety from not knowing where they would be taken. As we can see, then, women did not freely chose to move into Facility A on the basis of information provided or select it from a range of options. As noted, Facility A is not for involuntary admission. Users supposedly enter of their free will by contractual agreement. But although they may have agreed to sign a contract after observing the facility, when they have been brought in by a caseworker with the power to decide their eligibility for public assistance, they may have little choice in the matter. Furthermore, the limited number of facilities available to women, and the limited number of spaces within them, means there was in fact almost no choice. Thus, even though in theory users entered Facility A by voluntary contract, in effect admission was almost always compulsory, determined by the authority of the caseworkers.

Determining client needs and type of support to provide

Facility A is a transitional facility. A "space where...clients prepare themselves for a new life in the community," its purpose is to help its users transition to life in a local community. Almost all of its residents receive public assistance, and ultimately, it is up to the caseworker from the welfare office to decide, taking into account the client's wishes and issues, whether the client can receive public assistance and what direction her life takes after she leaves the facility. Since how the client does from day to day at Facility A is an important factor in making these decisions, clients had contact as needed with caseworkers while living there. The direction of the client's life after leaving was thus determined through ongoing three-way negotiations between the client, the caseworker(s), and Facility A. Based on what plan of action was decided upon, Facility A provided services designed to help her adjust to life after leaving. However, for some individuals, no clear plan was ever established for what to do after leaving. This was probably because caseworkers, pressed by their daily job responsibilities, did not go out of their way to contact the facility or the client unless there was a particular problem. Furthermore, it was often the case that clients in apparently similar situations were treated differently based on factors like welfare office policies and the caseworkers' different understandings of the problems.

The largest category of users of Facility A was those waiting for an opening at another facility such as a critical care nursing home or a Rehabilitation Facility. These individuals generally suffered from illness or disability and would go for outpatient treatment or be seen at Facility A by visiting doctors or nurses. Four were elderly women certified as needing care (at required care levels 1–3 on a scale of 1–5, with 5 indicating the greatest need), who received care from home helpers or went out for daytime care provided by long-term care insurance. However, because the waiting period to get into critical care nursing homes is often long for elderly people with low required care levels, they tended to remain in Facility A for a long period. Clients with mental and intellectual disabilities or addictive disorders would go out to community workshops and to see self-help groups and counselors. However, because there are few facilities that take in people with these kinds of issues, it was difficult to establish a plan of action, which resulted in their stay at

Facility A being extended. Some users of Facility A also used their time there to try to establish a healthy rhythm in their life and get experience working, in order to live independently in an apartment after leaving.

During the study period there were ten people who moved out of Facility A. Four of them left when openings came up in facilities for which they were waitlisted. Two went to live in ordinary housing while continuing to receive public assistance. Two were transferred by ambulance to a hospital when their condition deteriorated, one entered a psychiatric hospital, and one left of her own accord. The average length of stay was nine and a half months.

We will now look at the four individuals discussed previously to get a concrete picture of how the residents of Facility A view their lives there, what vision they have of the future, and how the form and direction of their assistance is determined.

Sumiko had separated from her husband in order to receive public assistance and moved into Facility A with much anxiety. I asked about her first impression of the place. She replied that she liked the staff members at the time, and repeatedly expressed her gratitude towards them.

> [Q: What was your first impression?] My first impression was of
> —————, the director, and she was an amazing person... All the people
> in the office were great... I have nothing bad to say about Facility A.
> It was good from the beginning, and the director was wonderful...
> I'm very grateful.

These expressions of gratitude were partly out of consideration for myself (the author), since I was working as a staff member, but they nevertheless indicate that how she was treated by staff members shaped her first impression of Facility A.

When Sumiko first moved into Facility A, the original plan was for her to move into a nursing home together with her husband, who was then in a separate free or low-rent housing facility. However, despite their old age Sumiko and her husband did not require care, so it was likely that they would have a long wait. At some point the director told her, "If you worked you'd have more spending money," and "since I was in good shape," the director began looking for employers who were recruiting older workers. She went to an Employment Stability Office several times but was not able to find a suitable job. She was then told by the director that another housing facility run by the same nonprofit organization that ran Facility A was looking for meal servers.

> The director asked if I wanted to work, and I said yes… I asked her to set it up for me. I am glad to be working there.

As a result, Sumiko began going to work twice a week, although limiting her hours so her extra income did not exceed the exempted amount of 8,000 yen (~USD 68) per month that can be taken home without resulting in a reduction of her public assistance benefits.[10] Unlike men of working age receiving benefits, who are expected to look for work, a seventy-year-old woman receiving benefits would normally not be expected to work. However, following a suggestion to increase her spending money by working, she decided that she wanted to work, and helped by her reputation at Facility A for being a reliable person, she was able to find a job.

Sometime later, Sumiko's husband, who had been staying in a different housing facility, was evicted from the facility for breaking the rules prohibiting drinking and gambling. He was also deprived of his public assistance benefits. Sumiko was shocked at this, and defended him, saying that he was not a bad person.

> They say that he was drinking and playing pachinko and things. A staff member of his dormitory called the caseworker and told them. And the caseworker there got a very bad impression of him, as a drinker and gambler. But he's not so bad – I know it sounds like I'm praising him because he's my husband, but he's really not that bad.

Having lost his benefits, Sumiko's husband returned to living on the streets. She reported that he would sometimes call her, and they would sometimes arrange to meet at places like parks. Sumiko said that initially she was very concerned about her husband living by himself as a rough sleeper, and thought of going to be with him. However, as she got used to living at Facility A, and influenced by the advice of staff members, she said she eventually more or less let go of the idea of living with him – "my husband can worry about himself" – and focused on her own life.

I'm OK with him taking care of himself. I've been living apart from him for a year, more than a year, and I've gotten used to it. The director told me at the beginning not to think about him too much, that worrying wouldn't help. I'm comfortable with the situation now, and he can live his own life as far as I'm concerned – I'm not stuck on being with him anymore.

According to Sumiko, she discussed her husband's loss of benefits any number of times at first, but recently, she had stopped bringing it up because it would injure his pride as a man. In other words, she used the gendered concept "man" in expressing her concern for him.

So if I mention what happened before or what Facility A has done for me [implying the burden that his losing his benefits placed on Facility A], he gets angry and tells me not to bring it up. And I don't want to talk about it either. I mean, he brought it on himself. I know men get mad when you tell them something like that, so though I used to mention it a lot I don't anymore.

Sumiko's original wish when she moved into Facility A was to live in a nursing home where she could be with her husband. But as a result of her husband's problems, she told her caseworker that since she was still in good shape physically she no longer wanted to move to a nursing home. And although she still felt, following the traditional ideal of a family, that "a married couple should live together," she said that if that was impossible, she wanted to continue living apart from him in Facility A for the time being.

I asked my caseworker, and (s)he said I don't have to go to a nursing home if I don't want to. My caseworker has taken me off the wait list for nursing homes... I'm still healthy, and I'm still, I can't say young, since I'm over seventy. If I was weak physically it would be another matter, but since I'm still in good condition, I asked to be taken off the list... [Q: Do you have an idea of what you want to do in the future?] Well, I don't think it's possible to be with my husband. I'd be happy to stay here for the time being. I'm satisfied at this point to be able to get together and talk with him once in a while. Though I do worry about him. I hope he'll be able to settle down somewhere. We are married, so ideally we should be living together, but with things the way they are, I've more or less given up on it, though that may sound coldhearted.

Later, when the director of Facility A suggested that she visit a Rehabilitation Facility to see what it was like, Sumiko refused. She was concerned about "getting along with people" if she moved to another facility, and preferred to stay at Facility A, which was familiar.

> I wish the people here at Facility A would stop telling me to leave. My caseworker told me I can stay here as long as I live, you know. So I won't know what to do if the Facility A people tell me, "Sumiko, you can't stay here anymore." I won't know what to do if they say they want me to leave. I don't want to move to another facility, anyway. They said it was only to go see what it was like, but I said I didn't want to go... When the previous director was still here, they said, "Sumiko, why don't you try a Rehabilitation Facility?" So I told them that I'd rather they let me stay here permanently than go somewhere else. I don't want to go somewhere else. I'll have to get along with new people if I do that. Yes, I know even if I stay here lots of people will come and go, but I'm comfortable here. I know it's not all about me, but I don't want to go to any other facility. That's being honest. I don't want to move.

Sumiko also said that she "tries to do whatever she can" to ensure that she is not made to leave Facility A, and repeatedly talked about her "gratitude" to Facility A. Although she wanted to live with her husband, since she understood that this was almost impossible while she was receiving public assistance, Sumiko wanted to stay at Facility A as long as possible. For that reason, she tried to make the best impression she could on the staff members, showing her gratitude and avoiding conflicts.

When Kazuko first moved into Facility A, she had borrowed a considerable amount of money that she had to repay, and expressed a desire to work. Although she went to some interviews, Kazuko, at the advanced age of sixty-eight and with impaired vision in one eye, could not find work. At a certain point, a plan was made for her to go on a waiting list for a nursing home while staying at Facility A. However, Kazuko had ongoing conflicts with the friend to whom she was paying back the money, and was often given warnings by her caseworker about her behavior when meeting the friend and other matters. This made Kazuko extremely concerned that she might lose her public assistance benefits. When I asked Kazuko what she hoped to do after leaving Facility A, she began to cry, and answered that she

wanted to stay there as long as possible, but if that was impossible
she had nowhere else to go.

[Q: What do you want to do after you leave here?] I don't have
anywhere to go if I leave here, so I don't know. I can't even handle
living on the streets – I'm not strong enough. This is more than I have
a right to anyway, living in a single room like this on taxpayer money,
right? [Q: How long would you like to stay here?] Well [laughing],
I can't exactly ask them to let me stay the rest of my life, can I? [Q:
If you could stay the rest of your life would you want to?] Sure, if I
could. If they say I can't do that, then where am I supposed to go? ...
I don't have the ability to take care of myself anyway. [Q: Does the
caseworker or anybody ever ask you where you want to go or what you
want to do with your life?] Uh, no, we've never talked about anything
that specific. It's really too much to expect, just being able to be here.
Someone like you has no idea. When they say you have to leave and
you have nowhere to go, there's nothing you can do. When you get to
be my age... [*begins to cry*]

One source of Kazuko's anxiety was probably insufficient communi-
cation with her caseworker to gain her understanding and agreement
on her plans for the future. She went on to say that it was thanks
to the caseworkers and staff that she was able to be at Facility A.

I feel it's more than I deserve, when there are people in greater need
than me. Having all this done for me [i.e., receiving public assistance
and staying at Facility A] ... I owe it to my caseworker that I can be
here. And the director...she's a really kind person.

However, Kazuko had also been warned repeatedly by staff about
problems with her behavior when she went out. She often failed to
return to the facility at the time she had promised, and was often late
to doctors' visits or meals without informing the facility. Kazuko
was aware that these were violations of Facility A's rules, and she
was clearly worried that her failure to follow the rules could lead
to her eviction.

I've certainly caused problems for the director. Like, I say that I'll be
right back and then stay out for hours [*laughs*]... [Q: You'd like to stay
here permanently?] Oh, yes. It's ridiculous, but I sometimes think I'd

be happy to stay here until I die. But from what I hear it's not possible
to stay that long... Not only that, I know that although I try to follow
the rules here, I sometimes break them. Like coming back when I said
I would [*laughs*]. It's not that I'm really such a reckless person, though.

As in Sumiko's case, Kazuko, too, depended on her caseworker to
decide whether she could receive public assistance. And since the
caseworker had never discussed plans with her, she was unable to
get a clear vision of what her future might be like, which filled her
with anxiety. As a result, she believed that causing as few problems
as possible at Facility A was important for continuing to receive
public assistance and continuing to stay at the facility.

As soon as Aki moved into Facility A, under directions from her
doctor, she began to attend a self-help group to treat her addiction.

> On the first day I went to observe [the self-help group] to see how it
> worked. And that same day I decided to join it right away. I had been
> told to do it, after all. I wanted to quit the gambling lifestyle, to get
> away from it. And I found out all the other people in the group had
> the same issues. I guess hearing that made me feel more comfortable.
> I started to think that if I worked with the group, I could get better.

As Aki reported, visiting the self-help group convinced her that
through it, she might be able to give up gambling. After that, she
began to go to meetings three times a day. The support plan for
Aki at that time was to use her stay at Facility A to figure out
whether she should live alone in ordinary housing, or move into
another facility.

> Until recently I wouldn't have even known what "addiction" meant.
> I thought my pachinko addiction was just being really into playing
> pachinko. That's what most people think, right? So I wouldn't
> think I had that kind of problem at all. But I also had a drinking
> problem, and of course I gambled, and was dependent on men, and
> had a codependency problem. And what that meant was that I had
> been addicted to these things for a long time – including to men
> I liked. [Q: And you realized this when people in the self-help
> group told you?] Well, I heard their stories and figured it out. It's
> not that they told me I was addicted, but I heard their stories... It's
> group therapy.

After being diagnosed by the doctor, and attending the self-help group, over time, Aki went from "just thinking I was really into pachinko" to recognizing that she had an addiction. She then began to realize that not only her gambling, but also her relationships with men could be understood as addictions. Even when Facility A was helping Aki to get through the process of her divorce and personal bankruptcy, she continued to attend the self-help group each day, becoming excited about the program and valuing her relationship with her fellow group members. Time continued to pass without her returning to gambling.

> I have a group of friends who understand what it's like. It gives me confidence that I can quit. That's why you go every day, whether it's early in the morning, whether it's raining. It's for me, after all... There were many times I badly wanted to get away, but I don't want to escape anymore. I've been treated well all along... My friends will wait for me, they believe in me... I can manage because of my friends, you know?

Aki hoped to live independently in an apartment after leaving Facility A. However, she felt that she needed to remain in Facility A until her doctor gave her permission to leave, and says that her caseworker said the same thing.

> So I won't be able to do what I want as long as they keep me here. But I can't leave until the doctor in charge at the clinic says I can move into an apartment, and the people at the welfare office also say I have to wait for the doctor's approval... [Q: So what if you could move into an apartment, if you did get approval...?] I would want to move in. I need to be able to live my own life.

Aki also said: "When I'm all better I'd like to get married again, happily. I want to have a family." "I don't want to be alone all my life." At the same time, since joining the self-help group, Aki realized that she had a problem with dependency on men, and felt that to treat her addiction disorder, she would have to approach relationships with men differently than she had before. There was one man in the self-help group who Aki had feelings for, and she had received a lot of advice on how to interact with him from one of the senior female members of the group.

She says it's fine to have feelings for someone, but not to start anything. Once you start something, you'll get stuck in a bad situation… I mean, it was terrible for me before. There was always someone at my side, without exception, some man. I had boyfriends, I had a husband, all my friends were men too. She tells me not to mess up anymore, that I can't afford to make a mistake.

Aki also said that her mentor advised her that she needs to learn to have good relationships with other women – "Since you're a woman yourself you have to make women friends." A senior member of the self-help group also advised her to attend women-only meetings of that group. The self-help group in general expects its members to abstain from relationships with men until they have refrained from gambling for three years and successfully transitioned to living independently. Aki said that she dreamed of the day when the three years of abstinence come to an end.

Well, people like my sponsor [the member of the self-help group who had been advising her] say we can't get married until we've been sober [free from gambling] for at least three years – three years is the yardstick. [Q: So after three years you're generally allowed to get married?] Yes, in theory, if someone says they want to, and the sponsor says, all right, it seems like you're about ready. We all see senior members who are married, and there are people in the group who got married after waiting for three years. That's what I want, if things were perfect.

Through participating in the self-help group, Aki rethought her relationships with men prior to that point, and picked up new views on what made up a good family or good relationships with men or friends. She was working to have a "good life" as described in the advice she got at the group. She would stay with the self-help group for the rest of her life, she said, to make sure she never went back to gambling.

I'll attend for the rest of my life. I can't stop moving forward. When people quit they always end up drinking, gambling, and some people even die. The senior members have explained how it is and I get it – they've shown me how it really is… They say you'll lose your mind if you stop going [to meetings]. Attending is what makes it possible to stay sober, because of the help of the group members. So I'll go the rest of my life.

Aki, as we can see, was greatly committed to the principles of the self-help group and tried to follow the group's guidance faithfully. Taking her doctor's diagnosis into account, she also held a clear vision of what kind of future she wanted for herself: to one day live independently, to treat her addiction disorder by participating in the self-help group, and, after some years, to get married again. She also had been doing physical training to help her to live independently despite her persistent paralysis.

To coordinate the various welfare entities involved in Aki's case, a meeting was held every three months between the public assistance caseworker, a women's counselor from the Women's Consultation Center, a nurse from the public health center, and a caseworker from the disability department. This gave the people working with her a clear picture of the challenges in her case and her future direction. And Aki herself, thanks to the self-help group, which gave her a daily venue for dealing with her problems, was able to think clearly and calmly about her future and what she needed to do now to achieve her goals. After the procedures for her divorce and personal bankruptcy were complete, after about a year living in Facility A, Aki moved to a women's housing facility that had been recently opened by the self-help group.

In the previous facility she had stayed in, Namie had a reputation for often having serious conflicts with other people. She moved to Facility A after a fight with another resident. She also exhibited problematic behavior at Facility A, such as not bathing for months. The original consensus was that because of her physical disability the most appropriate facility for her would be a Relief Facility that provides living assistance.

Namie liked to smoke, and consumed more than a pack of cigarettes a day. She used most of her monthly spending money on cigarettes and the occasional can of coffee. However, at a certain point, her public assistance was reduced so that she had less spending money, and could no longer buy as many cigarettes as she used to. As a result, when the end of the month came Namie would frequently ask fellow residents and staff members for money and cigarettes. The director, explained to her many times that her benefits had been reduced and that she would not be able to buy cigarettes in the same amount as before, but Namie did not seem to understand, getting angry and repeating her request for money.

Around this time the cigarettes belonging to another resident who left them in the smoking room disappeared, and a rumor started that Namie had them. Other residents also repeatedly found that cigarettes, sweets, and the like which they kept in their own rooms had gone missing. Namie was also witnessed several times leaving the rooms of other residents. When this happened she always said that she had gone into the wrong room by mistake, but it became obvious that she was stealing things. The director at Facility A concluded that if Namie continued stealing, they could no longer allow her to reside in the facility, and they had Namie sign an agreement that she would be evicted the next time she stole something from another resident's room. Namie's caseworker was informed of this development.

Some days later, Namie was once again seen leaving the room of another resident. True to the agreement, Namie was evicted from Facility A. The recommendation from Facility A was that Namie be moved to live by herself in ordinary housing and continue to receive support from an aftercare program for former residents of Facility A that was run by the same nonprofit organization. However, Namie's caseworker stated that Namie would not be approved for living in ordinary housing and would lose her public assistance. Namie said that in that case she would go back to sleeping rough. In the end, the caseworker found a psychiatric hospital that would take Namie, and she moved there, after about one year living in Facility A.

For practical purposes, Namie was forcibly evicted from Facility A for failing to keep her agreement. During the period in which I surveyed Facility A for this study, there were various incidents in which the prohibition on gambling or curfews were broken, or residents were caught shoplifting, but in no other case was a resident forcibly evicted. Although theft was not specifically mentioned in Facility A's rules, Namie's theft was a repeated infraction of the social code, which is presumably what led to her eviction. Another factor leading to different treatment than for other infractions was that her actions harmed other residents. Despite this, in the end Namie kept her public assistance, and her caseworker was able to find another facility that would take her. Although Namie considered going back to rough sleeping, unlike Sumiko's husband, who lost his public assistance due to his drinking and gambling, Namie did not lose her public assistance. This was probably because Namie's caseworker acted to prevent a disabled woman from becoming a rough sleeper. A difference may exist between men and women when it comes to the standard for cutting off public assistance.

The first thing to note from these accounts is how residents like Sumiko and Kazuko, when asked their impression of the facility, mentioned the way they were initially treated by staff members. Likewise, Sumiko's citation of relationships with other people as the primary reason that she didn't want to move to another facility indicates that personal relationships within the facility and the staff's treatment of residents played major roles in shaping their desire to stay in this facility. Also, Kazuko understood her public assistance as coming from "taxpayer money" and the hard work of the caseworkers who helped her obtain it. We can see, then, that welfare systems and facilities are not impersonal things, but were understood differently by the various individuals who operated and used them.

Another point is that the only rules given to the residents when they moved in were that drinking and gambling were prohibited and that curfews must be followed. However, in reality, a variety of expectations concerning behavior in daily life – such as returning at the promised time, in Kazuko's case, or bathing regularly, in Namie's case – were communicated in the form of "warnings." Failure to heed such warnings did not in itself lead to loss of benefits or eviction. But many users, like Sumiko and Kazuko, were not adequately informed by their caseworkers about what they could expect after leaving, and were uncertain about how long they would stay in Facility A. Hence, they tried to make a good impression by not causing problems and by expressing gratitude to the staff. We may conclude that it was not so much that residents obeyed the rules that had been formally presented to them as conditions for staying at Facility A or receiving welfare, as that they tried to adhere to what they, subjectively, believed to be the standards in order to avoid making trouble, based on uncertainty about what would happen to them in the future.

Further, it was caseworkers and the Facility A staff who decided whether benefits would be awarded, and users were expected to follow their directions. But there were others, too, whose advice had a major influence on what would happen to these women, including individuals from associated welfare and medical entities, such as doctors and self-help groups. A variety of expectations from a variety of perspectives set the context in which plans for support were decided.

In addition, in terms of different philosophies underlying support for men and women, generally, men of working age who apply for public assistance are expected to seek work. For women, although the situation varies based on age and health, the expectation for women to work is lower, and for this very reason, wages are low enough that it is difficult to be paid more than one would receive in public assistance benefits. Sumiko and Kazuko, despite being older women who were not expected to seek employment, nevertheless did so, just as a man of working age would. This was not so much because they were guided to do so by others as because they chose to.

Gender: one form of social expectation

As shown in Chapter 3, welfare systems available to homeless women were organized so as to pressure women to conform to prevailing social norms. However, when implemented, these systems give local governments and caseworkers much discretion; questions about which system or facility to use are determined by a variety of factors, including availability and local rules. Thus, they do not have uniform expectations for all women in terms of gender roles. In fact, in the process of determining what type of assistance would be provided, there were relatively few cases in which norms or standards were explicitly defined. On the contrary, in some cases, because women lacked a clear picture of what their future life would be like, and feared losing their benefits or being evicted, they tried very hard to be cooperative, submissive, and to avoid making trouble. In the discourse of welfare practice, there were, in fact, relatively few normative statements referring to gender as a category.

It is therefore incorrect to assume, as Passaro does, that the general direction in which the welfare system leads women is the same as the norms that homeless woman are expected to follow. The expectations for women using a welfare system are not necessarily defined in terms of gender. Gender-based expectations make up only one part of a wide variety of social expectations. These expectations are embodied in the decisions made by caseworkers as to whether benefits will be awarded and what type of services will be provided, and in the advice and diagnoses given by welfare and medical organizations. They are found in facility rules, staff warnings, and in interactions with other facility users. In some cases, the social expectations presented by various agents in various forms contradicted each other. The individual women staying in Facility A, for their part, differed greatly from one another in the sorts of statements they made related to gender. Passaro tends to essentialize gender in her interpretation of the differences between women who continue rough sleeping and those who use welfare services when she draws parallels between those who reject gender roles and those who do not. She overlooks the multiplicity and fluidity of norms as well as the individuality of women.

This should become even more obvious when we examine the practices of women who continue to live as rough sleepers. Passaro's argument implies an essential difference in gender identity between the women in Facility A and women rough sleepers. In the next chapter, I will challenge this assumption by examining cases of homeless women who sleep rough.

5 The world of women who sleep rough

Life histories of women who sleep rough

We will now turn our attention to the lives of women who have slept rough for a significant period. This chapter will begin by looking at the way that female rough sleepers live from day to day.

The diets, income sources, relationships, and other aspects of the lives of rough sleepers all vary greatly depending on whether they sleep outside at stations and roadsides or whether they have a fixed residence in tents and other shelters set up in places such as parks and riverbeds. This chapter will look at the case of the homeless women living in Park B, Tokyo prefecture, whom I surveyed in 2003. Park B is fairly large. At the time of my research, about 250 people were living there in tents. Out of the approximately ten women among them, I will discuss the four rough sleepers with whom I was able to become especially close. I will begin by describing, in order, how they became rough sleepers.

I met my first informant, Eiko (Chapter 2, Table 2.4, 29), when I was participating in a group for homeless women in Park B. She had a friendly, easygoing personality that made her the first woman rough sleeper at Park B I was able to get to know well. Although she gave her age as sixty, other interviewers recorded her age as fifty-four or sixty-six, so her exact age is uncertain.

Eiko came from a family of nine children in a prefecture that neighbors Tokyo prefecture. Her parents divorced when she was little, and she and her siblings were raised by her father. She reported that because of memory problems resulting from a serious illness at age two, and bullying she suffered as the child of a poor family, her school attendance fell off over time. To this day, she is virtually illiterate.

> Officially, I went to elementary school, but really I only went sometimes. When I went I would find they were far ahead of me. The

boys, especially, would be mean. They would get out of the way when
I came. They'd refuse to share their textbooks with me. They'd say I
was dirty. When I was going home from school, they'd run away from
me. "Get away, she's dirty. Dirty, dirty."

So I couldn't learn anything even if I tried... Sometimes I'd steal
[notebooks] from other kids. I wanted those things so much. I realize
now that it was wrong to do that, but I wanted them so much... They
were distributed at school, and you had to bring money, but I didn't
have money. And when I would manage to go to school, they were
so far ahead, I didn't understand what they were doing. Not at all. I
had to be with boys, and I didn't have anything to wear, and they'd
call me dirty and things. And I was shy and couldn't talk to people.
Finally I didn't want to go to school anymore.

After being permitted to graduate from elementary school in form only,
she worked at places like Japanese inns. She was married between
her late twenties and her late forties, when her husband died. She did
not have children. After her husband passed away, she worked while
receiving public assistance. Her inability to read or work competently
with numbers held her back in daily life as well as at work, and she
was often mistreated as a result. She says that these experiences gave
her a sense of inferiority that made her feel very discouraged.

I mean, I haven't been to school. I don't have an education. I can't get
a job anywhere because I can't fill out a resume. They need a resume.
I wish I could write one, but I can't... Since you have to be able to
write for these jobs, I never think I can get one.

I worked part-time for a company that sold smoked foods... I went
there part-time. Do you know those scales for weighing things? You
have five food items, and a box, and you subtract the weight of the
packaging to get the weight of the food. But I don't know how to do
it [arithmetic]. People really tormented me for that... I have no idea, I
can't do math... It was awful. I wished I knew how, but they wouldn't
teach me. They don't say "this is how to do it." It really hurt, being
looked down on like that. I wished I could do math.

Later, she began living with her older sister and her public assistance
was cut off. According to Eiko, she began sleeping rough after
coming to Tokyo to get a job at a company her sister had introduced
to her. She got lost on the way and ran out of money trying to find her

Photo 5.1: Tamako's tent, where she allowed me to stay.

destination. At the time of the survey, she claimed to be in her tenth year of rough sleeping. For the first three years, she lived vagabond-style with no fixed place to stay. After that she began staying in a tent in a fixed location. At some point the tent was destroyed by a fire, and four years ago, together with other rough sleepers in the area, she moved to Park B.

My acquaintance with Yūko, my second informant (Chapter 2, Table 2.4, 6), was also through the group for women rough sleepers. I started out visiting Eiko in her tent, and since Yūko often came there to see Eiko, I gradually got to know her as well.

Yūko was sixty at the time of the survey. She was one of four sisters, and grew up in a motherless household after the death of her mother when Yūko was ten. After graduating from an evening high school, she got a job at a trading company. In her twenties she married a man who she met at work, but she did not get along with his family, and they divorced after several years. She has lived alone since then. She has no children. Yūko is proud that she worked alongside men on an equal basis and sometimes used being a woman to her advantage. She readily discussed her work, often connecting it to her identity as a woman.

In that sense, if I had the desire...being a woman, it was easier to get what I wanted. But I paid the price. I had to struggle to learn on the job... They wouldn't explain things, so I would take the Shinkansen [high-speed train] to Yokohama to learn more... I would go to the customs office and have them explain things... I'd go to Yokoyama to observe them loading and unloading cargo. No one else would do that kind of thing!

In terms of doing work, there have been lots of advantages to being a woman up till now. It's not that I took advantage of it, but...I'm glad to be a woman! I would hate to have been born a man [*Laughs*]. And being a woman always gives you a way out. You kind of learn that naturally – it's not that you purposely try to use being a woman, but it comes naturally, so I think on some level you know what you're doing.

During the "bubble economy" period of the late 1980s, Yūko formed her own trading company, with herself as president and two employees. At age fifty-two, she met, at a favorite restaurant-pub, a man who worked as a carpenter, and they lived together as husband and wife. However, as the bubble collapsed neither her company nor her husband could get work. Falling behind in the rent, they moved out of their apartment. After sleeping rough at train stations and elsewhere with her husband, five years ago she began living in a tent at Park B.

The group for women rough sleepers was also where I met my third informant, Tamako (Chapter 2, Table 2.4, 30). At the time of the survey Tamako was thirty-six years old. In 2003, when few rough sleepers were young, Tamako was the youngest person in the park. She appeared uncomfortable speaking in front of people, and rarely spoke at the group, inevitably leaving after a short time. I first began speaking to Tamako after being introduced to her by Eiko. When I was alone with her she spoke a great deal and laughed a lot.

Although it is not immediately evident, Tamako has a mild intellectual disability, and has a class 4 Rehabilitation Certificate (the lowest grade). However, because her parents were unable to accept that she had a disability, and refused to admit it for a long time, she did not enter a special school for the disabled until her second year of middle school. Because of this, she was unable to follow what was being learned at elementary school, and says her academic ability is at the lower elementary school level. The many text messages that Tamako sent me regularly contained writing errors.

Kids who have an intellectual disability when they're in elementary school usually go to one of those places, you know, a school for disabled children. But I couldn't go to one of those. I went to a regular school, so I couldn't understand what they were doing [in class], and since I just pretended to do the work, in the end I didn't learn anything. I couldn't keep up with the work. [Q: Did you go to a regular school because your parents didn't realize you had an intellectual disability? Or did they know but still wanted to send you to a regular school?] Yeah, I think so. Basically, I think they did it because they didn't want people to know that I was mentally slow. Because they didn't send me to a special school until the second year of middle school. It would have been better just to send me there from the start. [Q: You're the one who had to suffer, right?] Right. I had gone through the regular grades without learning anything. They wouldn't let me go anywhere, and I couldn't ride the subway by myself, because I was always with my parents.

After graduating from middle school, an introduction by the school she had attended brought Tamako a job at a garment factory. Her parents, concerned about her handicap, monitored her closely, accompanying her on the way to work and involving themselves in her social life. She began to resent the interference. Moreover, her father became violent with her. Tamako began to feel uncomfortable and restricted living with her parents and from the age of twenty-eight would leave home periodically. She reported that while away from home she would live off "spending money" received from men she met through a "telephone club" (*terefon kurabu/terekura*, telephone-based dating service in which men pay to talk to and sometimes meet women).

I couldn't stand it anymore. I felt stifled living at home. Like I'd suffocate... It was no fun being alive. I didn't have any freedom. And the reason I left home was because I wanted to make my parents understand. I couldn't tell my father directly. That's why I would leave, because I couldn't talk about myself or how I felt. [Q: About how long would you stay away from home?] I'd say about a month... [Q: Where would you go for that month or so?] Like I said, I'd always call in to the dating club... [Q: How did you spend your time when you were away from home?] All different ways. This and that.

You know why I called the phone club? I ran away so I didn't have any money. [Q: Did people give you money?] Well, you know, you can ask them for spending money. Some women do that. [Q: Did they give you money?] Sure. I didn't have anywhere to go.

Wanting, as she said, to get away from home, she got married at age twenty-nine to a man in his forties she had met through the club. According to Tamako, she liked children, but was advised by her parents, doctors, and others not to have any because she could not raise them with her intellectual disability. Thus, she had no children. Her husband soon took to gambling night and day, and she once again began leaving home. One time she was away, she was nearly forced to use amphetamines by a man she knew, and was rescued by the man who she now lives with as her husband, who she says is a former *yakuza* gang member. After divorcing her first husband, she stayed with this common-law husband at a friend's home, but when they could not find anywhere else to live they began sleeping rough in Park B. Tamako says that she had no idea she would live as a rough sleeper until her husband brought her to Park B, but that she had no big problem with the idea. She has been sleeping rough for a year and a half.

> My husband didn't tell me anything, I didn't know before I came here [that they would live outdoors]. I had no idea. We didn't have a room to stay in. And he didn't explain, so I didn't know before I got here. I wasn't expecting to live this way. [Q: Did you think you were going to an apartment?] Yeah. And then it was like, "Here it is!" and I thought, well, why not? It won't make any difference if we can live the way we always do. People can think what they think. But I realized if you worry about what people think you'll never be able to manage.

My fourth informant was Fujiko (Chapter 2, Table 2.4, 3). I met Fujiko while staying in Tamako's tent. At the time of the survey she was forty-eight, and had no siblings. She was brought up, she says, by parents whose attitude was that as a woman, she didn't need more education than necessary to marry and take care of household finances.

> My parents used to say – because I'm an only child – I don't remember them ever telling me to study. Because we were a family with a girl... What people used to say in the past was that someone who was born a girl...should get married once in her life even if she ended up coming back home after a week... A girl doesn't need to study. She only needs,

Photo 5.2: The area in front of Tamako's tent. Many people would come to visit. When it rained, blue tarp was laid over it to keep it dry.

> you know arithmetic, not math, just arithmetic. To be able to use the money well that her husband earns at work. To keep the household accounts, that kind of thing, if she takes good care of money, that's all she needs to know. To use the money well that her husband brings home and write it down every day... Take care of it like that, planning it out. All a woman needs to know is how to calculate. Besides that... you have to keep up with washing dishes. Wash them right after you cook... Don't let the laundry pile up.

After graduating from high school, she worked at a hospital calculating patient expenses. Later, she married a taxi driver who she had met at work, but had no children. Continuing working with medical records until age thirty-five, she then became a full-time housewife. She also worked part-time for a period at a supermarket. At some point her husband became the guarantor for a loan taken out by a friend, and when the friend disappeared, he had to take responsibility for the loan. Unable to pay it, he declared personal bankruptcy. She then traveled with her husband to Tokyo, where they hoped to make a new start in a place where they were not known. After sleeping for about a week by a train station, about two months before I surveyed her, they began coming to Park B only in the evenings, to sleep on cardboard sheets. When she found a tent that was available, she settled down in the park.

The hardship of rough sleeping

Next, we will look at the hardships faced by female rough sleepers on a day-to-day basis, focusing mainly on the four women discussed above.

Most rough sleepers suffer from severe poverty and material want. Most rough sleepers start out losing their home, and commence rough sleeping with a tiny amount of cash and a few basic necessities in their possession. Especially at the beginning, they may not know how to find food, a place to sleep, or even the minimal things they need. When Eiko first began sleeping rough, she says that many days she was unable to sleep or eat.

> I hadn't eaten anything... And I hadn't slept, so... I just sat like this, because it was winter. Just like this, sitting on a bench... I hadn't slept, hadn't slept for four or five days, so...

Even after finding a place to sleep, rough sleepers also need to obtain food every day to stay alive. But they often lack food and other necessities, which can lead to health problems. According to a 2012 national survey, 26.7% of rough sleepers responded that their health was poor (MHLW 2012). Fujiko spoke of a time when her husband became ill when they were sleeping rough in severe conditions.

> [Q: Your husband got sick and was taken away in an ambulance?] Yeah. [Q: Had he been sick prior to that?] If he did, there was no sign of it before then... Living like this exhausts you mentally. He wasn't sleeping. I think he couldn't sleep because I was with him [and he worried about me]... At most he would just snooze for about an hour. And so...he got a fever of about 40° [104° F].

Apart from the material privation rough sleepers face, they are also subject to constant pressure from government, businesses, and local residents who want them off the streets. Since the enactment of the Self-Help Act, which explicitly called for the removal of rough sleepers from public places, cases of rough sleepers being forced out of their living spaces and having their belongings confiscated have occurred throughout the country.

Rough sleepers also suffer from harassment and attacks. Every year the media reports assaults by young people on rough sleepers, which result in injuries, and sometimes death. There are countless other, unreported, incidents in which stones are thrown at tents, fireworks set off, and tents and belongings set on fire. Rough sleepers live in public spaces, where they are exposed and defenseless. Danger is a constant companion.

Besides the threat of physical violence, rough sleepers also are subject to verbal abuse and harsh looks expressing prejudice and discrimination. The danger of such harassment and violence is far greater for rough sleepers who stay near train stations and roadsides than to those staying long-term in tents that shield them from view, like the rough sleepers of Park B. Yūko spoke of the ordeal of being exposed to the gaze of passersby when she was sleeping at a station.

> At that time I was staying on sheets of cardboard. During the day there was no place to sleep. At night they'd let you make it into a kind of tent to sleep in, but during the day you had to move them out of the way. And some people would stop and look at you as they passed by. They could see your face clearly even without trying to look. Some people would stare and stare at you. They'd say so you could hear, "Look at her, she's got some nerve smoking those expensive cigarettes." What's wrong with that? I bought them, didn't I? Or, "What do you eat?" When I was sleeping on cardboard, I felt so ashamed, really pathetic.

At the time, in 2003, rough sleeping was tacitly permitted, with no efforts made to forcibly remove tents from Park B. However, since tents had recently been cleared out from neighboring parks, the residents of Park B feared that the same thing would happen to them. The attendant at Park B patrolled the park twice a day, giving rough sleepers detailed directives on how to conduct their daily routine. These directives ranged from where they could hang their laundry and how large their baggage could be, to how to keep the park clean. The attendant was familiar with every tent in the park, and residents had to follow rules such as covering the outside of tents with blue tarp and limiting their height. Setting up new tents in the park was prohibited.

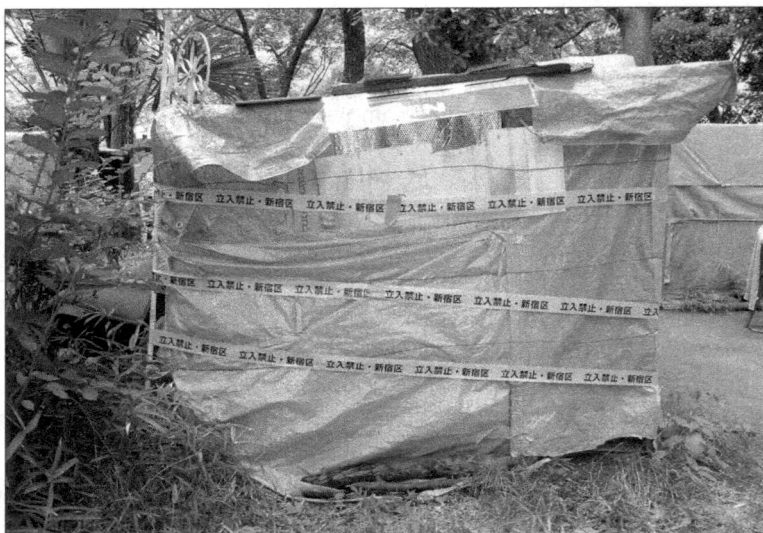

Photo 5.3: An abandoned tent, about to be removed by authorities.

Residents in one particular section of Park B had to be ready to move their tents to a predetermined alternate location when notified by the attendant. The order for this transfer was given regularly, about once a month, although the tents would always be returned to the original place after several days. A reason was always given for the order, such as the need to lay wood chips on the ground, but residents believed that it was partly a form of harassment designed to prevent them from making their tents too big or accumulating too many possessions. And in fact, the tents in this area were set up to enable frequent relocation, and generally were compact in structure compared to other locations.

Even when they are not victims of violence or forced removal, the simple presence of strangers near one's personal living space can be a source of fear. When I asked women rough sleepers what made them afraid living in a park, most immediately replied that using the toilet at night frightened them. Tamako, who lived with her male partner, emphasized the condition of living as a woman surrounded by men. She said that when she was by herself it could be frightening not only at night but even in the daytime.

Oh yeah, as a woman here by yourself, you feel afraid. Sure, once
you get used to it it's usually all right. I have my husband here so
it's not so bad. But honestly, at night even I'm scared... When I
have to use the toilet I wake him up... [Q: Are you sometimes afraid
even with him around?] No, not really, but when he's not around,
when he's not around it's frightening to be by myself, even during
the day.

With all the dangers they are exposed to, women who sleep rough
say that the approach of any stranger, especially a man, is a fearful
moment. Some men may be volunteers who have come to deliver
food or supplies, or to visit the tents to check on the residents'
safety and health. But, says Eiko, since you can't know their
intent until they speak to you, even the sound of their footsteps
approaching makes you frightened. With this in mind, many support
organizations in various locales have made a policy of having
only female representatives approach female rough sleepers when
conducting outreach activities.

[Q: When support groups are patrolling the area, and they go where
women are staying, do they ever give women the job of talking
to women?] Oh yes... When they all meet they talk about how it
would be better for women to talk to women... [Q: And are women
sometimes frightened when it's a man?] Sure. Even I would get scared
when I was staying in the underground passage of a subway station.
[Q: Of the patrol person?] Right. [Q: Because you have no idea who
it is.] Right, no idea.

Women rough sleepers were sometimes subjected to bullying
and violence, not only from passersby, but from other rough
sleepers in the neighborhood. In particular, the testimony of
Eiko, a single woman living in an overwhelmingly male society
of rough sleepers, indicates extensive experience of not only
the fear of violence but actual injury due to violence.[1] Eiko
explains that she suffered violence due to the fact that she was a
"weak person."

There was someone threatening me with violence...so I ran away, in
the middle of the night. To the park, at night, I ran away... [Q: Did you
get hit?] I couldn't afford to get broken bones, so I ran away to the park.

She was asked by other rough sleepers to go on an errand to buy alcohol.

> I didn't know how to do it. And I didn't know where the place was that sold alcohol...when I got back...it was horrible. They hit me. It was horrible... I got hit with a piece of concrete. I should have refused [to do the errand], but I didn't know, so I couldn't refuse. I didn't mind going, but I didn't know the way. When I finally figured it out and bought the alcohol, then I didn't know how to get back, and finally it was dawn. And they all asked me if I'd run away with the money... they got really angry. It was terrible!
>
> They're really aggressive... Unbelievable... Really violent. They get mean when they drink. [Q: Do they treat everyone that way?] Like I said, they do it to the weak ones.

Although she spoke only briefly about it, Eiko also discussed being threatened with sexual harassment and sexual violence. Such sexual harassment and violence was mainly a theme in the testimonies of single female rough sleepers who lived alone. When Eiko discussed this experience, she mentioned that it confused and upset her because it violated the ideal of chastity that had been instilled in her by her parents.

> It was terrible... Those days were unbelievable. Unbelievable. Everyone there was a big drinker... A man touched me on the backside and came after me, saying something to try to persuade me... I ran away from him... My parents had warned me about it when I was little...it wasn't right...

There were also women who were physically abused by their partners in their tents; Yūko, for one, was regularly beaten and kicked by her husband. For a while, Yūko's face was constantly puffed and swollen, and she once suffered a cracked cervical disk after her husband hit her. She had to wear a brace on her neck for several months. When it happened, her husband was drunk, and the people living in the tents around them just watched it happen without intervening. Yūko said that after her husband went to work she stayed alone in the tent, unable to eat or go to the toilet or even go to the hospital to treat her injuries.

I was still wet from bleeding. And in that state…I had to crawl to the toilet, I'm not kidding… I couldn't speak. [Eiko:] Didn't anyone say anything? [Yūko:] No, they stayed where they were, because they were scared. Because he would have said, "Come on, all of you, I'll fight you!"…No one could do anything to stop him! … If anyone got involved, who knows what he'd do? So they just watched… I couldn't even go to the toilet when I needed to. I couldn't eat… I couldn't go to the hospital, so how could I get better? And then…my husband got some work, and he left for work, and I was left alone. I couldn't fix a meal, and he certainly didn't leave me anything to eat, or leave me any money… I had no desire to eat or drink, didn't even have any water, so I didn't need to use the toilet.

The words and behavior of these women bore the marks of multiple, accumulated traumatic experiences, from the discrimination and poor treatment they received before becoming rough sleepers, to living constraints that denied them access to even minimal necessities, governmental pressure to vacate their living space, attacks by passersby and other dangers, and the violence and sexual harassment suffered at the hands of rough sleeping men. These conditions were unavoidable as long as they were sleeping rough. Clearly, once they got caught up in these oppressive conditions, they had no choice but to come to terms with them if they were to survive.

Living strategies of women rough sleepers

However, there is more to these stories than being passively caught up in oppressive circumstances. Even when unable to change their basic situation, their daily practices reveal a wide variety of living strategies to reduce their hardships and survive the rough sleeping lifestyle. They coped with unsatisfactory situations by using their intelligence and various practical tactics. These strategies are not necessarily decided on actively and willfully by the individuals who use them. But rough sleeping is a desperately harsh situation in which death awaits those who do not adapt, and some of the strategies used by rough sleepers are employed without conscious intent. People who are new to rough sleeping may not yet have adequately mastered them. But over time, as the period of rough sleeping extends to long-term, these strategies are refined and incorporated into their everyday lives, as they are instructed by, or imitate, other rough sleepers.

People who have just begun rough sleeping often start out sleeping on pieces of cardboard in stations, underground shopping areas, or roadsides. Normally it is only possible to stay in such places at night; in the morning they must move on. People in these places generally live a "vagabond" lifestyle.

Hence, they can only keep a minimal number of personal belongings – as many as they can carry around. Under these constraints, over time, rough sleepers learn techniques for sleeping more securely. Fujiko spoke of how, on her first day of rough sleeping, she was taught some basics by another rough sleeper.

> I happened to meet someone nice that [first] day [of rough sleeping]. I didn't know about blankets, or how to get cardboard, and then someone explained it to me. [Q: Did they approach you first?] Yes. At first, naturally, I didn't know what to do, and I was just looking, trying to figure it out. Then he came over to talk to me. And he told me about using blankets, or how it was better to put a blanket on top of cardboard for sleeping, things like that.

In due course, most rough sleepers gradually transition from living vagabond-style to living in a fixed location. Today there are fewer and fewer places in urban areas where rough sleepers can settle down in tents, but when I conducted my research in 2003 there were still many tents to be seen. Compared to other urban locations like train stations, fixed living in tents like those in Park B was out of sight of strangers, making it both safer and possible to keep more possessions. This set the basis for a more stable lifestyle. Once residents had a full set of bedding, they could sleep more comfortably; it was possible to earn some income from collecting abandoned items; and cooking was possible if one had utensils. Yūko, comparing vagabond living with settled living, spoke of how much more stable settled living was.

> Sometimes I'd be all worked up about where I'd sleep that day – what to do if it rained, or if someone took my space and left me nowhere to go. Compared to that, this [living in a tent] is like living in heaven. I mean, I can stretch out my legs and lie down when I get back. And I don't have to put away the cardboard... In fact, if you get yourself a space like that you can even get work and do other things... I mean, I

sell books, so I have a place to set them out, but with cardboard there's no place to put books... Since I have a kind of home base I can go to find books when I want to. I can take a nap in the daytime... And when it comes to eating, [without a tent] you eat boxed lunches and things like that... Convenience store items. [Since you can't cook for yourself] you have to eat things people have thrown away, so you can't have a balanced diet at all. You damage your health. No vegetables or stuff like that.

There were about 250 rough sleepers living in Park B at the time of the study, most of them in tents at a fixed location. They lived in structures such as plywood huts, tents made of blue tarp, and, in locales where frequent movement was necessary, camping tents were common; every type of structure was covered with blue tarp. Following changes in management in Park B under the Park Management Division, no new tents were permitted to be set up. To prevent tents that had been vacated by their owners to be discovered by park authorities and taken down, they were managed by a rough sleeper who played the role of "boss" in the neighborhood. Under this system, if the rough sleepers in the area approved, a new arrival to Park B like Fujiko could move into an empty tent without the knowledge of park authorities and eventually settle down there. These tents averaged about eight square meters in area and were used to store clothing and other necessities. Some tents even had electric power from generators, or battery-powered televisions.

Most rough sleepers were not completely without income, and were able to obtain cash in a variety of ways. Some performed regular wage labor as day workers or at part-time jobs. Yūko, based in her tent, had done jobs such as selling insurance and cleaning in office buildings. Yūko's husband had also done day labor in the construction industry. Other people collected abandoned items such as aluminum cans, magazines, and large discarded items. Yūko's husband sometimes collected discarded magazines. When that happened, they would perform a sexual division of labor: while he went out to gather magazines, Yūko would remain at the tent cleaning off the magazines and performing other "domestic" tasks.

Sometimes it went really well. We would make about 7,000 yen (~USD 60) each time. He would leave at about 2:00 a.m. and get back by 10:00 a.m. Then the books have to be cleaned with sandpaper.

Photo 5.4: Magazines recovered by rough sleepers from station trash bins, sold on the roadside at cheap prices.

[Q: Who does that? Your husband? Or you?] I would do that, then take them all over to be sold. [Q: You used sandpaper to clean the books? ... So, your husband collected them and you cleaned them?] Right, well after he came back we did it together... [Q: Where did you take them? To a used bookstore?] You know, Bookoff [a national chain bookstore that buys and sells used books]. [Q: Including magazines?] That's right, magazines too.

"Line-standing" was another type of job done by rough sleepers. This job, which is not legal, involves waiting in line to buy tickets for concerts and sporting events, which will be resold by ticket scalpers. Rough sleepers are employed to purchase tickets, for which they receive a set compensation. Because they stand in line to buy tickets, they are called "line-standers." Line-standing occurs, with seasonal variation, several times a month, and standers are compensated about 1,500 yen (~USD 13) each time. At Park B, between several dozen and several hundred rough sleepers were summoned each time line-standing took place. Among these "line-standers" were some who worked as "chief buyers," employed by the scalpers to assemble the required number of buyers, buy the tickets from them, and sell them to the scalpers. Tamako reported that her husband would receive a commission of 500 yen (~USD 4) per person that he recruited in this role. In addition, Eiko regularly received payment for media interviews. Some rough sleepers use the address of a place where they do not actually live to apply for and receive certain benefits, which require the recipient to have an official certificate of residence. Yūko, using the address of a friend, received pension payments. Tamako received a disability payment of 8,000 yen (~USD 68) per month, using the address of a friend who lived in a city ward with a particularly good disability allowance rate.

Many people who have just begun rough sleeping buy meals with cash they have at hand or find discarded food. But over time, they learn methods for obtaining meals from other rough sleepers, who tell them the best times and places for getting discarded food, how to get food items distributed by welfare offices, and the times and places where soup kitchens are open.

[Yūko:] Well, we'd get up at about 2 a.m., the time when someone comes to pick up the garbage from the convenience stores. We'd go before the truck came. The garbage would be out there. And some of it was...food. [Q: And you knew what time a particular store had pickup, things like that?] Yes, most places seem to do it at a definite time. But neither my husband or I knew that at first. We'd walk around randomly, going, "Oh, they haven't left anything today" or "Where does everyone go to get the food?" And after a while – and most of the other rough sleepers won't tell you what time to go, because people will come and grab all the food – if you walk around, you find someone who will tell you about what time.

[Eiko:] So, I go to look for food...in trash bins. It sounds disgusting, but the stuff isn't really dirty. There's nothing wrong with it. You can judge it by looking at it. People throw away a lot of food. [Q: Did you use soup kitchens or things like that?] No, at the time we didn't know anything about that. We had no idea they existed. Over time, we found out...our friends would tell us... Over time we learned. You'd wait in line, go through it once, get the food, and hurry to the end of the line, and wait, and get it again. After a while you'd get the hang of it...

Park B is a large park located in a very publicly visible part of Tokyo prefecture, so it has attracted various groups that provide services to rough sleepers, such as grocery handouts and soup kitchens, each day. At a nearby welfare office hard biscuits were handed out every weekday at 9:00 a.m., and a certain church distributed rice balls or baked goods year-round every morning at 5:00 a.m. on a street near Park B. In addition, a volunteer group handed out cooked rice at 6:30 p.m. on Sundays, and on Mondays a soup kitchen was operated by one church at 8:30 a.m. and by another at 5:00 p.m. On Tuesdays, Thursdays, and Saturdays, residents living near the park distributed pork soup with rice, curry, and similar items to rough sleepers who came at 6:00 a.m. and helped clean up the park area. A soup kitchen was operated at Park B by a church on Wednesdays starting at 4:00 p.m. On Saturdays at 9:00 a.m., a group of volunteers operated a soup kitchen. Another church provided additional hot meals in the winter. Some of the church-run soup kitchens required users to listen to a sermon or sing hymns before giving out the food. With all of these services, the Park B area is a relatively good place for obtaining food. Some of its residents would also travel some distance to access soup kitchens in other neighborhoods.

In the soup kitchens at Park B, the sponsoring groups and rough sleepers attempted, in various ways, to give priority to women. The nature of these efforts varied according to the organization, but included practices such as:

- Allowing women to go to the front of the line at the soup kitchen;
- Allowing any woman who arrived before a certain time to go to the front of the line;
- Male rough sleepers assisting with the food distribution quietly prioritizing women by giving them number cards first; and
- Male rough sleepers waiting in line voluntarily sending women to the front of the line.

At Park B there was a broad, common, tacit understanding that women in rough sleeper society needed special treatment. Fujiko described this phenomenon as follows.

They send you to the front of the [soup kitchen] line. Otherwise a bunch of people just rush over and women can't get in. At first, Tamako and I would be standing in line, and they'd *always* say "Come up here!"

meaning to the front. "Stand here." Letting you in line. Tamako's husband would tell them to and they'd all let us into the line. [Q: Is every soup kitchen now the same way? Women go first?] "Women go first?" Well, sort of, not always, but it is at the Monday morning one if you go early. I mean, part of it is about coming early. If you're there before everyone lines up they'll naturally let you go in front. And on Monday evening, if you get there by 3:30 their policy is women first. And on the Wednesday one, if you find Mr. ——— [name of a rough sleeper helping run the kitchen] and ask him he'll let you in front. At first, we waited in line. If you do get in line they can't invite you to come up front, because everyone else is there. So he said to come to him and he'd give us tickets for the front. So we go early, before they give out all the tickets, and get the front ones.

Because most of the rough sleepers in Park B were settled residents, they often cooked for themselves. Using portable gas stoves, they would cook using ingredients they had purchased at the stores or received from volunteers. All four of my female informants cooked for themselves more often than utilizing soup kitchens. Rainy days, however, were said to be a problem for getting meals; soup kitchens were sometimes cancelled and the gas stoves outside the tents could not be used.

Many rough sleepers also kept pets: Eiko, Tamako, and Yūko all had cats. They obtained pet food from neighborhood animal lovers who walked their dogs in the park or from volunteers; otherwise, they bought it themselves.

A church also offered services such as free haircuts in Park B. Other services available included free medical consultations by volunteer physicians, and escort to welfare offices by volunteers. Rough sleepers who became ill used these services to get medical treatment. Rough sleepers receiving treatment would go to the welfare office to get their public benefit tickets permitting them to use a hospital, where they would be admitted or treated as outpatients as necessary. In Tokyo prefecture, rough sleepers are eligible to receive medical assistance, as a separate category of public assistance.[2] For instance, Fujiko's husband went for medical treatment three times a week using medical assistance benefits. She said that this was because he refused to be hospitalized, since that would leave her alone in the park. Fujiko's husband felt that

it was his job as a husband to "take care" of her. She also said
that it made her "really happy" that her husband cared about her
this way.

> At first he was told he had to be hospitalized, but ultimately, living
> the way we do...if he had to be hospitalized...even if someone was
> there [men who would be willing to protect Fujiko] there's no way
> they would really do it. He told me... "You can't be safe by yourself.
> However much ————— [name of a man who seemed like he would
> help] and the others help out, you won't feel safe... As a woman,
> alone, what if a bunch of men attack you? You can't fight them off
> by yourself. You may have ————— there but he can't be ready for
> what might happen. He can't be relied on for everything that could
> happen. As a woman, if you had an apartment you could live alone,
> but with you living in these conditions being hospitalized will just
> make me sicker. [Q: Meaning because of worrying?] Yes. So he said
> he wouldn't do it. And honestly, that made me really happy, that he
> was so concerned about me.

Rough sleepers made use of things distributed by volunteer groups,
such as clothing, futons, and blankets. For other necessities, they
would either purchase them or ask for them from church groups
or volunteers. One church gave out a numbered card to each rough
sleeper, and if a cardholder showed the card and wrote down what
item he or she needed on a form, the church would obtain that item
by the following week. In this way rough sleepers were able to
obtain hard-to-get items like glasses and shoes. Additionally, the
monthly meeting of the women rough sleepers' group mentioned
earlier was held at Park B. At these meetings women could obtain
items that it would be awkward to ask men for, such as feminine
hygiene products. In my case, women sometimes asked if I could
get items such as gas canisters for cooking, public bath tickets,
mosquito-repellent incense, and insect repellent, and I sometimes
obtained these items for them to thank them for allowing me to
interview them.

> [Q: I was wondering about how you get hold of feminine hygiene
> products.] [Fujiko:] ... When I had money I bought them. So when
> I ran out, I'd still have about two months' supply – the big kind and

the long thin kind… I'd have those as a backup for when I ran out. When I totally ran out, feminine hygiene products were the thing I needed first. That and baths… Otherwise, I'd ask "Hallelujah" [a church group]. You could go to the church and get them to write down what you needed on a form.

[Tamako:] If you went to the Women's Support Group meeting, you could ask ———— [woman volunteer] and she'd get them for you… I asked for those first of all. When I first met her, I had lots of requests.

Rough sleepers took baths at the nearby public bath, but all four women mentioned how they hated not being able to go more often because of the high entry fee. Male rough sleepers could strip down at the park and rinse their bodies with water from the public fountain, but women, when unable to use the public bath, would wash their hair and rinse their bodies at the public restroom. Fujiko described this activity as follows:

As far as bathing goes, frankly, you can wash your hair with cold water if you want to. You know that restroom that has the toilet sound blocker [*otohime*]. I used to wash my hair there, because you can fill the sink with water. Most people use that faucet [on a public fountain in the park], but when you do it there your hair touches the ground. I hate having my hair touch the ground when I wash it there… So I go to that restroom with the sound blocker, and fill the sink with water. Washing with cold water does leave your hair feeling a little rough, so I use extra conditioner. My hair feels nice and smooth… [Q: I know where you mean – the nice, clean place.] That's it. It even has a mirror. The mirror and all make it perfect.

Almost all of the rough sleepers washed their clothes by filling a basin with water from the park fountain and washing by hand, then hanging the clothes on lines or fences. Some also used coin laundries. Female rough sleepers did these things too, but Eiko said that she had had her underclothes stolen when she was young and was upset by it, and did not feel comfortable hanging out women's underwear where many men were present. Because of this, she would hide them with towels or hang them behind trees where they would not be seen.

You can't hang out your laundry here, with so many men around... I hate doing that. I had them stolen when I was young, my underwear... It costs 500 or 600 yen (~USD 4–5) to use the coin laundry. And you can't hang out your clothes there, bras and things like that. [Q: You mean you can't hang out underwear to dry.] No, someone will take it. With no other place to hang them, if you hang them here [under the tent], it takes about two days [to dry]. [Q: Where did you hang them?] In back, hiding them with towels.

Another strategy often used by women rough sleepers is to live together with a man. Kazuko's experience sleeping rough as a single woman was discussed in Chapter 4. To protect herself from the many dangers of sleeping rough, Kazuko had a practice of sleeping next to a certain man each evening. According to a study conducted in 2000 by the Urban Life Institute, eleven out of fifteen women rough sleepers were living with men; a 2001 study by the Osaka City University Institute on Urban Environmental Problems found twelve out of twenty to be doing this. In some cases, women transition into rough sleeping together with a male partner; in other cases, they meet a man when sleeping rough and begin living with him. Among my four female informants in Park B, only Eiko lived alone; the other three lived with male partners, all of whom they had been with since before becoming rough sleepers. Yūko said that she probably would not be a rough sleeper if she didn't have her husband; Fujiko and Tamako each said that their bonds with their husbands were strengthened by the hardships of rough sleeping. Both said that they felt that rough sleeping was particularly difficult for a single woman.

[Yūko:] Well, I think I do it because I'm with him. If I was by myself, I don't think so. I wouldn't do this by myself [*laughs*]. This is no way to live.

[Fujiko:] And so when it's time to sleep, my husband makes a point of sleeping outside. He never lets me be on the outside, even when we're just sitting. After a certain amount of time has passed he has me go inside. It's hard but it works. I think it even makes our relationship stronger. [Q: Are you closer than you were before?] I think so. We do fight sometimes, but...

[Tamako:] We do the same thing. It's the only way to get by. Living this way makes us close. You can't afford to fight when you're living here.

When I asked Eiko, who had been sleeping rough as a single woman, whether there were things she was careful about because of living alone, she replied that she had never really thought about it, but that she tried not to antagonize the people she interacted with. This was certainly one of Eiko's strategies for living alone.

[Q: Are there things you are careful about as a woman living alone?] Oh, not really, no. As long as you don't say things, as long as you don't antagonize people. Go along with them and it's fine... Just figure that's the way they are, and don't get angry.

Many of the strategies used by women rough sleepers, as we have seen, are common to rough sleepers of both genders, such as finding work and a place to live. However, women also spoke about hardships, and strategies for dealing with them, which they cited as being particular to women, such as how to bathe and do laundry and how to protect themselves from physical danger. At the same time, there was also special consideration for women shown by most people at Park B that gave them priority in receiving food at soup kitchens, and some women rough sleepers were able to use this to their advantage.

As we have seen, there was great variety among the women in how they viewed their identity as a woman and how they utilized it. There were differences between Eiko, who was single, and Tamako, Yūko, and Fujiko, who lived with their husbands, in what and how much they said about their experiences of violence and how they protected themselves from danger. Furthermore, there was a difference between Yūko's and Fujiko's attitudes about working with men. Yūko, based on having lived on her own for a long time and being economically self-sufficient, liked to speak of how she was "a woman who worked on an equal basis with men." Fujiko, in contrast, spoke of "housewives' know-how." From this, it should be clear that to explain the difference between women who receive welfare protection and those who live as rough sleepers on the basis of whether they are "renegades of gender or not" is to overlook significant individual differences.

6 Continuing and ending rough sleeping

Resistance and subjectivity of rough sleepers

By focusing on the world in which four women rough sleepers led their lives in Park B, we have sought to understand the hardships they faced and the various strategies they used to survive from day to day. We will now turn to the question of how these women ascribe meaning to their lives as rough sleepers, and the relationships they have with other people. We will also consider a closely related issue: the nature of "choice" in the decisions these women made about whether to continue rough sleeping or not.

Through examining these questions I hope to shed light on what may have been overlooked in previous research that focused on the subjectivity and resistance of rough sleepers. As noted in Chapter 1, prior research on rough sleepers, resisting the prevailing view of them as apathetic or lazy, emphasized their autonomous subjectivity and the fact that they work. However, the tacit assumption of this research was that rough sleepers were men, exemplified by *yoseba* laborers. This approach is undoubtedly a valid response to a society that marginalizes the homeless. But among the population of rough sleepers, there are also women, who are not necessarily expected to work, and other non-working people. Hence, the assumption that rough sleepers are working people, further marginalizes those who do not work.

This chapter will therefore consider the women rough sleepers who have been overlooked in prior research, looking at their practices at the day-to-day level.

The meaning of rough sleeping

People typically suffer a variety of disadvantages in society prior to becoming rough sleepers. And once they are rough sleepers, they live under a wide range of constraints. But the life of rough sleeping is not merely a site for the reproduction of dominant social values; it can also be a site for the construction of new values and meanings. In what follows, taking Eiko and Tamako as examples, I look at some creative ways that people who have long been structurally disempowered create their world anew.

Eiko, fearing being looked down on, said that she used to find it impossible to tell people she knew that she could not read or write.

> [Q: Were you able to tell people, say, at work that you couldn't read or write?] No, they would have thought I was stupid. I couldn't tell anybody unless it was somebody I really trusted. They looked down on me, yes, they did. Didn't try to understand. Just looked down on me even more.

Moreover, Eiko spoke repeatedly of the disadvantages and sense of inferiority that she felt were due to her illiteracy. These included being frequently looked down on by family and workplace acquaintances; difficulty in finding a job because of being unable to write a resume; and having to ask someone to help her get money from an ATM because she didn't know how to use it and having that person (she believed) take some of the money. When speaking of how she became a rough sleeper, she related why she was unable to read.

> My older sister...said that they [the company] would hire me any time I liked, so she wrote down the phone number for me. But it wasn't the company's idea to have me work, so they wouldn't come to pick me up. They would respond if you called them, but they wouldn't come meet you. Because it wasn't a case of them asking me to come. I got confused when I heard that, because I'm not smart. I mean, I can't even read. Eventually I ran out of money and had to sleep in the streets. I had that phone number and my belongings stolen... I had brought my bags, but they were all stolen. [Q: What kind of company was it?] It was a cleaning service. That's all I can do, since I didn't go to school.
>
> I was confused, had no sense of direction, didn't know where I was, totally confused... After a while my money ran out, and my phone money, and I didn't have my train fare to get home, and that's why I started sleeping outside here.

Eiko revealed her inability to read and write not only to me, but to many people she met, including reporters and volunteers. In particular, the story about how she became a rough sleeper seems to have always been a part of the interviews that she had done with news reporters and researchers. I had already read the transcripts of several interviews Eiko had done with other people, and although these interviews contained things that contradicted what Eiko had told me, the story of how she became a rough sleeper was always identical, as if it had been recorded. We may conclude that for Eiko, not being able to read and write was a symbol of the disadvantages she had suffered over time and a convincing reason she gave to people for why she had been forced into rough sleeping.

Eiko's narrative about the problems she suffered because of illiteracy was originally something she hid from others. However, when she was placed in the position of a rough sleeper with an audience looking for a rough sleeper's story, her narrative was reconstituted; illiteracy became something that she should actively speak about. Ken Plummer (Plummer 1995) argues that a story must be told at a particular time; when a previously untold story becomes a told story it is because a community appears to receive it. He further argues that communities are themselves formed through such stories. This is true of Eiko's story. Once she had a community of people made up of interviewers interested in rough sleepers, media reporters wanting to use her testimony in their reports, sympathetic volunteers, and a social movement to which she felt a sense of belonging, the story changed into something that should be told.

With the transformation of her story, and the growth of a new community in her life, Eiko's world expanded, and new relationships developed. Volunteers wrote postcards to her in the easier *katakana* phonetic script, which she could read; visitors came to deliver donated supplies to her; a stranger who had read a newspaper article about her sent her a dictionary to help with her study. The relationships that she developed after telling her story even brought her material support. And as a participant in the homeless movement, says Eiko, she learned to ride a train by herself, which she had been unable to do, and new opportunities opened for her to learn to read characters and words.

The pamphlets by ——— (a homeless support organization) use *hiragana* characters to show how to read the hard words. [Note: written Japanese contains many *Kanji* (Chinese characters) that children or less literate adults may be unable to read. To solve this problem, phonetic characters can be placed above the *Kanji* to assist with correct reading.] So I read them over and over. I've been getting them for a long time.

Being in the homeless movement has given me many good experiences. Like, I've learned to figure out where I am. In the countryside there's hardly any chance to ride a train. I always look at signs and things this way. Sometimes the characters are read one way, sometimes another way. You know, there are many different readings for one character, so I don't know how to read them. I get confused... But now I go to a lot of different places. The way to read them is given in *hiragana*. "Oh," I think, "this is how you read it."

For Eiko, the significance of being illiterate, which until then had been purely negative, changed when she became a rough sleeper. In becoming able to actively tell her story of these negative experiences, Eiko created a new community, and within this community, which recognized her story, she began to receive necessities and learning opportunities. Eiko said that before becoming a rough sleeper she was a shy person who rarely spoke, but afterwards, as she "came to understand more and more things," she "became stronger and stronger."

But you know, I was quiet just like Tamako. I didn't talk much. I was quiet. I spoke so little that my parents wondered whether I was mute. [Q: So you became able to speak after you became homeless?] I'm a gloomy type; I think things over for a long time. Here, I have to live with men around. Being around them has made me stronger. I thought, I have to be stronger, I can't keep acting this way. I have to get stronger, I thought... I would worry about being made fun of. And I was made fun of, being the way I am. I knew I had to be stronger in my life... You get stronger the more you learn. When you're the only woman there, you get stronger. [Q: If you don't speak up, you lose out.] Exactly! You naturally become stronger. [Q: What kind of thing did you learn that made you feel more powerful?] When you are going through life by yourself. You have to say something or people will think you're stupid. I would think "I have to keep on living. I'll die if I keep going on like this." And I did get stronger.

Eiko described herself as "quiet just like Tamako," and in fact, Tamako, too, said that she used to be unable to converse with people. Because her parents, ashamed of her intellectual disability, concealed it from other people, Tamako herself felt that her disability was a burden on others. Not only was she unable to tell people about it, she was unable to talk with people out of a fear of being laughed at.

> I was afraid I wouldn't be able to make friends. I have this disability, right? And that made me unable to socialize with people... I was afraid, how should I say this, if I spoke they'd all laugh at me, so I became afraid to speak. And I didn't feel like I knew the right things to say...

However, Tamako said that her current husband, rather than hiding her disability from people, made a point of telling them openly and trying to help them understand. Since meeting her husband, she said, she became able to converse with other people. And all of this was "since coming to the park." Rough sleepers generally suffer a great deal of discrimination and disadvantage both before and after becoming rough sleepers. Such discrimination and disadvantage is something they all have in common. As Fujiko put it, "All of us who live this way are in it together." Meeting a man who did not conceal her intellectual disability from other people was certainly part of how Tamako learned to talk with other people, but the feeling that "everyone is in it together" was also an important source of support. Tamako stated that Eiko, in particular, "treated me well," no doubt because of their similar life experience. As time went on, Tamako became able, of her own accord, to tell other people about her intellectual disability, which she regarded as her greatest misfortune. The first time I interviewed Tamako, she began by calmly taking out her Rehabilitation Certificate from her bag and showing it to me.

> [Q: Have you always been able to tell people about this intellectual disability?] To be honest, before, I never said the words intellectual disability. When I was living with my parents I never told anybody. It's since I met [my husband] that I became able to talk about it. I was worried. I was afraid my friends would reject me. I was afraid that if I said I had an intellectual disability they'd reject me. It's only been since I came to the park. [My husband] would tell people like Eiko. I could talk to them once they understood my situation. [My husband] also let ——— [another rough sleeper] know about it. "She has an intellectual disability, so you need to help her out." ...Eiko and the others treated me really well. [Q: But you told me about it yourself.]

> I did tell you myself. I said it myself for some reason. I'm surprised myself. I didn't used to be able to talk about it myself. [My husband] always told people for me.

This gave Tamako a community that accepted her even after she revealed her disability. Tamako became more "cheerful" because of this, which further expanded the community around her. Tamako's husband was one of the "boss" figures among the rough sleepers of Park B, which brought Tamako the respect of others at the park. Partly because of this, Tamako concerned herself with helping newly-arrived rough sleepers with such matters as shelter and food, and sometimes expressed a consciousness that she was "taking care" of them. Particularly when a woman first arrived, Tamako would give her special care, on the grounds that otherwise "she won't be able to survive as a woman."

> That woman [a woman rough sleeper newly arrived at Park B] was over on those steps under an umbrella like this. We went, and my husband got someone staying near her to ask how she was doing. We were afraid she wasn't eating anything. When they asked, it turned out she hadn't eaten, so we let her come eat at our place... Then she said she would take care of herself so she didn't need our help, and now she takes care of herself. I helped her out, but she said she'd take care of herself.
>
> We also brought all sorts of things [to Fujiko] when I heard her husband was ill. Because she said her husband was down with illness. Sick and couldn't get up. You know, they needed help and we wanted to give them things, so we brought them over, brought over lots of things. Then a tent became available. It was empty, so I wanted them to use it, and we got them settled there. We talked to ————— [one of the "bosses" who controls the use of empty tents] for them.
>
> I sometimes do it for women because I pity them, unlike men – men manage to get by somehow or other. Women can't get by in this place. Especially when it's all men.

Prior to becoming rough sleepers, Eiko and Tamako both experienced problems like illiteracy or an intellectual disability as purely negative things that gave them a sense of social inferiority. Living as rough sleepers, these things took on a different meaning. And with that change they developed an ability to speak out about disadvantages, which helped them to become "stronger" and "more cheerful." This kind of personal growth might have been possible in other contexts besides rough sleeping, but in the lives of these two women it was the first time for such a thing to happen. That it did shows the potential for the world of people who have up until now been victims to be transformed. This represents a creative side of the world of rough sleepers that must be acknowledged.

Emergent community

Iwata Masami has described rough sleepers as people who have lost "a place to live," as well as people with "a position in a particular social group" (Iwata 2000: 28). To be sure, in many cases people begin sleeping rough after the loss of important social relationships. However, the rough sleepers in Park B could also be found building new social connections. Since most of the rough sleepers at Park B lived in a fixed location for an extended period, conditions were ripe for building close relations with others. They greeted each other freely and regularly visited each other's tents. Rough sleepers spend much time together with others in activities such as waiting in line at a soup kitchen. Because it is necessary to leave one's tent and move around the park to use the water fountain and the toilet, there are frequent opportunities to see, greet, and converse with others. They are rarely rushed for time. As one put it, "The hard part is having nothing to do." Visiting one another and conversing was seen as a valuable way to spend time. A common sense of shared hardships among rough sleepers was part of what sustained this ethos, as expressed by Fujiko when she said: "All of us who live this way are in it together." In their daily interactions, rough sleepers often had all sorts of spontaneous conversations: small talk with no particular meaning; gossip about Park B; exchanging information about work and other matters, and silly jokes; as well as complaints about rough sleeping and personal tales of life's difficulties.

One expression of the rough sleepers' sense of a shared experience of disadvantage and material want was the active exchange of possessions that took place among them. Most of the rough sleepers at Park B regularly gave things to each other, including food, cigarettes, daily necessities, books, and objects with no obvious value such as dolls and toys. It was extremely common not only to give others objects that one did not need, but to sometimes share objects that one did need. For rough sleepers, who have no guarantee of being able to obtain what they need, the creation of a smoothly functioning system of gifts and donations can be considered a strategy for reducing risk. Being able to expect help when one is in trouble is important to feeling secure. Thus, for rough sleepers it is more logical to give unneeded items to someone else than to throw them away, even if the other person does not seem to really need them. There was an obligation to accept what was given, and an expectation that the gift would be reciprocated in some form. Tamako had the following to say about giving and receiving gifts among rough sleepers.

> The community in this neighborhood is very close, so most people are very helpful. Most people help each other out. I don't know about other places. I don't know about other places but here we help each other, so I get helped out a lot. They bring all kinds of things to me. You remember ———— who you just met. He's like that, he brings over things to eat. [Q: Like the eggplant a while ago.] It's a big help that people bring things like that. It really helps us out. He made us some grilled eggplant when we had nothing to eat.

There was also regular exchange of information about rough sleeping. The practical strategies indispensable to living in the rough, such as how to secure a place to sleep, the time and place unused food products were put out for collection, the days and times soup kitchens were operated, and how to find work, were shared among rough sleepers or learned by imitation. Even after these tactics were more or less understood, there was constant exchange of new information, such as the availability of a new "line standing" job, or which soup kitchen had the best food. As Fujiko explained in an account cited earlier, it was common for experienced rough sleepers to approach new ones and pass on these strategies. This information served the further function of building new relationships.

The give-and-take relationships among rough sleepers involved not only things and information, but also actions. At times, when a labor-intensive activity such as moving tents took place, many people would assist with the work and help each other. This mutual assistance was not limited to one-time projects like moving tents; there were also cases that persisted over time of more or less set groups in which one person would give an object to another, and that person would reciprocate with an action. This phenomenon was especially pronounced in cases like Fujiko's and Tamako's, where several rough sleepers formed a group that lived communally. Fujiko had meals almost every day with her husband, who lived in an adjoining tent, and seven other rough sleepers, including another couple. This group practiced a division of labor with each person in a fairly set role: contributing money or material such as food and daily items; doing "housekeeping" and other work; or a combination of these. The relations in such a group were not necessarily equal, but constituted a kind of internal class system for rough sleepers, with those providing money and objects on top, and those contributing work on the bottom. This, in turn, led to relationships in which one person "looked after" another, and some acquired boss-like status.

Because Fujiko's husband was recuperating from illness and unable to work for an income, and Fujiko was busy taking care of him, as a couple they had almost no cash income. However, she was able to receive things like meals and necessary items from other members of the group, and in return, actively did "what she was able to do," namely, "housewives' work," and in this way secured her position in the group and made it possible to sustain her life.

When we go out for a meal, F pays for the meal, and G takes care of the coffee. In general, if we need something, F will pay for it. Accepting help like that is the way we do things... We don't have any other choice. I mean, we don't have a way of paying people back for what they do. So, we just do something... In return for being helped, if we could go work we'd work and do something with the money we got, but for now there is no prospect of getting an income, so we just do what we can.

F paid for the public bath. But G is very realistic about it. He doesn't feel like he can let other people pay for him when he goes out for a meal. He's really resigned to that. So, when the group is doing something, let's say X is fixing a meal, well, Y always gets back from work late, and if we are cutting up food and things like that, G doesn't do any of it. But he does help clean up afterward. When we go to wash dishes G follows along offering to help carry them. We divide the tasks that way.

It's about everyone helping each other. So if you do whatever you can no one will complain to you... Over here, it's all men. So they're really happy when I do the kind of things a housewife can do well.

However, this role was not so much gender-determined as it was the result of the unequal distribution of resources. Even within this group, not only Fujiko, but also men who had few resources to contribute, including Fujiko's husband, tended to do chores. The same phenomenon occurred in Tamako's case. Tamako lived communally in a group of five rough sleepers, including herself, her husband, and three other men who lived in an adjoining tent. The tent used by the three men "belonged" to Tamako and her husband, and Tamako's husband regularly introduced the three men to work as "line standers" and gambling house "ticket buyers,"[1] making Tamako and her husband the most powerful members of the group. As a result, the group's everyday chores and tasks were done mainly by the three men, and not by Tamako, a woman. Although Tamako would sometimes cook when she felt like doing so, most of the tasks like cooking, cleaning, washing dishes, laundry, and taking care of pets was done by these three men.

> I've been too busy to play around since my foster family [the rough sleepers who cohabit with them] has grown... At night there are lots of people here. They keep coming from other places. As many as seven people. They come to eat. He's a caring person, [my husband] here. "Come get something to eat," he says... [Q: Do the people you know come to eat?] That's right. Well, only the ones who sleep here. There are others, though. [Q: Are there people who sleep with you?] Yes, two people... You know the two rooms [tents] on the other side? Those are ours. There are three of them. My husband and I use this one. Remember? There are two more on the opposite side. There's also a place on this side where there were two tents. One person sleeps there. And there's a person sleeping on this side. There's also a bed in front, so one more person can sleep there. And my husband and I look after them. And there is another person that we take care of, that person comes too. My husband is really good at taking care of others.

The members of this group were not fixed, as can be seen in Tamako's statements "at night more people come from other places" and "as many as seven people." Members came and went, and the group grew or shrank, depending on circumstances at the time.

But if relationships among rough sleepers were flexible, with individuals freely reaching out to one another and helping out those who showed need, these relationships could also become distant almost overnight. The information and things exchanged among rough sleepers easily became the basis for disputes when relationships were damaged and individuals grew distant. The failure to receive compensation for something one had given, or a delay in that compensation, affect feelings of security. As long as one can expect compensation at some time, life is less risky, and one feels more secure. When, in a time of difficulty, people failed to receive what they expected as compensation, the relationships they had built could easily be destroyed. In particular, when items being given and taken were perceived to be rare under the circumstances, unsatisfactory transactions were the cause of much trouble afterwards. Although I was unable to interview them for this study, there were some rough sleepers who adopted a strategy of deliberately distancing themselves from these unstable, rapidly changing relationships, preventing conflict by avoiding contact with others.

As shown by Tamako's report that she paid particular attention to women, women rough sleepers tended, whether consciously or not, to form connections with each other on an everyday basis. This includes the four informants discussed in this study, who knew each other and visited each other's tents. When Yūko spoke of her friendship with Eiko, she alluded to the fact that they were women in explaining the nature of the relationship.

> You know, before I met Eiko, I was really the only woman around. [Q: So you enjoy talking with other women like Eiko?] Yes. A man wouldn't understand what I had to say... Men and women think differently. Men don't like to talk about silly things... [Q: Is Eiko the one you're closest to now?] There isn't anyone else. All the other people are men. Before I met Eiko, since I had no one to talk to, I'd just read books or go to the library. Or walk around in the department store.

When Yūko suffered a fractured cervical disk inflicted by her husband, the other women rough sleepers, perhaps sensing that they were vulnerable to the same danger, were very concerned about her. When Yūko, who had left her tent to get away from her husband, came back to be with him again, she was advised by Eiko, Tamako, and others to leave him again. They also would invite her out of her house during the day in order to keep her apart from her husband as much as possible, and told her husband directly to stop hurting her.

[Eiko:] Yūko, you have to get away from there! You can't stick around in a place like that and get beat up. Everyone's worried about you... There are lots of good people around, I mean it. You'll be much better off without him... [Tamako:] He said he hit her... I said, if you want to find her [Yūko] so much, why don't you treat her better?... Yūko's husband came over, saying he wanted to talk with my husband, I don't know what about, anyway, he came. And he said his wife had left. And I... said I'd tell him what I thought about him. Well, he left in a good mood... He won't change. You should go somewhere else. You have to go somewhere else, Yūko! Unless you try you'll never know. You'd better go somewhere some distance from him [Yūko:] Maybe if I go stay somewhere for a couple months. [Tamako]: Two months isn't enough. It won't work. I hate to be the one to say this, but I really think you have to get away from him. Your body can't take getting hurt time after time like that... He won't ever change, I guarantee it. The kind of person who hits people never stops. That's what they're saying these days. [Eiko:] That's what I hear. That kind of man never, ever changes. He will never change in a month or two. Maybe a year or two would make sense, but even then, there's no guarantee he would get any better.

Despite this, the relationships among women rough sleepers were not necessarily firm or consistent. Later, after witnessing Yūko when she was drinking, and hearing from Yūko's husband that she couldn't do household chores properly when she drank, Eiko began to say that she felt she could understand why Yūko's husband wanted to hit her. Tamako, too, hearing this story, began saying that "the person being hit also was part of the problem" and began to distance herself from Yūko. As we can see, although they built relationships based on their identity as women rough sleepers, the dominant social discourse that expects women to do household tasks remained inscribed in this identity and was sometimes damaging to those relationships.

Drinking *shōchū* [a distilled alcoholic beverage] is a big problem with her. And she doesn't eat much, which makes it worse. She gets drunk fast. We cook with flames, so it's not safe. We tell her it's dangerous. She wouldn't be able to live in an apartment by herself... They say she used to live in an apartment. Her husband got back from work and the bath was boiling over, the water heater was just left on. The water was boiling from being left on. Starting a fire puts other people besides yourself at risk. That's what I told her. It was unbelievable. And everyone had been saying her husband was the bad one, you know? That's what they said but when you heard both sides of the story it wasn't true. He said he was worried...leaving her alone... So he was worried. You have to listen to both sides if you want to understand... When she has money, she gets drunk, apparently. She just lies down like this... Men, you know, they have a short temper, that's how they are. He [Yūko's husband] isn't a bad person. He says, "She's my wife, so sometimes we're going to hit each other." I agreed with him... Her husband gets worried... So I thought I could understand why he felt like hitting her. With her acting like that, it was natural for him to do what he did.

Despite this, Yūko continued to visit Eiko's tent occasionally for some reason, such as sharing leftover food. Their relationship was not completely broken, but remained in a perpetual state of flux.

There was another woman rough sleeper who used to live in the tent next to Eiko's; the two would help each other out. According to Eiko, this woman "bullied" her, and called a *panpan* (whore). She cited this as her most humiliating experience, referring to the ideal of chastity that her father had taught her when she was a small child. As these examples show, normative gender concepts were invoked by women rough sleepers as reasons both for building communal relationships and for the destruction of those relationships.

She bullied me, that woman. There was this nasty woman who bullied me. A nasty woman... She went too far, saying I was selling myself... If I was going to do it, I would have done it a long time ago, you know? So I hated meeting her... Saying I got drunk and prostituted myself... Treated me like dirt. My father had told me when I was little not to do that. It was so humiliating.

Their neighbors in Park B were not the only people with whom rough sleepers formed relationships. Many also formed cooperative relationships with religious and volunteer groups that provided services such as operating soup kitchens. Eiko, for example, participated daily in various support activities for rough sleepers. These activities, as discussed in Chapter 5, not only were personally rewarding for Eiko but also gave her opportunities to study and chances to acquire necessities. Volunteers from some of these groups actively tried to develop relationships with rough sleepers, making the rounds of the park and attempting to speak with the occupants of each tent. Some people who lived in the neighborhood around the park also brought things like food and clothing. People who used the park to walk their dogs would joke and share pet stories with rough sleepers who had pets, and regularly made gifts of pet food. Former Park B rough sleepers who had moved on with public assistance would also frequently visit and bring food or other gifts.

As we can see, then, although a breakdown of social relations may have been what brought rough sleepers to Park B, they did not live in individual isolation, but rather built a loosely-organized community. This type of community is similar to the "invisible community" that Nishizawa Akihiko (1995) identified in social relationships at *yoseba*. At *yoseba*, an important norm governing social interactions is that people do not inquire into anyone else's past. This norm serves both to enable relationships, by rendering them relatively safe to enter, and to inhibit relationships, by ensuring distance is maintained. Because relationships at *yoseba* are neither fixed nor recurrent, they are not easy to recognize visually. This norm, by invoking a common understanding of a hidden "past," builds a sort of collective consciousness and group solidarity among the inhabitants of the *yoseba*. This is an example of what Nishizawa called "invisible community."

The same norm applies in the rough sleepers' community. Rough sleepers almost never referred to another person's past unless she brought it up of her own accord. As with the *yoseba*, this functioned to create a group consciousness, based on shared experience. This group consciousness included common experiences with the hardships of rough sleeping. However, the sense of community was not limited to those with first-hand experience as rough sleepers; it also could be found among local residents and volunteers who sympathized with the difficulties experienced by the rough sleepers. This community is neither an aggregate of independent, isolated individuals, nor something to which every individual belongs, nor something that unites every person. Rather, the common experiences of oppression and material want led to new relationships between people, and community came into being newly formed in each new situation, as the sum of these relationships.

Their "choices"

I asked Eiko while she was living in Park B what she wished to do in the future. She responded that she would like to continue rough sleeping as long as her health allowed. Her reason was that when she was receiving public assistance benefits in the past, she felt humiliated. However, the desire to continue rough sleeping that she spoke of was not merely a passive response based on a dislike of the stigma of receiving benefits; it was founded on the positive significance she had given to her lifestyle. At Park B, many people who cared about her "came to visit," and this life gave her a pleasure that she could not find living alone in an apartment and receiving benefits. The homeless movement, which she participated in of her own will and in which her participation was welcome, gave her "many things to do" and brought a sense of meaning to her life. The first thing she mentioned after saying "my life now is much better" was the other people who supported her as a rough sleeper. When speaking of this active wish to continue rough sleeping, she always expressed awareness of the crucial roles played by others.

> [Q: Eiko, don't you want to receive public assistance?] No. It would be too lonely living by myself in an apartment. I'd go senile. Here, everyone comes to see me.
>
> [Q: Would you like to live in a group home?] Not now. I have so many things to do [in the homeless movement]... And there are a lot of other things I want to do.
>
> This is still better [than living with her older sister]. I'm glad I came here. Lots of people help me out, they call me by name, they're good to me. It's far better now than before. ———— [a volunteer] and everyone else help me out [i.e. bring food and useful items]... They brought stuff the other day, all of them do it, and I'm so grateful that they help out... So happy... I'm thankful for all the things people bring. Getting all this help makes me happy, and grateful.

Eiko had suffered numerous disadvantages and had long felt herself inferior to others. Now, she was able to speak openly of the main cause of the feeling – being unable to read – and yet feel needed and acknowledged by others. This was the rough sleeping life she wished to continue. She was able to continue sleeping rough, and experience it as meaningful, precisely because of the indispensable presence of others who, sympathizing with her difficulties, gave her things she needed and helped her to feel valued. It seems incorrect to consider this "choice" by Eiko to continue sleeping rough to be based on autonomous "subjectivity" or "resistance at the individual level" (Nakane 2001:16–17); rather, it was continuously and provisionally determined in the context of relationships with others.

In comparison, when I asked Fujiko whether she was considering going on public assistance, she replied that she intended to continue living at Park B for some time. She gave several reasons, including still being able to work and being able to receive national pension payments in three years. However, she also said that she was basically following her husband's wishes. According to Fujiko, she personally wanted to get public assistance, but men were reluctant to use social welfare, and she gave priority to her husband's feelings in this matter.

> [Q: Have you considered receiving public assistance?] I want to, but my husband doesn't. You know, men seem to resist accepting it.

Fujiko's "choice" to continue rough sleeping was, in effect, a submission to her husband's desires. By comparison, as discussed in Chapter 4, Sumiko, in Facility A, also had a husband and also made an effort to submit. However, Sumiko submitted to Facility A rather than her husband. Fujiko, who continued rough sleeping, and Sumiko, who moved into a facility, were each faced with a similar "double bind" dilemma: they had to choose between the welfare system and a husband. Each made a different choice, based on the circumstances at the time, to connect to one or the other.

After being physically assaulted by her husband, Yūko left the tent where she had been staying with him in Park B. Taking a friend's advice, she went alone to seek help at a welfare office. There it was decided that she would go directly to a Women's Consultation Center for temporary emergency protection, without the knowledge of her husband. At the end of the two-week limit for temporary protection, in accordance with the welfare policies described in Chapter 4, she transferred to a Women's Protection Facility. However, when she returned to Park B to see how her husband was doing, she found he was not eating. Fearing that this probably meant that he also was not feeding their cat, she said that she returned to the park.

My friend told me to go to that government office, and I went to the welfare office, then to the Women's Consultation Center, and then I moved into the dorm [Women's Protection Facility]. The director there...said she didn't want me to leave. But I came back to the park because I was worried about the cat. But the dorm was really great!... I went to check on my husband and he said he hadn't eaten for three days. Three days! He was all thin from not eating. So I left him some money and told him to get something to eat. With him like that, the cat probably wasn't eating either, you know?... I finally came back... The dorm mother and director both wanted me to stay a little longer [in the protection facility]. But with my husband saying he wasn't eating, I thought, he must not be feeding the cat either, and it scared me. I couldn't stand the cat not being fed... At the [Women's Consultation] Center they said, "I can tell you love your husband." [Laughs] "Why do you love someone like that?" they said. I said, "It was the cat – I realized I needed to take care of the cat." "It's not the cat – you love your husband!" they said. Well, once you've been with someone, you can't break up just like that. I have to make sure my husband has something to eat... I can't just leave him that easily. Everyone thinks I'm a fool. They don't say anything, but it comes out later. That [I stay with him] when he doesn't even work. Once you're together with someone – I mean – you know how it is. You promise you'll support him. [Laughs] Remember, I worked for a long time. So I'm strong enough to do that... Because I had to do everything myself. Sometimes I could do work better than a lazy guy like that.

Yūko was not unhappy with the welfare system or facilities. To the contrary, her impressions of the Women's Protection Facility were entirely positive, "really great," in terms of staff and interpersonal relations. After returning to Park B, she said, she missed the facility and sometimes went to visit. Nevertheless, she returned to a husband who was violent to her and "didn't even work," believing that she had to "take care of him," and explaining this in terms of her "manlike" character, derived from life experiences.

Domestic violence is generally rooted in women's low status in the social structure, and is reportedly experienced by women regardless of factors such as education level or income (Society for survey of abuse by husbands [partners]), 2002). Yūko and her husband lived primarily on Yūko's national pension money. Most likely, she could have left her husband and stopped living as a rough sleeper. However, because, as she put it, "when you've been with someone you can't break up just like that," she returned to her violent husband. However, this should not be seen to imply dependence on her husband, as indicated by her statement that she has to support him.

As discussed in Chapter 1, Passaro argues that women using the welfare system are compliant with gender norms, while those who continue sleeping rough are rejecting them. But as we have seen in the cases of Fujiko and Yūko, prevailing gender norms prescribed that women should submit not only to the expectations of the welfare system, as Passaro observes, but also to her their husbands – even one living on the streets. Faced with multiple and contradictory normative discourses, they act in accordance with the circumstances at the time, even if they were partly compelled to do so. This meant affiliating themselves with the person or people who they were most comfortable affiliating with at the time. In each case, the result – leaving rough sleeping or continuing it – was the reality they "chose." The differences between their "choices," and the results of their choices, cannot truly be explained as a simple result of either conforming to or rebelling against prevailing gender norms.

Tamako, who lived at Park B, drifted back and forth between these two states. Asked what she hoped to do in the future, her answers were varied and inconsistent. Sometimes she said that rough sleeping was uncomfortable and that she wanted to live in an apartment, or that she wanted to try living on her own. At other times she said that she wanted to live with her husband on public assistance.

When a couple who are both rough sleepers want to get public assistance, some say it is easier if they apply separately, with the wife applying first. Taking advantage of the relative ease single women have in receiving benefits, the wife can temporarily enter a facility, and when her assessment is completed, transfer to independent living in an apartment. If the husband then moves into her apartment, it is easy to receive approval for two rough sleepers to receive benefits as a couple.

In the past, after discussing it with her husband, Tamako had tried to take this route. However, she could not tolerate living by herself in a facility, separated from her husband, even though she, her husband, and her caseworker all understood it to be temporary. On the first day in the facility, she suddenly panicked, and ran away. Since that time, Tamako said that she did not believe it was possible for her to go on public assistance since she could not accept being separated from her husband even temporarily. At the same time, she expressed her frustration at her lack of information about the public assistance system and the fact that the results of her assessment did not guarantee that she could live in an apartment with her husband as she wished. She also said that she liked rough sleeping, speaking of how carefree it was and how she was happy that her very best friend lived in Park B. Ultimately, she continued living in Park B with her husband as before.

After I had completed the main work for my research at Park B and had been back in Kyoto for some time, I heard from Tamako that her husband had been caught procuring work for "line-standers" and gone into detention. Tamako, unable to be on her own, stayed for some time in Fujiko's tent, and over time grew close to F, a male rough sleeper who lived nearby. When rumors about her relationship with F spread around the park, Tamako, unable to tolerate staying there, suddenly left Park B on her own. Later, she moved into a hotel with F using income from his job. From then on, Tamako's thinking became very unstable. She would call me nearly every day with different stories about her plans. Sometimes she said she planned to marry F and live with him in an apartment. At other times, she said that she would wait at Park B for her husband to get out of jail; or go on public assistance benefits by herself; or return to the home of her parents, with whom she had had no contact for a long time.

> I have this disability, you know, and because of it I can't stay by myself, so I find someone to depend on. I depend on someone, because I'm afraid of living with my disability. Like now, I'm depending on F. Because I'm afraid. I can't wait by myself, I can't wait by myself for my husband to come back, so I find someone to depend on. [Q: Can that person be either a man or a woman?] Either one. It can be a man or a woman. [Q: Would someone like ———— [a woman rough sleeper] be OK?] Sure, she's got herself together... I have to get myself together too, with this disability... If someone would let me stay with them, that would be great. [Tamako seems to be hinting that she wants me to let her stay with me.] I just need someone to depend on. I end up depending on a man. I depend on someone because it's lonely otherwise. For me it always ends up being a man. I always end up depending on a man. I mean, even now I'm still depending on F. I just depend on men. [Q: Why men?] I don't know. I just can't think clearly. When I ran away [i.e., left Park B] my mind just panicked...

> I have a disability, so when I'm here by myself I think about all kinds
> of things... I couldn't go to my parents' home even if I wanted to. Well,
> I do want to. I don't want to be a burden.

Citing her disability, Tamako repeatedly stated her need to depend
on some other person, and spoke of the fear this created. When I
asked her whether this person could be either a man or a woman, she
first responded that it didn't matter, then admitted afterwards that
she always turned to a man. I responded by telling Tamako what
options were available, explaining how welfare worked, and trying
to convey that she had my support no matter what option she chose.
I took her phone calls, which sometimes came late at night, and gave
her the chance to speak her mind.

One day, two and a half months after Tamako had left the park,
she called to say she was at a welfare office. According to Tamako,
when she was living with F in the hotel and completely dependent
on his income, she always had to be careful to keep him in a good
mood. Tamako had suddenly become anxious about this, decided to
go on public assistance by herself, and gone to a welfare office. The
result of the interview, she said, was for her to check into a temporary
emergency facility, and she was now on her way to that facility. I
could sense, on the other end of the phone, her relief at being able
to receive public assistance. "If it's this easy to do, I should have
done it sooner."

> Since I have this chance I decided to just go ahead and take it... I mean,
> I have to be able to take care of myself. I really didn't think I could
> go by myself... They say you get three meals. If it's this easy to do, I
> should have done it sooner. I can't believe how easy it is!

However, that very same day, right after she arrived at the facility,
she received a phone call from one of the rough sleepers at Park B
who had been part of her community. He had been arrested together
with Tamako's husband and had gotten out of jail a little before him.
Having learned this, Tamako left the facility and returned to the
hotel where F was staying. Some days later, hearing that her husband
had gotten out of jail and returned to Park B, Tamako went back to
rough sleeping at the park.

As in other cases, Tamako's "choices" to be a rough sleeper or stop
being a rough sleeper were the result of actions that were situation-

contingent and provisional, made in the context of her relationships with people like her husband, F, the facility, her parents, and myself, and constrained by a web of normative discourses. Arguably, the varied and contradictory language that she used to explain the meaning of starting or stopping rough sleeping, and her relationships with others, were explanations adapted to particular situations that served as a "vocabulary of motives" to label particular "choices" she made as the result of the actions of that time.

Fragmented realities

Previous studies of rough sleepers have resisted the view of rough sleepers as persons in need of rehabilitation or as subjects of aid and relief, instead arguing for the need to recognize their autonomy, which these studies see as holding the potential to reform society. As I have argued, one problem with this approach is that it ignored those people, including women rough sleepers, who did not fit the mold of the hard-working, male *yoseba* worker. Furthermore, the sort of practices we have seen by the women in this study, which change in response to the state of everyday relationships, are overlooked by an approach that, in order to oppose an "ideology of exclusion," emphasizes rough sleepers' "volitional resistance" at the "individual level." From the point of view of these women, such "resistance" had little to do with what course they took. Whether they continued rough sleeping based on their conscious intent, or used life strategies, perhaps unconsciously, to survive as rough sleepers, or used welfare to leave rough sleeping, they carried out their practices in their daily lives on a case-to-case basis, in the context of relationships that were constantly being formed and re-formed. In the process in which one person moves into and out of rough sleeping, there is little evidence of "resistance" or of some autonomous "subject" playing a clear role in determining what decision is made.

Might it not be the case that previous research, with its excessive interest in the subjectivity of rough sleepers and the idea of their resistance, has assumed a subject that chooses to act rationally based on a consistent, independent volition? If so, this may be why such research failed to fully apprehend the nature of the performed life practices of rough sleepers – practices that emerge in the context of dependent relationships formed with others, in a process of responding daily to changing circumstances. Practices that can be interpreted as subjective or resistant make up only a part of the daily lives of homeless persons. Sometimes they accept the rule of authority, sometimes they directly resist it, and sometimes they use creative tactics to avoid its grip. Hence, representations of rough sleeping as the consequence of the actions performed by a hypothetical independent subject based on individual volition is highly problematic. Unfortunately, with the Homeless Self-Help Act declaring the rough sleeper's own volition to be the screening standard for determining whether he or she can receive aid, such representations may in practice function to legitimize exclusion, contrary to the original intent of researchers who set out to oppose an "ideology of exclusion." Indeed, the researchers' desire to find a subject that performs resistance may have led to an excessive focus on rough sleeping, which is only a temporary phase in the course of these practices. This focus may well have contributed to a failure to acknowledge the existence of women rough sleepers, the sort of practices we have observed in these case studies, and their way of life.

Dipesh Chakrabarty, referring to Gramsci's work on subalternity, writes that subaltern history is "necessarily fragmented and episodic" (Chakrabarty 1995: 757). The practices of the women rough sleepers we have observed, too, occurred only in fragmentary fashion, lacking the consistency that comes from taking a long-term perspective. In other words, the practices of women like Eiko, who expressed a desire to continue rough sleeping provided that her relationships continued to thrive, or Tamako, who repeated a cycle of starting, then escaping from, rough sleeping, displayed what appears to be inconsistency or reactivity. This was because the actions they performed took place under the constraint of limited resources and violence and in accordance with traditionally expected roles for women. The fragmentary form of the lives of these women aptly symbolizes the position into which they were forced, being marginalized both as rough sleepers and as women. Yet this fragmentary quality is neither inherent nor exclusive to women rough sleepers. Rather, it would seem to be particularly prominent in the case of women due to the traditional imposition on women of negative values and practices that are incompatible with being independent and rational. A new focus on the fragmentary, inconsistent practices of women rough sleepers, such as those we have observed, may be the key to reconsidering the validity of "knowledge" that insists on finding an independent subject within the daily situations in which people live their lives.

7 The process of change

The influence of support over time

In Chapters 5 and 6 we have looked at the daily lives of women rough sleepers living in Park B. Living under numerous oppressive conditions and unable to meet their basic needs, they devised strategies and formed relationships to get by.

In this chapter, I will look at the Women's Support Group, a group of women rough sleepers and women supporters in the city of Osaka in which I participated for some time, focusing on its activities and the rough sleepers who have been involved with it. The supporters, including myself, had an influence on the life choices of the rough sleepers and sometimes actively intervened. In the more than nine years that this group has been active, there have been many changes in the daily lives of the rough sleepers. At Park B in Tokyo prefecture, as described in Chapters 5 and 6, my role was solely that of a bystander observing the world of these women. Moreover, the investigation was conducted over a period of only 10 months, so Chapters 5 and 6 essentially serve as a cross-section of these women's lives taken over a limited period of time. This chapter, on the other hand, will cover a period lasting a number of years to portray the way that supporters involved themselves with women rough sleepers, and the ways those women changed.

The purpose of investigating the activities and members of the Support Group will be to understand the process by which the women rough sleepers make decisions. As noted in Chapter 1, many previous sociological studies of rough sleepers have been motivated by opposition to the view of rough sleepers as objects to be reformed. Instead, they emphasized points such as rough sleepers' resistance to society based on their own volitional will, or the autonomy and creativity behind their everyday living strategies. Likewise, feminist research rejected the "human rights" approach to prostitution with approaches such as sex work theory, which argued that women who do sex work do so willingly and autonomously. What is presupposed in such approaches, whether rough sleeper research or sex work theory, is an individual "self," isolated from others, that determines its actions autonomously and rationally. However, when we observe their lives over time, it becomes clear that in fact, the lives of women rough sleepers are determined in the context of a continuous process of change, in which interventions by other people and relationships with acquaintances play an important role.

This chapter will look at the ways that supporters, including myself, involved ourselves in the lives and decisions of women rough sleepers over a period of time, and how these women changed in the process.

"The Women's Support Group"

The Women's Support Group is a group for women rough sleepers and women supporters that was formed in the city of Osaka in July 2003. Its basic activity is monthly meetings in which rough sleepers, former rough sleepers, and supporters, all women, meet over meals and tea to talk. The Support Group has, at the time of writing, been active for over thirteen years. The Women's Support Group was formed after a woman rough sleeper complained that there were no opportunities to get advice about women's problems. It was instigated by a woman active in assisting rough sleepers in their decision-making, and consisted of women sleeping rough in Park C in Osaka as well as women already involved in support activities who responded to the call for members. Some participants volunteered for the Women's Support Group while working as doctors, nurses, and staff members of women's facilities. I have participated from the beginning.

As the group's main activity, once a month they would meet outdoors, sitting on rush matting, and talking over sweets and meals. Amidst casual conversation, participants spoke of difficulties women experienced living in an overwhelmingly male environment, and of problems in daily life. When someone had a problem – for instance, receiving inadequate support from an organization due to being a woman – and there seemed to be a good solution, members would think of measures to take and the group would make a request or proposal to the organization involved. The group tried to conduct relationships on a basis of equality as much as possible. In some cases, strategies to prevent harassment and other problems experienced not only by rough sleepers but also by supporters during their support activities were discussed by the entire group as issues commonly faced by women. To create a space where women could feel safe, participation in the monthly meetings was in principle limited to women.[1]

People involved in support activities for rough sleepers can typically be divided into those who consider rough sleeping as something that should end and those who consider continuing it to be acceptable. Most participants in the Women's Support Group are of the latter opinion. Therefore, the group is flexible in the type of support offered, based on an individual's wishes. For women who wish to continue rough sleeping for the time being, the group works to make this possible, and for women who want to end rough sleeping, they help in various ways, such as accompanying them to apply for benefits. Members sometimes visit women receiving public assistance who have moved to ordinary housing and work to sustain relationships with them, offering help to cope with the various problems they experience.

A variety of activities have been conducted by the group over the years, depending on the time and the people involved. For instance, in response to frequent requests by rough sleepers to supporters for loans of money, at one time the group ran a microlending operation. It lent small amounts of money in the name of the Support Group, which were to be repaid each month. There was also a period in which supporters and rough sleepers together conducted outreach to women sleeping rough outside of Park C, approaching women in other parks and stations, checking on their safety and whereabouts, and inviting them to the monthly meetings. Some other activities have included *karaoke* singing, movie viewings, attending gatherings with other rough sleeper support groups, and visits by rough sleeping members to university classes to speak of their experiences. The funds needed for running the group are donated by supporter members.

For the first two years, the monthly meetings were held at Park C. Later, as the tents of one member after another were cleared out of the park, the club stopped meeting at a fixed location and instead moved among several parks. In recent years, the main locations of meetings have been the D riverside park, rented indoor spaces, and the homes of members. Over more than ten years of the Women's Support Group's activities, there have been about ten rough sleepers who participated regularly over a period of time, and about ten others who joined in only once or twice. At present, most of the participants are former rough sleepers who have moved to facilities and regular housing. Among the supporters, five or six individuals, including me, did the main work of running the group; about ten people participated regularly for a length of time; and about thirty participated only once or twice. There were also numerous women rough sleepers who received individual help from supporters in the Women's Support Group. These supporters did things such as helping individuals to apply for public assistance and keeping in contact with them.

The lives of women rough sleepers

In this section, out of the many women who participated in the Women's Support Group, I have selected three whom I was able to interview in detail about their lives and with whom I was able to form long-lasting relationships. Here, I will introduce their life histories and describe their lives as rough sleepers.

Keiko (Chapter 2, Table 2.4, 20) lived in Park C in a tent with a male partner. She was the only member of the Women's Support Group who had participated consistently from the time the group was founded. At the time that I interviewed Keiko, who came from the Hokuriku region in northwestern Japan, she was forty-four years old. She grew up in a farming family with five children, and said that growing up she was bullied by schoolmates as well as by her siblings. After graduating from middle school, she moved to the Kansai region to work at a factory, helped by a cousin living there; after this, she worked at various restaurants in the Kantō area near Tokyo. When she was twenty-three, her parents persuaded her to return to her hometown to get married, to a farmer about twenty years her senior. Unable to tolerate his heavy drinking and the lack of sexual relations, she divorced him after only one month. After this, she moved about the Kantō area, working as a live-in food server at workers' lodgings. When she was thirty-seven, she began sleeping rough for the first time at a park in Tokyo prefecture. After six years of sleeping rough, she made her way to the city of Osaka, where she began sleeping near a station using cardboard. She said that she chose a space to sleep in that was near a restroom and was bustling with people, because she felt "unsafe" in deserted areas.

> Women need access to a restroom. It had to be a place with a restroom...
> I felt bad about bothering people with my presence, having people look
> down on you like that... Even though people see you...that was the
> only place with a restroom. So that's where I had to be. I'd be afraid
> in other kinds of places.

Eventually she set up a tent in the same place. At the time, she says, she got meals through helping out at a soup kitchen run by a rough sleeper support group, and got income from donations from passersby and from acts of prostitution. Describing how she performed sexual acts solicited by passersby, Keiko put it this way: "For me, it was fooling around. I thought I'd just amuse myself with them." Here, Keiko presented it as if she were a subject who was in control of the relationships.

> In the area around the station, somehow or other you manage to find
> someone who will help you. Of course, there are also some people
> who propose doing something nasty. [Q: Really? What kind of thing?]
> Well, you know, if you're woman, they want what a woman's got. [Q:
> Are some of these rough sleepers? Or do you mean office workers or
> people like that?] Office workers. [Q: What do they say when they
> approach you?] Well, maybe I shouldn't say it, but you know, about
> men's physical needs. [Q: And what do they say when they ask for
> that?] Not directly, they say something like let's go get something to
> eat. [Q: I see! And about how much do they say they'll pay?] Oh, well,
> you know, "How about I give you this much?" [Q: About how much?]
> Oh, sometimes 1,000 yen, sometimes 3,000 yen (~USD 10–30). As
> they say these days, I was like a *fūdoru*, a sex worker. But from my
> point of view, I was treating them like playthings. I thought I'd just
> play around with them. I was still young, you know.

After one year, Keiko was evicted from the area when it became a construction site, and moved to Park C. There, she moved into a tent with a man in his 70s whom she had known previously, along with a cat. When I met her, Keiko was still getting her meals and daily supplies through helping out at a soup kitchen run by a rough sleeper support group.

Midori (Chapter 2, Table 2.4, 18) lived in a small park in the city of Osaka. When a Women's Support Group meeting was held there, she began attending each month. Midori was cheerful and talkative. Among the rough sleeping women I met, she expressed her thoughts and memories with unusual articulation and clarity.

Midori was born in Kyūshū, in southern Japan, to a family of eight children. When I interviewed her, she was fifty-one. After leaving high school without graduating, she became a nursing trainee, but dropped out, and at age eighteen moved to the Kansai area to work in the nighttime entertainment industry. At twenty-five, she married a former customer more than a decade older than she was. Her husband had a child from a previous marriage, but that child was already grown and working independently, so she did not live with the child. At the time her husband was living on worker's compensation and did not have a regular job. After their daughter was born, Midori continued to work in the entertainment business as the main breadwinner for the family. However, problems developed after the Great Hanshin Earthquake of 1995, when the family of one of her husband's relatives moved in with them and her relationship with her husband, which had never been harmonious, deteriorated. After sixteen years of marriage, Midori left home. She remained single and supported herself on jobs such as domestic helper, construction worker, and live-in waitress at a *ryokan* inn. Her last job was at a well-known hot spring inn, but as she grew older it became physically hard to continue the strenuous work involved in being a waitress. Due to being a capable worker, many responsibilities were heaped on her, and eventually she developed health problems and had to leave the job. She decided for the time being to return to her family home, but on the way there, all her money and identification cards were stolen at a sauna where she was staying. In a state of despair, she was sitting in a park when she noticed a rough sleeper collecting aluminum cans.

It started out when I was sitting in a park, feeling really bad, so bad that I might as well be dead. I didn't care what happened to me. And while I was sitting there that first day, I saw someone picking up cans. There was talk on TV about homeless people, but it was my first time to actually see one. When I looked at what these homeless people were doing, I saw them with cans, different kinds of cans, sitting in a chair doing something with them. I realized that you could collect cans and sell them like that.

Photo 7.1: Midori's bicycle, loaded up with aluminum cans.

Midori realized that this was something she might be able to do. She began sleeping rough by observing and imitating what she saw.

With the help of other rough sleepers, she set up a tent in a park where about thirty people were living. While collecting cans, she met a man who taught her the tricks of the trade – for instance, how it was more effective to collect cans on the days recyclable waste was picked up, and what places yielded the most cans, and how to collect them. Eventually, she was able to make 1,500 to 2,000 yen (~USD 13–18) per day.[2] Leaving her tent in the morning while it was still dark, she rode her bicycle to a residential area. Sorting the cans collected and taking them to sell took about eight hours of work daily. If she met the caretaker at an apartment complex she greeted him and received some aluminum cans; in return, she helped with cleaning or sorting trash. She always greeted neighborhood people who passed by while she was working with a "Good morning" or "See you later." She thus developed new acquaintances, some of whom brought her cans or something to eat. She said that one elderly individual came every week to help out just to pass the time, and on those days she made twice as much money as usual.

I can collect more cans than other people now because of what I've
been taught. Also, I get a lot of help from people who don't do it
as a job. You know, regular people... An older man comes to help
out, bringing cans from his apartment complex. He brings cans
collected from his apartment complex... It's easy for retired older
men to just stay home. He was in really bad health. Well, after a
while he started talking to a lady in the neighborhood, and then to
————[a male rough sleeper friendly with Midori]. Now, ————
is originally from Osaka so he knows the whole city. So he takes the
older man to a bunch of different places by bicycle. And the man's
health got much, much better. Physically better with a smile on his
face. Everyone says his complexion is much healthier looking. So
after a while they finally started coming where I am, ————and
this man. And the man said he preferred talking to me. [Laughs] So
according to ————, the old man always says, I want to go with
her. With her!

As she established set collection routes for each day of the week,
she was able to collect more and more cans, and her life became
more stable. Because, Midori said, she needed to keep the trust of
the people who support her work, she worked every day without
fail, even in rain or snow.

Midori had relationships with many other neighborhood
residents. For instance, when she learned that a person who always
brought aluminum cans for her was collecting pull-tabs for a
charitable organization, Midori began pulling off every tab from
the large number of cans she collected every day and giving them
to that person in thanks for always bringing cans. (In Japan, charity
organizations collect pull-tabs to be recycled. They exchange the
tabs for wheelchairs, which are donated to the needy.) Although
this was time-consuming and reduced her income in proportion to
the weight of the pull-tabs, Midori wanted to pay back this person
for their help and has continued to do it. There are also people who
come to Midori while she is sorting out cans in a residential area,
wanting her to listen to their problems.

There was a kid in his twenties who worked part-time. He praised the
way I work so hard. He was getting off the night shift and offered to
buy me coffee. Then...he sat next to me and said... "people in these

Photo 7.2: A collection of pull-tabs that have been removed from aluminum cans. On the left are collections of stickers taken from the cans, which can be exchanged for prizes. These are sold for 1 yen each.

apartments don't like me." "Why not?" I said. "I think it's because I always say what I think." I said, who cares if they don't like you?

Once, when an elderly person told her about being abused, Midori informed a representative from a government office who was making rounds at the park, acting as a go-between for the welfare office.

Midori's life, then, was enhanced through her relationships with the people around her, whether fellow rough sleepers with whom she shared information and food, or with neighborhood residents who helped her in her work. Midori expressed pride from living on her own income, giving her self-respect even as a rough sleeper. She also said that this was what made relationships with other people possible. These relationships, in turn, helped her to maintain her income.

I think [people respect me] because I speak to them as an equal... Homeless people sometimes act too humble. They look down when they talk to people. I never want to be that way. I know what I do – I

live in a park, I'm definitely not an ordinary person. But by collecting
cans I can buy the food I need for myself, and use the public bath...
If I look straight at people when I talk to them, they always treat me
normally... I make sure I have goodwill to them...talk to them like
I like them.

Midori's mode of living on her own earnings certainly fits the model
story for self-sufficient rough sleepers as portrayed by previous
activism and research. Hers is a case study that belies the stereotype
of rough sleepers as "lazy," and provides a living example of a rough
sleeper who, despite the difficulty of her circumstances, lives an
ordinary life much like everyone else. However, her self-supporting
way of life appears more complicated when her gender is brought
into the picture. Although it may seem to conform to some ideal
model for a rough sleeper, in many respects it does not conform to
the prevailing norms for a woman.

Even after marrying and having a child, Midori supported her
family, as her husband did not work; after leaving her family, she
continued to live on her own earnings. She was proud of the fact that
when she worked at construction sites, she did so on an equal basis
with men in a predominantly-male environment. She was also proud
that after becoming a rough sleeper, she earned money for herself
with no help from a man. Midori expressed her feelings this way:
"It's so much easier if you have a man to help you out." One could
sense a hint of envy for women who were in a position to depend
on a man economically.

Even if you're homeless...it's easier if you have a man to help you
out... I'm sure it's easier that way, you know. Your partner takes care
of you, and all you have to do is some daily chores.

Although Midori herself was proud of the way she had always worked
"like a man," some rough sleeping men she knew took a negative view
of that fact. Some, she heard, would say behind her back that she was
"not a woman." Many male rough sleepers strongly expressed the
view that there should be a sexual division of labor; they expected
women to perform "women's roles." Some men living in the same
park as Midori disapproved of women doing jobs like collecting
discarded articles. Indeed, there were even quite a few cases in which
a man would be bothered to see a woman sleeping in the rough by

herself and, not feeling he could overlook it, share food and money with her, with the result that the two began living together. In such a milieu, a woman like Midori, who earned a living working "like a man," was in the minority. Midori even said of herself: "I don't think of myself as a woman."

Midori also invoked this idea in explaining the reason she left the home where her husband lived. Her body, she said, stopped being able to accept having a relationship with a man that was more than just friendship. She expressed this condition by referring to herself as a "man." According to her, this was the main reason that she abandoned her daughter and husband and left home.

> I would get chills when my husband came up next to me wanting to do that. Remember, I told you, I couldn't accept a man physically anymore. I couldn't stand it. And my husband would always say, "You're with some other man, right?" I decided that was enough [and left home]. I couldn't do it after I had a child... My body changed, I became a man. [Laughs]

When some other women rough sleepers said they dreamed of remarrying in the future, Midori reacted scornfully. "What's the use of a man when you're homeless?"

> I don't think it makes sense. When you're homeless, what's the use of a man? Everyone talks about it, but really they just can't get away from them!... Going off somewhere with some guy and getting paid for it... They need to do it to live.

Although she expressed a belief that "women need to be that way to live," Midori considered herself to be different from dependent women. In fact, although some women rough sleepers do sometimes earn income like Midori, many of the women surveyed here took on the role of housewives, even when living on the streets. Rather than going out to earn money, they remained at the tent sites and performed household labor. Midori also noted, that some of them had sexual relationships with men in exchange for money.

I first met Itsuko (Chapter 2, Table 2.4, 9) during outreach activities with members of the Women's Support Group. She lived with her husband in a finely-made hut in Riverbed D. Itsuko, a sociable person, immediately accepted the invitation to the monthly meetings, saying: "I like that kind of thing," and attended regularly thereafter.

Itsuko was sixty-nine years old. She was born in a prefecture in the Chūbu region of central Japan. Later, her parents were assigned to work in Taiwan, and Itsuko remained in Japan to be raised by her grandparents. She describes herself as a lively, spirited girl, something of a tomboy.

> I was a mischief-maker, and a bold talker. The boys couldn't handle me. I mean, I'd knock them over and say "Don't mess with me!" You couldn't tell if I was a boy or a girl then.

Itsuko rarely attended elementary school, and left middle school after one year. As a result, she has poor literacy skills to this day. At age thirteen she began working in a match factory. She married a fellow worker when she was fifteen, and they had two sons. However, Itsuko says that she had relationships with a variety of men, and since she continued to work at a canning factory after marriage, she did not spend much time taking care of her children. When she was twenty-six she asked her husband to "set her free," and they divorced. The children remained with their father, and Itsuko left to become a *geisha*. She gave little in response to repeated questions about what happened after that, but did admit that she had spent time in jail. She began sleeping rough at a riverbed when she was in her fifties, with a man she met working at a pachinko parlor in Kamagasaki. Since then, they had lived fifteen years as husband and wife in a tent with two dogs. About fifteen people lived in tents along this part of the riverbed.

Itsuko's younger husband regularly worked as a day laborer, which gave them enough income to purchase most of their food and daily necessities. The tent they lived in was well-furnished, with an electric generator that powered a TV and fluorescent lighting. They had another hut that they used for storage space. When her husband was out working, Itsuko would remain at the hut doing housework and waiting for him to return. Despite sleeping rough, her life was much the same as that of any other full-time housewife. Her husband took care of their finances; he worked, and when there was enough money, if he felt like it he would give Itsuko up to 10,000 yen (~USD 90), which she would use to pay for things like food, daily items, doing laundry, and dog food. Her husband would also, at times, stock up on necessities. However, whatever remained of her husband's income he would use for his personal entertainment, like playing pachinko. Itsuko also liked pachinko, but she said that out of deference to her husband, she rarely went.

According to Itsuko, "Sometimes he gives me spending money and sometimes he doesn't." Therefore, she collected aluminum cans on a small scale to supplement her income as much as possible.

After her husband went to work, Itsuko would walk the dogs and then go out to collect aluminum cans. Although she used to travel some distance by bicycle, she had lost the stamina for this as she grew older, and now did all her collecting in the neighborhood on foot. After accumulating a certain quantity of cans, she went out to sell them once every few weeks. She sold them to a junk dealer located close to their home, out of loyalty, although she was aware that she could get more money selling them to someone farther away. Itsuko said she did not make much money from the cans, but since her husband controlled how they spent the money he earned, this gave her a small sum to spend as she wished.

When there was still not enough for living expenses and spending money, Itsuko said that she would sometimes sell sex for money. She appears to have had a couple of repeat customers. One was a male rough sleeper living in a nearby tent who worked and had income; another was a man living in a nearby apartment who had set up a hut at the riverbed (where Itsuko lived) to keep his pets in, and regularly came to take care of the pets. Her price for sex was 5,000 yen (~USD 45) each time.

> There's this driver, you know? He offered me 5,000 yen. [Q: A driver?] Yes, he lives nearby. He's at a company, he works. I can't afford to stop seeing him. So, I do what I have to do... Otherwise, you know how it is [I couldn't get by]. It [sex] is over in a second, anyway...

Moving to a regular home

I met these three women through the Women's Support Group, and as part of the group's activities as well as on a private basis, maintained relationships with them that have lasted for years. As one would expect, over time, their lives and their understanding of their lives went through changes. We will now look at how those changes occurred over time, and what part the Women's Support Group played, including my own role.

It was right after the formation of the Women's Support Group that Keiko, who lived in Park C, suddenly disappeared. Concerned members of the group looked for her high and low and finally found her staying with a male acquaintance in Kamagasaki. Apparently, a male rough sleeper she had met when volunteering for a rough sleeper support group had forced his way into her tent and had stalked her. The man in his 70s who had been living with her fled somewhere as a result, and she fled to Kamagasaki. She had been sleeping rough in a cardboard structure for a while when a male acquaintance from a support group approached her.

> I was sleeping near the Airin Labor and Welfare Center [a government office that provides jobs and welfare to day-laborers]. People had helped me put up some cardboard. [Q: You were by yourself?] Yes, I was alone. [Q: Wasn't that dangerous?] No, not really, it wasn't that dangerous… So ———— came along on his way home, saw me, and asked if I'd like to cook for him. I said, not now, and told him to come at such-and-such a time. I didn't think he'd really come. With it raining I didn't think he'd come, but he did come that evening! It was 4 or 5 o'clock, and I was so surprised, I said, "I can't believe you came!" [*Laughs*] [Q: So that was the first time you'd met him?] No, before that we'd eaten together at the soup kitchen. As I said, when I first started living there I was helping out at the soup kitchen. That's where I met him. But he'd never talked to me before. [Q: So, he asked you to cook something for him.] Right, right. I said, what do you usually do? He said, "I always eat out. I can't cook myself, can't cook at all. I don't cook anything but rice. Nothing to go with the rice." Can you believe it? Even children cook!

With this request to cook food, Keiko began living at the man's house. While living there, she learned about an opportunity to earn money selling copies of a magazine called *The Big Issue*,[3] and eventually decided to move out and make a living selling magazines. She began sleeping in a cardboard structure by a train station, and, when she had the money, sleeping at a 24-hour café. Gifted with a friendly manner, Keiko said that her magazines sold well, netting her about 1,800 yen (~USD 16) per day. However, with train travel to the selling location costing at least 600 yen (~USD 5), and with the money needed for food and for using the overnight café, she was barely able to get by. To obtain the magazines to sell, she borrowed 5,000 yen (~USD 46) from the microcredit fund that the Women's Support Group had just started, which she paid back in installments out of the money she made. However, the long hours on her feet every day, and not enough sleep at night, made this life unsustainable. With the winter cold, she became ill, and three months later was hospitalized.

Keiko, knowing from her interactions with the homeless support group that rough sleepers could apply for public assistance for hospital treatment, went to the welfare office alone when she got sick, applied for medical assistance, and checked into the hospital where she was treated for chronic diabetes. According to Keiko, when she began rough sleeping, eating nothing but hamburgers she picked out of the trash at fast-food restaurants made her diabetes worse. Supporters from the Support Group, including me, worried about Keiko's wellbeing after she was discharged from the hospital, visited her frequently to offer advice and support. Keiko had trouble figuring out what to do next, sometimes saying she would return to rough sleeping and sometimes saying she wanted to go on public assistance and live in ordinary housing.

At the time, there was no place for hospitalized rough sleepers to go after they were discharged, so most ended up returning to rough sleeping. Since Keiko's caseworker had not helped to plan what she would do after leaving the hospital, if Keiko had not asserted herself, she too probably would have returned to the streets. Even if her caseworker had been interested in preventing this, and made the arrangements for her to continue receiving benefits post-hospitalization, the expectation was that she would live long-term in a facility. However, Keiko said that she did not want to live in a facility. She discussed the situation with her supporter from the Women's Support Group. It was decided that if she had a doctor write a report on her state of health that declared her unable to work, and if, when she left the hospital, she applied at a welfare office to change her benefit status so she could move from the hospital to living in an ordinary home, she could probably live in ordinary housing while receiving public benefits.

About three months into Keiko's hospitalization, I suddenly received a call from her. She said it appeared that she would be discharged the next day. She could not accept such a sudden notice of discharge, and wanted to go right to the welfare office to apply to change her benefit status so she could move into an ordinary home. Could I go with her? Unable to see her immediately on such short notice, and uncertain whether, with my lack of experience dealing with hospitals and welfare offices, I could successfully negotiate the result she desired, I told her I would find someone else to go with her, and ended the conversation. However, I could not find anyone right away. About two hours later I called Keiko and said that now I would go with her. Keiko was in low spirits, perhaps sensing my lack of confidence at negotiation. Her application to receive benefits at home would never be accepted, she said over and over; she was going back to rough sleeping. I repeatedly tried to persuade her that even if unsuccessful it was worth applying. But Keiko had already given up, and was getting ready to resume rough sleeping.

Right after this, though, another supporter called Keiko. While I had lacked confidence in the application process, this individual believed that changing her benefits was Keiko's right and that there was no reason for her application to be rejected. She telephoned the hospital and asked them to postpone Keiko's discharge a few days and write a report on her state of health. Keiko was cheered by this and again decided to apply for the benefit, echoing the supporter's words: "There's no reason for me to be rejected."

A few days later, the supporter, Keiko, and I went together to the welfare office to apply for housing assistance. We explained her situation: how she could not return to rough sleeping in her state of health; how she was not yet ready to work; how she wished to receive public assistance while living in ordinary housing. We were told that if she entered a temporary emergency protection facility for women and tried to find housing during her two-week stay, her application for housing assistance should be approved before the end of this period. Keiko checked out of the hospital and was admitted to the facility as planned. During her two-week stay, accompanied by a supporter from the Women's Support Group, Keiko looked for housing and successfully contracted a place to stay. Two weeks later, Keiko's nine years of rough sleeping came to an end, as she began living in ordinary housing.

For Midori, life as an unattached rough sleeper, making a living collecting cans, was both stable and sustainable. Thus, she was clear and consistent about her goal for the immediate future: to continue her present life as a rough sleeper.

> This is the right life for me. I know, it's crazy. [Laughs] It's crazy to me, too. Actually, I do have a plan to move into a Self-Help Center in

the next year. I have that in mind. But I also like living here... My life
now is interesting. Collecting cans and things is interesting. I get to
meet all kinds of people.

Midori hoped, eventually, to move into a self-help facility, and using
that as her address, look for work, and finally move into an apartment.
Her dream was to get a job as a caregiver for the elderly. She had
prior experience with this and thought it would satisfy her interest
in helping people. She gathered information on options available
after ending rough sleeping, reading flyers handed out by support
organizations and talking with representatives of welfare offices
when they came to the area where she lived. She actively looked into
what sort of facility she should enter to get qualified to be a caregiver.

> I don't hesitate to ask. You have to ask! I mean, I have to figure out for
> myself what I'd need to do if something bad happened to me.

And yet, despite having this clear vision for the future, Midori said
that for now she was enjoying her present life. With the help of many
people, she was able to live by her own efforts, and enjoy unexpected
encounters with new people.

However, in reality, it was becoming harder and harder to live
in a tent in an urban park as Midori did. In the city of Osaka, tents
were forcibly removed from Osaka Castle Park and Utsubo Park in
2006 and Nagai Park in 2007. This was the beginning of a process
of pressuring rough sleepers to leave wherever they could be
found, whether through persuasion, intimidation, or other means.
In Midori's park, local public servants who managed the park and
others who offered counseling on welfare frequently went around
advising rough sleepers to move into public facilities.

> Someone came to talk to me just today... They told me to check into
> a facility so I could treat my health problems... That would make
> it possible to work, they said. I said, I'm already working here, so I
> don't want to do that... I'm working now collecting cans!... And I
> like working. Working is better than sitting around doing nothing.

To the government office worker who advised her to enter a facility
and look for work, Midori replied that she did not want to go to a
facility. She might be a rough sleeper, she argued, but she already

had a job. If she was forcibly evicted from the park where she lived, Midori said she was ready to put away her tent, move into a facility, and look for a job.

> But I'll stay there until that happens. When it does, I'm ready to move into a facility somewhere. But otherwise, I told the Park Department person that I'd be the last to leave… No way I will leave before that. I'll stay till everyone else leaves. If one person leaves, everyone else might have to leave too. So if one person fights to stay, other people might be able to do the same. That's what I told the city government person. But you never really know what will happen. I don't know how long I can stay. I want to stay as long as I can, and when something happens, if my health goes or something, when that happens I'm ready to move into a facility.

At Midori's age, re-employment was still a possibility. As a woman, she would be given priority for admission to welfare facilities, and she was confident in her ability to adapt. For these reasons, she felt that she could cope with having her tent removed. What she said about staying in the park was out of concern for the others who could not manage in the same way, knowing that they would have nowhere to go.

Although she said she sometimes lost confidence, Midori always expressed a consistent vision for the future. Midori had built a life for herself working while sleeping rough, and had a clear goal for herself, which she communicated to welfare workers and other relevant parties. It is very unusual to find a rough sleeper, especially a woman, who can do this.

With this stated plan of moving into a facility within the year, Midori subsequently continued her rough sleeping life without disruption for a total of more than two years. But one year later, despite the clear vision she had described, she moved into ordinary housing under public assistance. While I did not learn exactly how this happened, it seems that when her chronic high blood pressure grew worse, a city welfare worker persuaded her to look for housing and she subsequently moved into an apartment.

Itsuko was heavily dependent on her husband, who controlled their finances, and had to be careful not to make him unhappy. Their relationship grew more and more distant over time, and as he aged, her husband was not able to work as often, and Itsuko had little spending money. For the first time, they were running out of food. As they grew more and more desperate, Itsuko began to think seriously about putting an end to fifteen years of rough sleeping. However, because her husband was still relatively young and working, they could not receive public assistance as a couple. Although she insisted, "It's our fate to be together; I don't think I can leave him," she also admitted that she was conflicted and thinking of separating from her husband and going on public assistance. Another thing that worried her was what would become of her pet dog, which she was not allowed to keep while receiving public assistance.

> I think about what to do, and I wonder whether we really have to be together the rest of our lives ...I'm sorry about it, but I'm thinking of leaving... Just taking my clothes, and leaving the other stuff packed in a corner. If I just do what's good for me, he'll do whatever he has to. I feel bad about it, but it might be the thing to do... I'm so tired... It makes my head hurt to think about it. My dog is young and healthy, it would be cruel to leave it behind. I worry a lot about these things.

Contributing to this change of heart was the ever-increasing pressure for rough sleepers to take down their tents. She was also unhappy with the physical abuse that she had suffered from her husband for many years.

> We might stay together if the tents were going to stay where they are... I don't really want to leave him without warning, but I can't stand the violence. If he was someone who would listen, I could say, "Well, we've been together for a long time. I'm very sorry, but I want to be free." If he would listen then I'd be happy to talk to him. I wouldn't have to make this decision. But...if I say anything, smack! He smacks me on my head... Every time I try to talk to him. It's really bad.

Based on what Itsuko said, supporters from the Women's Support Group, including me, offered to help her apply for public assistance if needed, but Itsuko was not yet able to make up her mind.

Soon thereafter, a vehicle belonging to Organization E passed Itsuko's hut. Itsuko remembered the driver previously visiting her hut and asking if she wanted to talk about her situation. So she stopped the car, opened up about her troubles, and was invited to the group's office. After consultation, it was immediately arranged for

Organization E to support Itsuko in applying for public assistance. Organization E had an established system for this support. A rough sleeper would initially move rent-free into an apartment owned by a participating landlord. Using that address as a base the individual would apply for public assistance, and when it was received it would be used to pay the security deposit and rent. This practice facilitated the approval of public assistance to rough sleepers, whose lack of an address tended to disqualify them. It made it possible to bypass the usual process for rough sleepers, which consisted of first moving into a facility and then searching for an apartment. Thus, the individual could begin living in ordinary housing immediately. However, there were problems with this system. Public assistance was not provided for deposit money or furnishings,[4] so Itsuko had to borrow money for these and repay it in monthly installments of 20,000 yen (~USD 183), taken out of her monthly benefit of 80,000 yen (~USD 734), for over a year. Another problem was that the apartment provided for her was close to the area where she used to sleep, so there was a risk that her husband would find her.

I learned about her new situation three days before Itsuko moved out of her hut, when, worried about her indecision over getting public assistance, I visited her with another supporter from the Women's Support Group. Itsuko explained that she was on her way to receiving public assistance with the help of Organization E, but although her application had been approved, she did not know when the benefit money would begin to come, which made her uneasy. Itsuko's explanation did not make much sense, and it was evident that she did not fully understand the complicated process for awarding welfare, so the supporter and I went with her to the welfare office to find out where she was in the process.

At the welfare office, we learned that prior to taking on the help of Organization E, Itsuko had gone by herself to the welfare office to ask about receiving public assistance. The welfare worker explained that due to her age, she should easily be eligible for public assistance if she applied as a single person. If she did, in view of her wish to escape from her husband's abuse, the best plan would be for her to first enter a two-week temporary emergency protection facility. From there she would look for an apartment far away from Riverbed D, where there was no danger of being found by her husband. When the apartment was found, deposit and furnishing money would be provided and she could begin living there under housing benefits.

However, Itsuko could not bring herself to make the decision that day to leave her husband and begin a new life. She was told to come back when she made that decision, and did not actually apply for benefits.

The pathway to living in ordinary housing presented by the welfare office seems preferable to living with the support of Organization E. If she could tolerate the two-week stay in a facility, money for the deposit and furnishings would be provided through her public assistance, so she would not have to pay it herself. Moreover, there was less danger her husband would find her. Since Itsuko did not understand these points, the supporter and I explained the situation carefully. At this, Etsuko complained that from now on she would have to help out at Organization E to repay them for their assistance, and expressed regret at accepting their support.

> I should have gone to the welfare office before joining Organization E! It's my fault for not deciding earlier.

Unfortunately, Itsuko had already signed a contract for the apartment introduced to her by Organization E, and it could not be modified.

Organization E, the welfare office, and the Women's Support Group offered advice to Itsuko to help her transition out of rough sleeping. Unfortunately, their activities were separate and uncoordinated. It seems that Itsuko, not wanting to squander the good will of each of the many entities offering support, and unable to understand the welfare office's explanations of their procedures, could not figure out whom to rely on.

> I couldn't decide which one to choose. I went to the welfare office, didn't know whether to go with the supporters, or ask at the welfare office, so I ended up running to Organization E... That's how it ended up, after all that confusion and worry.

Itsuko said that deciding to accept the support of Organization E came after struggling for a long time over what to do. However, it was not as much a clear, rational decision as it was a spur of the moment impulse to entrust her case to Organization E, which happened to be passing by at her moment of need, and responded to her needs promptly, offering a smooth path to residence in an apartment. Some days later, Itsuko left her hut without telling her husband, carrying only the most basic possessions, and moved to an apartment with the support of Organization E.

As time went on, Itsuko was often short of the money she needed to live on, and at one point, after she hurt her knee, it looked as if she might not be able to continue living in ordinary housing. Nevertheless, she did continue living in her apartment, helping with Organization E's activities while receiving their support, and attending the Women's Support Group.

Keiko and Itsuko, as we have seen, each made the transition from rough sleeping to living in ordinary housing through a process filled with hesitation and false starts. A variety of supporters were involved, including welfare office staff, local government workers who patrolled public areas, and members of the support organization such as the Women's Support Group and organization E. These various individuals and organizations strongly influenced the decisions that Keiko and Itsuko made. As for Midori, despite her clear and consistent plan for the future, when her health was compromised, she moved to ordinary housing at the advice of the welfare office, following a plan that she did not originally anticipate.

In search of the "will"

In the three cases of women rough sleepers we have met so far who were involved with the Women's Support Group, the group was able to build long and supportive relationships and hear their stories directly. There were other women for whom this was not the case. With some, for instance, it was difficult even to hold a conversation or learn their wishes.

A member of the Support Group first met Eri by chance while walking in town. Although it was mid-winter, she had no warm coverings and was sitting by the side of the road. Concerned with this elderly and frail woman who was unable to stand up, several supporters came out to see her. Eri had a clear awareness of things around her and was able to speak, but her statements suggested that she was suffering from delusions. For example, she said that she could not leave the place where she was because "I have to go work at the Embassy." From this, one of the supporters from the group who was a physician concluded that she suffered from a disability or illness of some sort. Unable to stand and walk by herself, she was only able to eat when other concerned rough sleepers occasionally brought her something. Clearly, her life was at risk if she was left here. However, she stubbornly rejected repeated appeals to allow herself to be hospitalized. Given her refusal to move, it seemed that the only thing to be done was to watch over her, so group members decided to take turns going to see her, and to ask the relevant local government office to take on her case.

Several days later, one of the supporters noticed that Eri was wet below the waist. Fearing that she would freeze to death if she remained in this state, the supporter brought a change of clothing for her. When Eri, who could not stand, had her clothes removed, not only were her underwear filled with excrement, but because she had been holding back, she began to defecate involuntarily. After the supporter managed to change her clothes and clean up, Eri thanked her repeatedly. The supporter recommended hospitalization once again, and this time Eri said, "I'll think about it."

Just when it seemed that it might be possible to help Eri to get over her mistrust of hospitals and other people, Eri was hospitalized, more or less by force, at the direction of a local government welfare consultant who had been contacted by the supporters from the Women's Support Group. Reportedly, this consultant tried to persuade Eri to go to the hospital while an ambulance and police officers stood by. As soon as she gave a sign of lowering her resistance, Eri was loaded into the ambulance.

A supporter who later visited Eri in the hospital found that she had recovered her strength and was able to walk. However, according to the supporter, Eri repeatedly complained that she had not wanted to be hospitalized; she had been living in the streets after running away from a psychiatric hospital. This supporter later said that although she was relieved that Eri's life had been saved, she was troubled that she may not have done the right thing. The Support Group members who had worked with Eri shared a deep sense of remorse. Could there have been some way, without using force, to respect Eri's dignity by gaining her voluntary consent?

Yoriko's is another case the group was involved in that led to similar feelings of remorse. A supporter spotted Yoriko crouching on the ground near a train station at night and called out to her. She was sleeping alone in the rough with almost no belongings at hand. Yoriko said that rough sleeping was hard to tolerate, so the Women's Support Group decided to support her in applying for public assistance and looking for housing. Based on speaking with Yoriko and learning her life history and issues, it was decided that she would move into a welfare apartment[5] in Kamagasaki where about 100 persons on public benefits lived.

Yoriko was seventy-three years old. She responded readily to questions and was able to take care of herself, but her memory of the past was poor, and she could not remember many aspects of her life history (for this reason, she is not included in Table 2.4, Chapter 2). She had no children and had been living with her common-law husband on public assistance, but she said he had died about half a year earlier. She said she had no education past the third grade of elementary school and could not read or write at all; she had trouble writing even her own name. However, she could do simple calculations and could do tasks like shopping with no trouble.

After Yoriko had been living in the welfare apartment for some time, it emerged that she was also receiving public assistance from a different locale. She had been living there, not in ordinary housing, but in a facility with staff who provided help in daily life, and she had left suddenly without warning. Her room there had been left untouched. Asked whether she wished to live in that previous facility or in Kamagasaki, she said that she preferred to continue living in the welfare apartment in Kamagasaki. The staff at the Kamagasaki welfare apartment then made arrangements to have the benefits at the previous location terminated.

The supporter from the Women's Support Group who had initially approached Yoriko worked as a doctor. She frequently visited Yoriko at the welfare apartment, and apart from writing prescriptions for medicine, listened to her and offered advice, brought furniture for her room, and generally helped in the large and small activities of daily living. Yoriko placed great trust in this supporter, and often spoke of how grateful she was to the supporter for reaching out to her when she was suffering as a rough sleeper.

> There I was, sitting on layers of cardboard... I almost wanted to die then, I really didn't know what to do... I thought and thought and couldn't think of anything... And that's when ———— [the supporter from the Women's Support Group] came over, and I'm so glad she came and talked to me... It wouldn't be so bad if I could sit there in one place all the time, but I couldn't stand the drunks and people like that coming over. I had to move all over the place. That day was

awful, it was the worst. [Q: What did you do for food and things when you were there?] Oh, you know, that Christian group, they'd come on certain days of the week, and bring things like rice balls and boiled eggs. But when they brought those things, sometimes I'd be there and sometimes I wouldn't, so I wouldn't see them every day. So often I wouldn't eat. Since I'd go completely without food or drink, it was so bad I couldn't walk. I was ready to drop. I was so glad when ———— came. What she did for me, I'm so grateful, it brings tears to my eyes.

Although Yoriko seemed to trust the staff at the welfare apartment, who cared for her in all sorts of ways, she had not managed to form good relationships with the other residents. At the communal bathing area, no one replied to her greetings, which led her to start going to a public bath paying 400 yen (~USD 3.6). She also began to believe that the man living next door to her was saying bad things about her to other people.

Yoriko had been living in the welfare apartment for three months when she disappeared. The supporter filed a missing person search request with the police, and several weeks later learned that Yoriko was living at a different location and receiving public assistance under a different name. Apparently, she was sleeping in the rough when a member of a religious organization came to talk to her, and with the support of that person she rented a room run by the organization. When asked why she had left the welfare apartment, she insisted that the man next door was saying bad things about her. She said she had left the public assistance money she had saved up with a staff member, making no attempt to get it back, and left the welfare apartment carrying only 7,000 yen (~USD 63), "planning to end my life."

At the discretion of the welfare apartment, Yoriko's room had been left as it was when she disappeared, so at her own request she returned to the apartment for a while. After discussions with Yoriko about what to do next, it was decided that because of her concerns about her interactions with the man next door and the other residents of the welfare apartment, it would be better for Yoriko to live on her own than to keep living in a group setting. Arrangements were then made for her to move to another apartment nearby, and live there with assistance from her supporter from the Women's Support Group. The new apartment was fully furnished, and with the generous help of her supporter, Yoriko lived there for about three months – until one day, she again disappeared without warning. Because the supporter had filed two missing persons reports, her room was left untouched for a while in case she came back. But this time, she was not found, and so the furniture and household items, only recently placed in the new apartment, were all disposed of.

More than six months after this disappearance, a message arrived from the Tokyo metropolitan police informing that they had Yoriko in their custody. Yoriko reportedly cried tears of joy when she saw the supporter from the Women's Support Group who had traveled all the way to Tokyo to meet her. I asked Yoriko what had happened during the past six months, but her memories were jumbled and difficult to make sense of. However, based on bits and pieces of what she told me, it seemed that while continuing to sleep in the rough, she would travel to Kyoto, Tokyo, Yokohama, and other places, and, in the cases of Tokyo and Yokohama, stay in facilities for rough sleepers and the elderly. No matter how many times I asked, though, Yoriko, a woman over seventy carrying almost no money who did not know how to ride a train by herself, would not explain how she was able to travel this distance between cities in her condition.

After the death of her common-law husband, and with the onset of serious delusions of persecution, she could not keep on living on her own. She would run away and begin rough sleeping until she fell into an intolerable condition and had to be rescued, repeating a cycle of going on public assistance at various locations and then running away without warning. Even though it was always Yoriko herself who would leave her life on public assistance to begin rough sleeping, she spoke repeatedly of how hard rough sleeping was, and was not able to explain why she would run away without notice. She did not seem to truly understand the reason herself. It may be that for Yoriko, who had a hard time negotiating things and saying "no" to unwanted offers, the only way to express her wishes was simply to escape from an unacceptable situation any way she could.

Accompanied by her supporter from the Women's Support Group, Yoriko left Tokyo to return to Osaka. Thinking that this time it might be better to be in an environment where there were people to watch over her than to live alone, she began living in a welfare facility in Kamagasaki while receiving public assistance. With her quiet personality, living in a shared space was hard for Yoriko. Although she sometimes stayed away from the facility for several days to avoid problems in her relationships with other residents, she managed to continue living there, and after five months, she moved into an apartment located close by the facility. She was able to live on her own, which had been her dream. When that was decided, she said she was so happy she couldn't sleep.

However, two days after moving into the new apartment, Yoriko vanished yet again, leaving behind the apartment she had dreamed about with all the furnishings that had been purchased with the assistance of the facility. A week later, Yoriko was found in police custody. Yoriko said that she had gone into a panic when the cord to the television didn't reach the wall; she did not know how to use the extension cord. The supporter from the Women's Support Group, a doctor who lived nearby, paid her many visits, and with the generous help of the facility staff, she began living there again. However, after that, on several occasions she disappeared for several days. Every time this happened, Yoriko would give a reason for leaving: she had panicked after not being able to open the automatic lock to her door to get in her room when the building manager was off duty, or her neighbors made too much noise. Finally, two months after beginning to live on her own, Yoriko once again vanished, and this time never came back. The supporters from the Women's Support Group, not wanting to continue repeating the cycle, did not file a missing person report, and she was never located again.

The process of becoming a subject

Today, most of the women I met and got to know through the Women's Support Group are no longer rough sleepers. Although there are individuals like Yoriko who have vanished and cannot be contacted, most of them, over the years that I have known them, found an occasion to transition out of rough sleeping. Even Midori, who consistently said she had a clear vision for the future and wished to continue rough sleeping, ended up moving into ordinary housing due to developments that could not have been predicted when I was interviewing her.

Relationships with and efforts by others had a major influence on these women in the process of leaving rough sleeping, sometimes in a short period of time, as in the case of Keiko on the day she was about to be discharged from the hospital. Keiko had been ready to give up on applying for public assistance and return to living on the streets after talking to me. She was influenced by my inner lack of confidence that I would be able to arrange for her to move to ordinary housing after ending her hospital stay, even as I promised to work on it. When she spoke to another supporter, who firmly believed in applying with the attitude that the applicant is a subject with rights, she changed her decision in a space of several hours.

The lives of rough sleeping women who made the transition to ordinary housing, such as Keiko and Itsuko, were not always stable. Itsuko, unaccustomed to planning how to use the set amount of money she received each month, invariably used up the bulk of her approximately 80,000 yen (~USD 735) in benefits within days of receiving it, leaving her with only 5,000 yen (~USD 45) or so to last the twenty days that remained in the month. She repeatedly commented that she had no idea what she used the money for. This worried the members of the Women's Support Group. Itsuko said these hard experiences made her often think of returning to her husband. Itsuko also had other money problems that persisted in one form after another. Nevertheless, Itsuko has managed to continue living in ordinary housing for over five years, with the help of Organization E, the Women's Support Group, friends, and neighbors. She says that being able to sleep without worry makes this the happiest time of her life.

Naturally, there are times that these relationships do not go well. Eri, who refused to use the welfare system even though continuing to sleep rough meant risking her life, was forcibly hospitalized against her "will." Although Eri seemed to be coming closer to accepting being hospitalized, in the end, the Women's Support Group was unable to support her decision. Later, when Eri was in a psychiatric hospital again, she reportedly told her visitors that she "didn't want to come to a place like this."

Yoriko repeated many times a cycle of living in facilities or housing while receiving public assistance, leaving it all behind to sleep in the rough, then returning to benefits. The physician supporter from the Women's Support Group cared for her with great devotion, trying to support her decisions, and Yoriko, for her part, highly trusted this supporter. For this reason, despite Yoriko's frequent disappearances, she would be located and would return to where she was staying, sometimes of her own accord, sometimes because of the request for a missing person search. The Women's Support Group was involved with Yoriko for one year and three months, but in the end she went away and was never located again.

For women in Eri and Yoriko's condition, it was probably difficult to be aware of one's own needs, to communicate those to other people through one's own actions, and to fulfill those chosen goals by oneself. Through the Women's Support Group, supporters maintained relationships with them. Although it was ultimately impossible to support their decisions, in the course of relationships it was possible to sense their "will," and there were moments when it seemed possible to support making that will into reality.

How should we conceive of choice and subjectivity in cases of people like Eri and Yoriko, or someone like Itsuko who managed to sustain a life in ordinary housing with the support of others, despite serious problems? The subject, I suggest, is not something that exists autonomously in advance. Rather, it emerges in an unending process of choosing with difficulty among multiple options, making choices that may come partly by chance. In the context of relationships with others, and a process of trial and error, this subject sustains these choices and brings them to fruition over time.

8 Resisting the spell of the autonomous subject

The focus on subjects and the exclusion of women

In the foregoing examination of a wide range of discourses on homeless women, and case studies of their daily lives, I have tried to highlight what has been overlooked by previous research on homelessness that has focused on ideals like resistance and the autonomous subject – to develop an understanding that can account for specific cases. These cases have included, for example, women such as Eiko and Tamako in Chapter 6 who decided whether to continue rough sleeping or not based on their relationships with others, and Keiko and Itsuko in Chapter 7, whose desire to continue sleeping rough changed over time.

However, these case studies cannot in themselves answer one of the central questions of this book: Why have homeless women been overlooked in the research to date? The exclusion of women in research on homelessness is not solely due to the small number of homeless women; the root of the problem lies in the assumptions – such as resistance and autonomous subjectivity – on which the research is based. The present study is an explicitly feminist work, challenging the underlying assumptions of previous research. It seeks not only to incorporate women into the research field, but to fundamentally challenge the perspective of research that has focused almost exclusively on men.

In this chapter, while addressing the question of what, exactly, has been missing from previous studies, I will discuss the problems with focusing on issues such as autonomy and resistance, and how this has helped lead to the exclusion of women.

The problem with the autonomous subject

We will begin by taking another look at the rough sleepers' legal situation. As discussed in Chapter 1, the 2002 Self-Help Act for

Homeless People marked the beginning of national governmental policies to support rough sleepers. Since its enactment, there has been a major shift in the policy landscape, focusing on the people who live on the streets for an extended period and do not receive public benefits.

Since the Self-Help Act was passed, more options have become available for those who wish to transition out of rough sleeping. A growing number of self-support centers offer employment assistance to rough sleepers, and thanks to the persistent efforts of various support groups, rough sleepers have gradually become eligible for public assistance, which had previously been denied to people with no fixed address. Finally, with the economic recession set off by the 2008 Lehmann Brothers bankruptcy, and the significant increase in poverty in the ensuing years, the number of people on public assistance has grown, reaching a postwar high of over 2,110,000 in 2012 (MHLW 2012). One response to this situation has been the continued expansion of support policies to help rough sleepers get off the streets.

Expanding support policies that create options for leaving rough sleeping is, of course, a positive development. However, as more options become available, this exacerbates the tendency to challenge and question the "free will" of those individuals who forego such options and remain on the streets. Indeed, the Self-Help Act stipulates "the desire to become independent" as a condition for receiving support. The law characterizes people who persist in rough sleeping as "persons who avoid participating in the life of regular society," and specifies that they may be subject to forcible removal. From this perspective, whether someone achieves "independence" or continues rough sleeping is a matter of the rough sleeper's individual will to become "independent." In other words, the problem is framed in terms of individual responsibility.

For women rough sleepers, this delineation of the problem was nothing new. After all, for women, options for leaving rough sleeping, if desired, have long been comparatively easy to find. However, as policies on rough sleepers have developed over time, the problem has ceased to be of concern for women alone. Under these circumstances, the question is not so much whether support policies are adequate, but rather: what is the nature of the "will" of those who choose of their own accord to remain in the streets?

Judith Butler's concern in her theoretical work on gender, discussed in Chapter 1, was how to understand the human subject who possesses this sort of will. Butler considers laws to be rules and norms that have power to compel people to follow them without questioning their origins. She denies that a subject called "woman" exists prior to being invoked by such laws. For if a subject existed prior to the discursive practice of normative laws, this would mean that a subject would be able to choose whether to follow or reject discourses that command it to be a particular gender. But gender is not acquired by conscious choice, but instead unwittingly and unconsciously. Therefore, the subject, invoked by the law, is constructed such that it appears to be an essence or natural object that precedes the law.

Butler's purpose is not to deny the existence of a subject. Rather, she argues that treating the subject as a pre-determined given deprives us of a valuable opportunity to "ask after the process of its construction and the political meaning and consequentiality of taking the subject as a requirement or presupposition of theory" (Butler 1995: 36).

Butler's ideas concerning subject are highly pertinent to debates on homelessness. If, with Butler, we consider the subject to be constructed by social discourse in such a way as to appear to have some sort of essence that precedes its construction, we can similarly understand that the "will" of those "persons who avoid participating in the life of regular society" is constructed as a post-facto explanation of their actions. The institutionalized provision of support services for ending rough sleeping imposes the choice to use or not use those services upon each individual. In other words, the law's demand to stop rough sleeping functions to construct a choosing subject, whether the subject conforms or resists.

This is not to deny the value of cultivating subjects who resist the forces of displacement. It is rather to point out that prior to the imposition of options or choices, there does not exist an autonomous subject capable of judging and making decisions about them. The autonomous subject can emerge only as a consequence of concealing matters about which no real "decision" is possible and situations that are fundamentally contradictory. By bringing these issues back into the open, I aim to create a place, in the politics of homelessness, for the voices that are inevitably excluded during the process of subject construction – the voices of those who are neither taken into protection nor involved in resistance. This is a central aim of this book.

Imposing the choice of whether to utilize the expanded support programs to leave rough sleeping or not, and interpreting that choice strictly as a question of individual will, ignores the cases of women such as those examined in the preceding chapters. These women's circumstances continually changed, as they agonized and prevaricated on whether to continue rough sleeping. According to the Self-Help Act, they are "persons who avoid participating in the life of regular society," having chosen rough sleeping of their own free will. This, then, is the problem with subjectivation: it gives rise to the post-facto understanding that rough sleeping was chosen by a subject in possession of a will.

We will now consider in concrete terms what it means to be ignored and overlooked.

The ethics of care

When faced with the choice of whether to continue rough sleeping or not, it was relatively rare for the women surveyed in this book to express their own will in clear terms. They would, for example, give priority to their husbands' decisions over their own desires, or offer different, contradictory responses each time they were asked. The difficulty in capturing the voices of women like these who are faced with hard decisions is investigated in Carol Gilligan's admirable *In a Different Voice: Psychological Theory and Women's Development* (1982).

In studying how people decide what action to take when faced with a moral choice, Gilligan, a developmental psychologist, found that women tend to describe moral values and human relationships in different terms than men. This issue is symbolized in Gilligan's questioning of the well-known index of moral development known as the Heinz Dilemma. The Heinz Dilemma presents a woman who is dying of cancer, and asks whether her husband, Heinz, should, to save her life, steal a drug that is too expensive to buy. Gilligan states that men and women tend to give different answers to this question. Jake, an 11-year-old boy, answers clearly that Heinz should steal the drug. He reduces the question to one of rights, and judges that between property and life, life is more valuable. Amy, an 11-year-old girl, lacks confidence in her answer. Stealing the drug, and letting his wife die, are both wrong, and the druggist who owns the drug is wrong for not considering the couple's situation. To her, it is a question of responsibility. In traditional developmental theory, human development is thought to proceed gradually from consideration for others to a higher stage of following rules and principles of universal justice. Based on this, Amy is judged as immature compared to Jake. However, Gilligan argued that these traditional standards for moral development were based on male standards, and the very feature that had traditionally been considered a virtue for women, namely recognizing the wants of others, was responsible for this low evaluation of the moral development of women.

From here, Gilligan proceeds to develop a theoretical foundation for recognizing the voices of women that are difficult to hear. According to Gilligan, for women,

> [T]he moral problem arises from conflicting responsibilities rather than from competing rights and requires for its resolution a mode of thinking that is contextual and narrative rather than formal and abstract. This conception of morality as concerned with the activity of care centers moral development around the understanding of responsibility and relationships, just as the conception of morality as fairness ties moral development to the understanding of rights and rules. (Gilligan 1982: 19)

This is the fundamental difference between two different types of morality, which were later characterized as "the ethics of justice" and "the ethics of care." Behind these two moralities lie fundamentally different views of human nature: the ethics of justice, which emphasizes the importance of rights in decision-making, treats each individual as separate, while the ethics of care, which emphasizes responsibility, views human beings as living within a network of relationships.

The voices of the women who appear in Gilligan's book are analogous in tone to the voices of women rough sleepers. For example, one woman quoted in Gilligan says: "It's hard for me to think about myself without thinking about other people around me that I am giving to" (Gilligan 1982: 55). We saw quite similar sentiments expressed in Fujiko's case, in Chapters 5 and 6. Fujiko appeared to be unable to think of herself and her husband separately;

even when asked about herself, she quickly shifted to talking about her husband and what he said. Yūko's case was similar. Having fled her husband's physical abuse, and despite saying that she was comfortable in a facility, Yūko ended up returning to rough sleeping in the tent where he lived because she felt that she needed to care for her cat and husband. In these two cases we can see how some women, due to their acceptance of the gendered role that has long been expected of them – that of caregiver – have been unable to become economically self-sufficient and make the decision to leave rough sleeping. The image of the rough sleeper as a worker who becomes self-sufficient through paid labor, which was presupposed in previous research on homelessness in its emphasis on resistance and autonomous subjectivity, seems to have excluded other types of people as subjects of research: individuals who are dependent on others, or are unable to become self-sufficient due to assuming responsibility for the care of dependent people.

Further, says Gilligan, because the thoughts voiced by such women tend to depend on context rather than follow rules, "from a male perspective, a morality of responsibility appears inconclusive and diffuse, given its insistent contextual relativism" (Gilligan 1982: 22). Indeed, Amy's statements seem much less certain and coherent compared to Jake's, and are difficult to make sense of rationally. Gilligan thus exposes the hesitation and vacillation often shown by women when making a decision, not only concerning the result of the decision but also in their manner of describing the situation. However, she believes that this distinctively female way of talking about decisions is rooted in women's lack of confidence in judging and acting on matters by themselves, due to the long-held expectation that they respond and tend to the needs of others.

For instance, Gilligan, in discussing a woman named Denise who chose to have an abortion despite her wish not to, writes: "When thus caught between the passivity of dependence and the activity of care, the woman becomes suspended in a paralysis of initiative with respect to both action and thought. Thus Denise speaks of herself as 'just going along with the tide'" (Gilligan 1982: 82). This reminds us of the case of Itsuko, in Chapter 7, who, after much hesitation while considering her husband and dog, and seeking advice from various people about how to leave rough sleeping, ultimately just went with the flow of events and moved into an apartment.

Likewise, Eiko, in Chapters 5 and 6, stated that she wanted to continue rough sleeping because the people there understand her hardships and support her. As for Tamako, by relying on the men and welfare organizations that she judged the most trustworthy at the time, she repeated a cycle of beginning and then leaving rough sleeping numerous times. In all these cases, it appears that when women rough sleepers make a decision that is important to them personally, they do not decide on the basis of what is best for them as an individual, but in almost every case consider their relationships with others. These decision-making processes are not adequately accounted for in either the view of human beings as structurally defined objects, or that of autonomous human beings willfully performing acts of resistance. I would suggest that both approaches fail to recognize the importance of relationships with others, and thus fail to account for the practices of women rough sleepers, such as those surveyed in this book, which are deeply embedded in such relationships.

These qualities can likewise be seen among the many women who have been constricted and disempowered by a multitude of normative expectations.

Autonomy and dependence

Gilligan's view has been criticized for "gender essentialism" and reinforcing the male/female dichotomy (Ueno 1995: 8). However, Gilligan states quite clearly that it is not only women who speak "in a different voice." The "ethics of justice" may be more closely associated with men and the "ethics of care" with women, but each is found in both men and women; they are not mutually exclusive. It is not that women value responsibility and relationships because they are women. Rather, they need to consider these things due to being charged with the care of others, for the role of caring for others has regularly been relegated to women. Women's emphasis on the ethics of care is not an essential or inherent quality. Rather, it should be seen as a quality found comparatively more often in women due to the social environment in which they are typically found.

The ethics of care theory, first outlined by Gilligan, has reached beyond feminist theory into fields like political philosophy, not for its value in understanding the experience of women, but for its broader implications. The theory raises new questions about the nature of a society that tacitly normalizes a healthy, adult male, seen as an autonomous individual, isolated from others, and making rational judgments. It also sheds light on what sorts of responsibilities and relationships have sustained people in ways that make such a society possible.

Until recently, such an autonomous individual has been presumed by default in the public sphere. The fact that individuals take care of others and are sustained by the care of others has been ignored. Sequestering such activities in the "private sphere" has helped give rise to a shallow concept of autonomy. As previously mentioned, such assumptions characterize certain studies of homelessness: when arguing that rough sleeping is a choice taken in resistance to power, such studies presume the existence of autonomous individuals, separate from others, who perceive what they need and are able to rationally assert their needs. I have been arguing that these assumptions render invisible the type of women we have met in this book. To put it the opposite way, bracketing out such women and their qualities was a precondition for establishing the idea of the autonomous subject. This, in turn, led to the exclusion of women.

As noted in Chapter 1, individualist arguments, which opposed the view of human beings as passive objects with the idea of an autonomous, isolated individual who resists power, have been used not only in male-centered homelessness studies, but also in feminist research on prostitution. Why have the very arguments criticized in this book for leaving homeless women out of the picture been used not only in research focused on men but in feminist research as well?

This same issue underlies a long-standing conflict in feminist research, between those who take the individualistic "human rights" approach typical of contemporary liberalism, and those who take a more contemporary feminist approach that challenges some of the assumptions of liberalism. This not to say that feminism does not argue for rights. But the critique made within the field of feminist research of the nature of knowledge production accounts well for the problems involved in the construction of such an autonomous subject and of what is left out by this. As Ehara Yumiko has stated, the problem comes from the fact that existing academic fields were founded with males as the default topic of inquiry, and when women are being discussed the vocabulary must be borrowed from these fields. Regarding this "inherent problem of knowledge production," Ehara says, "I am not claiming that the problem is that academic fields and specialized knowledge were produced by male scholars with the motive of protecting their interests by controlling women. Rather, I am pointing out the bias that inevitably attaches to any knowledge produced in accordance with the topics, concepts, intentions, and problematics that are characteristic of the production of academic and specialized knowledge" (Ehara 2000:126). This may be why the language used to discuss prostitution in feminist research also takes the form of an autonomous subject asserting its rights just as is the case when the subjects of research are male.

Cultivating autonomy

According to the legal scholar Kamiya Masako:

> Modern law is based on the assumption of rational human beings. Reasonable human beings exist who, using consistent judgment, make free choices, and act based on these choices. They act, fundamentally, for their own benefit and goals, and take responsibility for the results. The theory of such legal subjects is taken to be a description of our understanding of natural realities, and forms the basis for modern law. (Kamiya 1997: 62).

This definition is more prescriptive than descriptive. It is not based on empirical observation, but instead expresses a modern convention, calling for the respect of people, understood as entities who are all equally capable of making free, autonomous judgments.

Human beings, of course, are not born this way. Rather, some people are taught to be active, while others are socialized to be passive; the former to make autonomous decisions – ideally based on rational judgment – and the latter to conform to social convention and external authority. Feminism has rightly been concerned with how these modes of being have been gendered in modern, patriarchal society, where in fact, *men* have been socialized to be active and autonomous, while *women* have been socialized to be passive and subordinate. These distinctions are deeply entwined in a web of distinctions. For instance, the public realm has been distinguished from the private, with men free to be actively engaged in the public realm, and women consigned to the private realm. Leaving aside who benefits from this schema, for our purposes, the point is that public benefits, even when they do not prescribe the behaviors of the fictional rational subject, are only accessible to those who are able to operate competently in the public sphere. This puts homeless women at a distinct disadvantage.

As we saw in Chapter 7, Eri refused to be hospitalized even when she was in danger of dying on the streets. Yoriko repeatedly went on public assistance and then returned to rough sleeping, even though she found the experience difficult and painful. Such women cannot be considered to be autonomous subjects who make well-informed, rational choices. Yet under the modern convention of treating people as autonomous subjects, people like Eri and Yoriko have been excluded from access social welfare, which is targeted at those who can navigate and negotiate *as if* they are autonomous subjects in the public domain.

For these women to decide how to live and to implement those decisions, relationships with and support from others beyond the private sphere are necessary, such as those provided by the Women's Support Group. Under these conditions, they may be presented with options, make choices – often based on emotion or chance as much as reason – and implement them over time. For many of them, this is when their capacity for autonomy first arises. Autonomy is not an inherent trait, but a human capacity that can be developed over time with the support of others. As Sasanuma Hiroshi puts it:

> Just as it is common for one first to encounter a thing and only afterward realize that one wants to have it, human needs are constructed after the fact. The ability to be mentally self-sufficient is first cultivated by the receipt of advice and recommendations, which create choices. Choices are not made in a state of mental self-sufficiency that exists in advance. Rather, it is through the performance of unconsciously-made choices that mental self-sufficiency is first formed (Sasanuma 2008: 54–55).

Visualizing the future

Much of the previous research on homelessness has tacitly assumed that homeless people are male. Thus, based on the image of a rough sleeper who achieves autonomy through work, it has focused on the resistance to power by rough sleepers and on their subjectivity. This was a justified response to earlier research, which tended to treat rough sleepers as objects in need of reform. But it has had the unfortunate effect of leaving a variety of people out of the picture, many, though not all, of whom are women: people unable to act independently due to their role caring for others; other people who are necessarily involved in decision-making; and people who need support on their way to becoming autonomous. The process of change undergone by such people is also overlooked. We might well conclude these oversights are results of the relegation of care to the private sphere, and the presumption of males who are separated from the network of human relationships as the subject of research. The near total lack of research on homeless women has not been due simply to the small number of such women. Obviously, women do not make up a majority of rough sleepers, but this does not justify excluding them as subjects of research.

As discussed in Chapter 1, the assumption of human beings who make rational choices by their own will has been made in previous, male-centered homelessness research, in Passaro's research on homeless women in the United States, and in research on prostitution in the field of women's studies. But as long as an approach is taken that insists on viewing human beings as autonomous subjects, whether in academic studies or in the legal system, the practices of the types of women discussed in this book will be excluded.

The utopian feminist Drucilla Cornell is one thinker who starts from the recognition that there are always areas of life that are excluded from the law, and speculates on a future world that has never experienced these limits. While politics from the modern period onward have assumed that all people have personhood, endowed with free will and the capacity to make choices, Cornell says that in reality no such personhood exists a priori. And precisely because it does not exist in advance, we need to conceptualize what sort of legal system would be needed to make it possible for us to achieve personhood. Achieving personhood is a process of taking what has been excluded within ourselves and reconfiguring it into our identity. This process is achieved only by securing a space to freely imagine the person one wishes to become, and the procurement of such territory should be pursued by law (Cornell 1995).

The women rough sleepers who, instead of using support policies to get out of rough sleeping, continued to live on the streets, cannot be thought of simply as choosing rough sleeping through "personhood endowed with free will and the capacity to make choices." This is the very reason that projects like the Women's Support Group have continued over long periods of time. Such activities are fueled by the hope that given the right opportunity, and supported by relationships with others, an individual may begin to conceptualize her own future and pursue it. The aim is to accompany such individuals in the long process of gaining respect as someone with personhood. This process will go beyond the conventional application of the law. The key to success will be formal as well as informal efforts to find the things and relationships needed at a given time, without the imposition of the value judgments of others and with tolerance for indecision and error. What is needed is to search for ways to achieve this potential. This means, for example, not demanding that an individual stop rough sleeping or prostitution, even for her own protection. Rather, if someone continues sleeping rough or engaging in prostitution, the aim is to help enable her to freely imagine the way she would like to live, and secure an environment in which that will be respected.

Homeless people are people who have slipped through the safety net that was supposed to be there to catch them. Rather than pressuring such individuals to either return to a protected situation or to resist power, the aim should be to rescue those who are excluded by this choice. What would a system look like that would respect their personhood? A determined search for the answer should lead to richer inquiry into the meaning of personhood, for homeless people and for all of us. The way that we conceive our future will depend on how well we listen to the voices of those still living on the streets.

Epilogue

This book has focused on homeless women, discussing welfare policy and observing the world of rough sleeping women. It was written with three main aims. My first aim has been to describe the unique experience of homeless women, on whom almost no studies have been previously done, including both rough sleepers and homeless women defined in a broader sense. My second aim has been to reconsider homeless studies itself, which developed on the assumption that its objects of study were male. I did this by bringing a gender perspective to the analytic framework. Finally, my third aim has been to reconsider conventional ways of understanding human subjectivity, which hitherto has generally been seen as male, by looking at the daily practices of homeless women. In the concluding sections that follow, I will return to the theoretical questions that motivated this study, revisiting arguments to show how they apply to the questions raised in Chapter 1.

As discussed in Chapter 1, rough sleepers began to appear in Japan in large numbers in the early 1990s. A major characteristic of these rough sleepers was that most of them were male, with no more than 3% female. In the developed nations of Europe and North America, in contrast, a considerably greater share of the homeless population are women – reportedly, about 30%. This difference comes mainly from different definitions of the term "homeless." Whereas in Japan the term refers exclusively to rough sleepers, in the West, the concept of homelessness is broader, including people with no fixed residence who live in shelters and other facilities. Many women in Japan can be considered homeless in this wider sense.

Throughout this study I have tried to accurately depict the lived reality of homeless women in Japan, which has been virtually undocumented until now. This was the first aim of the book. The low visibility of homeless women, as shown in Chapter 2, comes from the fact that labor markets and social welfare policies have been based on the model of the modern nuclear family. This model is so pervasive in the Japanese context that it has been difficult to even conceive of female-headed households, since they do not fit the model. Nevertheless, there are welfare policies in place to compensate for the disadvantages suffered by women living in poverty because they do not have a male partner who supports them. The Japanese welfare system has been relatively proficient at ensuring that most women who lose their homes, rather than sleeping on the streets, have been able to live semi-hidden lives in welfare facilities.

Chapter 3 examined the historical development of those welfare policies, focusing on the case of Osaka prefecture. As we have seen, welfare policies distinguished between women based on the extent to which they conformed to the model of the modern family. Single mothers were the earliest to be offered protection services. Single women who lived alone, on the other hand, were treated as being at risk of becoming prostitutes, and therefore were subject to protection and rehabilitation. Today, protection services prioritize victims of domestic violence, while women who live alone and lack a home continue to be placed in protection facilities prescribed by the Anti-Prostitution Act.

Chapter 4 describes the conditions of a welfare facility inhabited by single homeless women, based on fieldwork observations and interviews. Once a woman lost her home and became eligible for welfare protection, the type of facility she was placed in, and the long-term life orientation of the support she received, depended on various factors. These included not only the woman's personal circumstances, such as ability to work and state of health, but also external factors such as the availability of spaces in facilities, and the discretion of caseworkers, which was significant. Consequently, a wide variety of normative values were involved in determining such matters as the "choice" of an individual woman to use the welfare system to get housing or to not use it and continue rough sleeping, and the type of life that was considered desirable. Few normative statements made reference to gender. In other words, although welfare policies aimed at homeless women are systematized with the expectation that women will perform the roles appropriate for them in a modern family, when these policies are implemented in the field, so to speak, gender is only one of a number of social expectations. We saw this in concrete terms in the lives of the women described in Chapters 5, 6, and 7.

When women are singled out from the larger homeless population for observation, it soon becomes obvious that the previous framework for homeless research, limited to persons sleeping rough, is inadequate for understanding their situation. In other words, a broader definition of homelessness needs to be applied when the subject of study is women. This leads to the second aim of this study, which is to reassess the conventional framework for homeless studies itself by specifically including women as a subject of study. The study of homeless women requires not only the inclusion of women in the research framework, but also a thorough interrogation of the male-centered assumptions of that framework. Apart from reassessing the definition of homelessness, the mechanisms by which poverty occurs are also different, as shown in Chapter 2, where I documented processes for falling into homelessness that are unique to women. These processes cannot be described by taking men as the default subjects. It was also shown that methods of analysis centered on the subjects' employment history need to be reassessed if women are to be included in the discussion.

As noted in Chapter 1, rough sleepers were a permanent feature of the day-labor *yoseba* areas, in the form of workers who had reached the point of being unable to work. The *yoseba* research from the late 1990s criticized previous studies which had treated the existence of unemployed and homeless *yoseba* laborers as a social pathology. Because of the way they interpreted the problems of *yoseba* and their orientation toward trying to solve those perceived problems, they tended to overlook the concrete realties of the people who lived there, and to over-emphasize their low status. These critics argued, instead, in favor of highlighting the subjectivity of *yoseba* workers, an active subjectivity that sought to reform personal and social conditions. Later, with the deepening economic recession of the 1990s, the presence of rough sleepers overflowed the *yoseba* districts, spreading throughout urban areas. The growing number of rough sleepers included a new cohort of ordinary working people. Accordingly, *yoseba* research shifted its focus from day laborers to rough sleepers, but the underlying assumptions of male subjects remained unchanged in the new research framework. This resulted in an increasing emphasis in sociological studies of rough sleepers on their will, individuality, and resistance to dominant social norms. In challenging the positionality of researchers who tried to understand and analyze the problem of rough sleeping objectively, and in asserting the need to look at society from the perspective of marginalized people, these studies were extremely valuable. However, their assumptions of self-determination and intentional resistance – of a rough sleeper who works for wages, and who rationally chooses his actions based on a conscious, autonomous will – is highly problematic.

This brings us to the third aim of this book: a reassessment of the idea of subjectivity. As shown in Chapters 5, 6, and 7, when the daily practices of women rough sleepers were examined at the micro level, it was apparent that they did not live in solitude, but in a context of deep relationships with other people. An "ethic of care," typically thought to be a feminine virtue of caring for others, could be seen in these women's intimate relationships with male partners, pets, and others. These relationships were fundamental to these women's sense of self when deciding whether to continue rough sleeping or to leave. The choices made in the context of these relationships, because of their connected nature, could alternate between entering facilities and returning to the streets; they were part of a continually changing process, influenced by others and by events.

Thus, there is a problem in the stance taken by researchers who, not yet having observed the world of such women in microscopic detail, assume that their research subjects are autonomous individuals possessed of reason and free will, and therefore assume that rough sleeping is itself an expression of resistance to social norms or of a desire to reform society. In the process, they consider the act of sleeping rough in isolation from the other performative practices that occur in the context of changes over time. They thus may overlook the ongoing process that results: a series of sometimes discontinuous practices in the lives of people who may repeat a cycle of sleeping rough sometimes and living as a homeless person in a welfare facility at other times.

The discourse on homelessness, as seen, for instance, in the existing academic studies of homelessness discussed here and in a legal tradition that forces a choice between autonomy and exclusion, has been conducted under the assumption that individual people are autonomous subjects capable of making rational choices. However, as this study has shown, most homeless women do not live their lives like that. It is precisely because this is not the case that we need to continually ask what, exactly, is required for someone to become an autonomous subject. A better approach would be to consider the subject not as something that is autonomous from the start, but rather as something that emerges in a process. Becoming a subject, for a rough sleeper, would begin with her choice to end rough sleeping and move to ordinary housing; she would have to sustain this choice over a long period of time, making mistakes along the way, supported by other people, in an unending process. To discover what is needed to become a subject, closer engagement with the individual practices of real woman will surely help give us the clues we seek.

Afterword

It has been fourteen years since I first visited Kamagasaki and eleven years since I began researching homeless women.

It started in my third year as an undergraduate. My attention had been caught by a poster I had seen on campus advertising a tour of Kamagasaki organized by a student group that was active in the area. I decided to participate. The streets, lined with vendor's stalls, were thronged with people, some walking, some standing around talking, some sitting in a circle drinking, some sprawled out sleeping on the roadside. Cyclists and stray dogs ambled through the crowd. There were voices laughing, talking, shouting angrily; strangers approached out of nowhere to talk. In the midst of the chaos I imagined for a moment that I was a tourist in some other country in Asia. The people were very human. Eating, sleeping, relieving themselves, happy, sad, or angry – this place, I thought, teemed with these very human actions and emotions. That alone was enough to make me like Kamagasaki.

Having become very fond of the place, I began working regularly at a Kamagasaki soup kitchen as part of the fieldwork for my thesis on volunteer activities. While volunteering on a weekly basis, I interviewed other participants about their motives for doing so. With the generous help of many people, my study about the meaning of volunteer work was genuinely fun to do. Motivated by the opportunity my studies gave me to share in the life experiences of all sorts of people I would never meet in a university environment, I decided to pursue graduate studies.

What followed, though, were many hard days that were painful even to think about. A day laborer I had become friendly with in Kamagasaki took a romantic interest in me. I turned him down right away, and he resented me for it. A series of misunderstandings made it worse, until he was threatening to kill me. This was shortly before my thesis was due. If I asked people where he lived to help me with this problem, it could ruin his life before he got a chance to make a new start after losing his home and job. Nevertheless, knowing that I had to at least finish my thesis, I cautiously returned several times to

my study field, showed my completed thesis to the people who had
helped me, and then fled from the site. Leaving the field that had been
so important to me – I had visited it weekly for three years and wanted
to continue going there – in this ignominious way, I was overwhelmed
by a sense that my first research project had been a failure. For some
time after that, every time I heard the voice of a loud man, I would
tremble with the fear that it was him.

And yet, I had a place to go home to. I could choose to stay away
from Kamagasaki if I wished. The women rough sleepers I saw
from time to time probably did not have that choice. What kind
of hardships did these women face, and what were their lives like,
living in a community made up almost entirely of men? Looking
back, it seems that my ongoing quest to answer these questions – so
important to this book – was inseparable from my own process of
getting to understand my identity as a women, and through that,
to make sense of what I had experienced at Kamagasaki. But my
sense of failure with my study made it impossible to see any value
in what I was doing. Although I had gotten to know women rough
sleepers, it was a long time before I felt like I had the right to ask
them to tell me about themselves. In the midst of my frustrations,
a certain woman – the one described in the introduction to this
book – came to help me out.

Since then, I have been able to meet and hear the stories of many
women, even if the process has not always been smooth. This book
represents my best effort to collect and present these stories.

This book is a revised and expanded version of my doctoral
dissertation, *The Sociology of Homelessness and Gender* (*Hōmuresu
to jendā no shakaigaku*), which was submitted to the Graduate
School of Letters, Kyoto University, and approved in November 2010.
Due to rapid changes in the conditions and policies that concern
homelessness in Japan, there are parts that no longer apply to the
current situation that I was unable to fully revise. My dissertation
was based on the following previously published articles, which are
listed by chapter.

- Foreword: Newly written
- Chapter 1: Newly written
- Chapter 2: "The Gendered Process of Exclusion: The Problem
  of Homeless Women" (Jendā-ka sareta haijo no katei: josei
  hōmuresu to iu mondai), Aoki Hideo ed., *Homeless Studies:*

The Reality of Exclusion and Inclusion (Hōmuresu sutadīzu: haijo to hōsetsu no riariti), Mineruva Shobō, p. 202–232, 2010.

- Chapter 3: "The Position of Women in Poverty Policy: A Case Study of Osaka in the Prewar and Postwar Periods" (Hinkon seisaku ni okeru josei no ichi: senzen sengo no *Ōsaka no jirei kenkyū*), *Jutsu: Kinki Daigaku Kokusai Jinbun Kagaku Kenkyūjo kiyō* 2, p. 152–171, 2008.
- Chapter 4: Newly written. In revising and expanding my doctoral dissertation, I made use of the same materials that were used in the following article, and the descriptions and data in this chapter partially overlap with it. "The Spread of Poverty and the Role of Women's Protection Facilities" (Hinkon no hirogari to fujin hogo shisetsu no yakuwari), in Miyamoto Setsuko and Sudō Yachiyo ed., *Supporting Women: The Role of Women's Protection Facilities* (Josei o shien suru to iu koto: fujin hogo shisetsu to iu basho), Akashi Shobō, p. 253–286, 2013.
- Chapter 5: Newly written.
- Chapter 6: "Resistance and Subjectivity in Rough Sleeping: A View from the Daily Practices of Women Rough Sleepers" (Nojukusha no teikō to shutaisei: josei nojukusha no nichijōteki jissen kara), *Sociological Review* (Shakaigaku hyōron) 56(4), p. 898–914, 2006.
- Chapter 7: "In the Shadow of Autonomy: On Support for Autonomy of Homeless Persons" (Jiritsu no kage de: hōmuresu no jiritsu shien o megutte), *Contemporary Thought* (Gendai shisō) 34(14), p. 196–203, 2006.
- Chapter 8: "Women Living on the Streets: Life Practices of Women Rough Sleepers" (Sutorīto de ikiru josei tachi: josei nojukusha no jissen), Sekine Yasumasa ed., *The anthropology of the street: report on a survey by the National Museum of Ethnology* (Sutorīto no jinruigaku: kokuritsu minzokugaku hakubutsukan chōsa hōkoku) 80, p. 185–201, 2009; and "Neither Free Nor Coerced" (Jiyū de mo naku kyōsei de mo naku), *Contemporary Thought* (Gendai shisō) 34(9), p. 211–221, 2006.
- Epilogue: Newly written

I would like to thank all of my teachers at the Graduate School of Letters at Kyoto University who have helped me so much between my early undergraduate years and the completion of my doctoral dissertation. I feel particularly fortunate for the generous guidance of Matsuda Motoji, who supported me in pursuing my research goals. The approach to fieldwork that I learned from Professor Matsuda is the foundation for all of my research. My undergraduate and master's program teacher, Hōgetsu Makoto, pushed me to take my project further by urging me: "Try living as a rough sleeper yourself!" Ochiai Emiko offered me much encouragement as a fellow woman scholar. I cannot begin to express my gratitude to Tarōmaru Hiroshi, who took on the burdensome task of peer-reviewing this study.

The kindness of the following individuals enriched my life as a researcher in countless ways: Sylvia Novac of the University of Toronto, during my doctoral years; Nishizawa Akihiko of Kobe University, after I completed the doctoral program; and Ruth Lister, of Loughborough University, during my stay in England. Since 2010, I have held a position at the Faculty of Social Sciences at Ritsumeikan University. I feel grateful to be surrounded by colleagues whose wide range of research interests is a great source of inspiration.

I greatly treasure my relationships with those in the Department of Sociology at Kyoto University with whom I spent so much time. The members of the Homelessness Study Group, starting with Aoki Hideo, pushed each other in a friendly way to improve; this was of invaluable help to me as I pursued a less popular research theme largely on my own. Through Sakai Takashi, Sekine Yasumasa, Sudō *Yachi*yo, and the study groups that they led, I made many valuable acquaintances.

Although I cannot name them all here, I wish to express my gratitude to the many people working in support of homeless people and women who helped me in the course of this study. In particular, I wish to mention the staff and managers of Facility A and of the nonprofit organization that ran the facility, who showed me the effort and devotion it took to care for individuals living at a facility twenty-four hours a day (my acquaintances then had been limited to women I met on the streets). Members of the Women's Support Group, especially Shimada Mika, Moriishi Kaori, Ogawa Yūko, and the late Yajima Sachiko were always there for me, as comrades in working with women rough sleepers and as friends, and were a constant source of strength and comfort. I also thank my mother, who watched over me patiently during my long years as a student, and my late father, who passed away before my project could be completed, still concerned about the future of my career track.

Ichimura Misako drew the wonderful pictures in this book that convey so well the reality of sleeping rough as a woman. Minematsu Ayako of Sekaishisōsha put up with many delays in the publishing schedule on my part. It is thanks to her careful, conscientious work that I was able to complete this book. I would like to express my thanks for a grant from the Ritsumeikan University Program for Promotion of Academic Publication that aided in the publication of this book.

Finally, my heartfelt thanks go to the women who told me their stories and answered my questions with such patience. I am truly grateful to you.

Maruyama Satomi
February 2013

Notes

Foreword to the English-Language Edition

1 *Josei hōmuresu to shite ikiru: hinkon to haijo no shakaigaku* (Living as a homeless woman: the sociology of poverty and exclusion). Sekai shisōsha, 2013.

Foreword to the Original Edition

1 Kamagasaki is a *yoseba* – a day-laborer market – located in Nishinari ward, Osaka city. The official administrative name for the area is the Airin Chiku district, but it is popularly called Kamagasaki, and in this book it will mainly be referred to as such.

Chapter 1

1 At the end of the ten-year term, in 2012, the Self-Help Act was extended for an additional five years. In 2017, it was extended for another ten years.
2 Women who sleep outside tend to choose hard-to-spot places to reduce the dangers to which they are exposed. Further, the 2012 MHLW numerical survey classifies 3.5% of the rough sleepers as "gender undetermined." It is not unlikely that this figure includes an indeterminate proportion of women who conceal their gender to protect their safety (Passaro 1996: 86). It therefore reasonable to assume that the proportion of rough sleepers who are women is slightly higher. Nevertheless, women almost certainly constitute less than 10% of all rough sleepers.
3 Another work, by Noyori Tomoko, based on interviews with female and young rough sleepers, discusses how those excluded from the normative "male breadwinner model" can become homeless (Noyori 2011).
4 Martha Burt and Barbara Cohen conducted interviews with 1700 homeless individuals at shelters and soup kitchens in the U.S., and found that 73% were single men, 9% were single women, and 9% were mothers and their children. Homeless men typically slept rough while women typically used shelters. Further, most homeless women were non-white and had a shorter period of homelessness than men. Single women had the highest level of education, and those with the lowest level were the women accompanied by their children. The study found that more women than men had been

married, and more suffered from mental illness, while a higher proportion of men had a history of imprisonment (Burt and Cohen 1989).

5 According to the *Survey on the Conditions of the Homeless* (Urban Life Institute 2000), out of fourteen female rough sleepers, four (19%) lived alone, two (14%) lived with friends or acquaintances, and eight (57%) lived with spouses or relatives. According to the *Report on the General Survey of Rough Sleepers* (Osaka City University Institute on Urban Environmental Problems, 2001), out of twenty women, seven (35%) lived alone, one (5%) lived with friends or acquaintances, and twelve (60%) lived with spouses or relatives.

6 Among the female rough sleepers I have met was one who, as an ethnic Korean-Japanese and a lesbian had long lived on the margins of society. She eventually entered a women's welfare facility. The staff members of this facility reported problems and concerns in dealing with sexual minorities like this woman.

7 Some researchers, such Aoyama Kaoru (2007), have attempted to bridge the gap between the "human rights" and "civil rights" approaches to prostitution.

8 A free or low-rent housing facility is a Type 2 social welfare service facility that provides lodging for free or at reduced rates for low-income individuals. Because these facilities can be created fairly easily by applying to the government for permission, in recent years they have been set up by a wide variety of organizations, mainly nonprofits.

9 There are others whose lifestyle falls in between that of the fixed-location and vagabond types, clearing their bed and leaving only their belongings there during the day, and returning at night to sleep in a set location.

10 This project (its Japanese name literally means "project to support transition to community life) was initiated in 2004 by Tokyo prefecture with the aim of reducing the number of tents, restricting its target to rough sleepers living in tents in designated parks within the prefecture. The prefecture rented empty rooms and rented them out for a period of two years at 3000 yen (~ USD 25) per month, with the aim of fostering economic self-sufficiency.

Chapter 2

1 Hasegawa Takahiko conducted a study of homelessness policies of seven developed countries and compared the definitions of homeless used in each. Hasegawa found that (1) Japan alone used the narrowest definition; (2) the United States, United Kingdom, Germany, and Norway used a somewhat broader definition; and (3) Finland and Australia used the broadest definition (Hasegawa 2005).

2 Workers' lodgings are unstable compared to ordinary housing because the worker loses his or her housing after becoming unemployed or changing jobs. The *National Survey on the Conditions of the Homeless* found that 33.4% of them had gone from workers' lodgings to living on the streets (MHLW 2012).

3 A survey of "Internet café refugees" in Tokyo found that apart from Internet cafés, places often used by respondents included: the streets (29.5%), fast food restaurants (23.7%), and saunas (23.2%) (MHLW 2007).

4 Welfare facilities come in two types: those run as Type 1 social welfare projects and those run as Type 2 social welfare projects. Type 1 projects are "projects which, because of their large impact on their users, require stable operating conditions for providing care." The residential facilities shown in Table 2.1 are run by these projects. Facilities run by Type 1 projects must be run by governmental bodies or by social welfare nonprofit organizations and are thus largely public in nature. As a result, the expenses incurred in running the facility and providing revenues are covered by national and local governments and regional public organizations. Type 2 projects are "projects which, because their impact on users is comparatively low, have a lower need for public regulation," and because of this there are no restrictions on who can run them. The only requirement for opening a facility is to register it with the local government. As a result, many nonprofits and other organizations have perceived a need for residential facilities for homeless people and have opened such facilities.

5 A survey of "Internet café refugees" has found 17.4% of them to be women (MHLW Employment Stability Bureau 2007), which further indicates the large number of women among the "hidden homeless" not seen in the streets.

6 Divorce rates for some other advanced countries are: U.S., 6.8; U.K., 2.0; Sweden, 2.5; and Russia, 4.5.

7 Kimoto Kimiko and Hagiwara Kumiko have studied the feminization of poverty that has occurred in Japan in recent years. They argue that although women's poverty has surfaced in such forms as single-mother families and elderly women who live alone, it has not yet materialized in Japan in the sense of most poor households being female-headed, as is the case in the U.S. However, they also note that married women in Japan are very susceptible to poverty when they lose their partner, and if this is taken into account, the feminization of poverty in a broader sense has indeed taken place there (Kimoto and Hagiwara 2010).

8 This treatment violates the original ideal of public aid, which was intended for persons suffering from poverty. Recently, partly because of severe economic conditions, it has become easier for men to receive public assistance if there is no work available.

9 Facilities for the support of single-mother families provide housing and assistance with daily life, but the number of households participating is a small proportion of the total number of single-mother households, with only 3.0% currently using or having used such facilities.

10 Because these thirty-three women were selected for their willingness and ability to provide detailed life stories, they are unlikely to have severe cognitive or psychological disorders. However, it should be noted that these conditions are relatively common among homeless women.

11 The MHLW's 2007 *National Survey on the Conditions of the Homeless* states that in the cross tabulation of statistics, "in order to give the analysis a clearer perspective, *sampling was limited to male subjects*" (p. 4; emphasis added). At present, although most studies do not separate

the figures for men and women, this is the only one that presents figures that apply exclusively to male rough sleepers. It is therefore appropriate for the comparisons made here.

12 Research on social mobility traditionally uses the status of the male head of household to determine the position of a woman, an approach which has been harshly criticized. Subsequently there has been debate over what index should be used to express a woman's status (Akagawa 2000 and others), but no viable method has yet been agreed upon. Hashimoto Setsuko (2003) argues that research taking social class as its subject goes no further than to look at work to reveal inequality; as such, women's issues are understood only as exclusion and alienation from work.

13 Homelessness is typically the result of multiple factors that have a complex relationship. I have narrowed these down to the major factors in my categorization.

Chapter 3

1 Compared to other advanced countries, Japan's welfare capture ratio is extremely low. For example, the ratio is 91.6% for France and 64.6% for Germany (National Congress to Promote Public Assistance Measures).

2 Japan is divided into 47 administrative prefectures. Osaka prefecture (Ōsaka-fu) is an "urban prefecture" with a population of about 8,860,000. The city of Osaka (Ōsaka-shi, population approximately 2,600,000) is located within the prefecture and is a separate governing body. In terms of welfare, the two units divide functions between them. For instance, Osaka city handles public assistance, but Women's Protection Services are administered by the prefecture.

3 As well as criticizing the anti-prostitution organizations for ignoring class oppression, Fujime Yuki has also criticized their complicity in colonial oppression by cooperating in Japanese aggression in Asia and willfully overlooking the forced prostitution of military "comfort women" (Fujime 1997).

4 Temporary protection is also sometimes provided by welfare facilities and privately-run shelters by contract with the Women's Consultation Center.

5 To help victims of domestic violence to gain independence, the prefecture began to provide housing which could be used for a six-month term.

6 In 2004, the city-government-authored "Project for Supporting the Independence of Rough Sleepers (Homeless) in the City of Osaka" specifically mentioned this Living Care Center as a facility to meet the needs of women rough sleepers.

7 The decrease in users after 2001 is likely due to the opening in 2002 of a facility providing temporary protective services run by the city of Osaka.

Chapter 4

1 Facilities used by homeless self-help enterprises based on the 2002 law have been excluded because most of them are limited to men.

2 Some free or low-rent housing facilities provide high quality service, offering private rooms to all and providing excellent casework. Because of this, some have recently argued that there is a need to rethink the role and meaning of Type 1 social welfare facilities, which, because of their public nature, are subsidized by the government (Mizuuchi 2010: 53; Fujita 2010: 83; Terao and Okuda 2010: 10; and others).

3 One new women's facility was opened in 2007 in response to a perceived shortage of such facilities.

4 Tables and charts were made using data from the following sources. (1) Rehabilitation Facilities and Accommodation Facilities: (a) "Business Summary of Facility Operations for Programs to Aid Rough Sleepers: Rehabilitation Facilities and Accommodation Facilities" (Special Ward Association for Personnel and Welfare, 2010); (b) "2010 Report on Activities" (Social Welfare Corporation Shin'eikai). (2) Women's Protection Facilities: "2008–2009 Fact-Finding Survey on Women's Protection Facilities" (Tokyo Metropolitan Government Council for Social Welfare, Women's Protection Panel, Survey Assessment Committee, 2010). (3) Mother-Child Living Support Facilities: "Current Conditions and Future Challenges for Mother-Child Living Support Facilities in Tokyo prefecture" (Tokyo Metropolitan Government Council for Social Welfare, Mother-Child Welfare Section, 2011). For Accommodation Facilities, data from one facility exclusively for males has been omitted.

5 Users of Rehabilitation Facilities who cite "lack of an address" most likely include women trying to escape domestic violence. Indeed, in a report for one of the three facilities, "fleeing domestic violence" is indicated in a note in the "lacking an address" section.

6 For Women's Protection Facilities, it is common for users to save money and move to their own home, but to begin receiving public assistance when the money runs out. By the end of the administrative year in which the users are surveyed, only half of those originally classified as "self-sufficient" remain without public assistance.

7 Although there are women with similar needs using both types of facility, there is a large difference in occupancy rates between Public Assistance Facilities and Women's Protection Facilities.

One reason for this is the different legal rationale between the two types of facility: public assistance that guarantees a minimal standard of living to needy persons, versus protection services for prostitutes and victims of domestic violence. Based on the different aims of the laws, caseworkers sometimes judge Women's Protection Facilities to be more appropriate than Public Assistance Facilities for helping needy women who have problems connected to sexual relations, e.g. prostitution or conflicts with male partners.

A second reason is that the form of welfare used can differ according to a region's social resources, the availability of services, and the material furnishing of facilities. Outside of the major urban areas, Women's Protection Facilities are often situated in Women's Consultation Centers in conjunction with short-term shelters and may be the only facilities in the region that cater specifically to women. This situation can result in

Women's Protection Facilities being underutilized, because of concerns about problems arising when women taking temporary refuge from violence share the same space with women who have been forcibly admitted, who typically suffer from disabilities and other serious issues. In contrast, in urban areas like Tokyo and Osaka, apart from Women's Protection Facilities, there are public assistance and other facilities that are exclusively for women. In this case it can be difficult to determine which welfare system – public assistance or Women's Protection Services – applies to a particular case. Local rules will sometimes decide this, based on factors like a facility's location and the areas of welfare practice in which it excels, as seen in the case of Osaka prefecture described in Chapter 3.

Third, the framing of the issues and the manner of administration differ depending on the value judgments and knowledge of the particular welfare service providers who administer these systems. When those deciding where a person will be placed make an "assesment" of what sort of casework is needed, various factors are considered, such as whether a facility has individual or shared rooms, whether the candidate for placement is able to work, facility location, the length of stay required, and whether the candidate has "sexual" issues; there is considerable variety in how cases are managed and thought about. In particular, since the Domestic Violence Act was implemented in 2002 as the foundation for Women's Protection Facilities, certain Women's Consultation Centers have made the protection of domestic violence victims a priority, tending to exclude other types of needy women.

A fourth issue is that placements for public assistance and for Women's Protection Services are made by different entities. For public assistance caseworkers, placement options are limited to either Public Assistance Facilities or to facilities categorized as home protection facilities (ordinary housing paid for by public assistance), such as free or low-rent housing and unregistered facilities. Only Women's Consultation Centers can place clients in Women's Protection Facilities. Thus, because public assistance caseworkers lack the authority to place clients in Women's Protection Facilities even if they deem that to be the best option, such women will normally end up in Public Assistance Facilities. Also, because the first place impoverished women usually go for help is a welfare office rather than a Women's Consultation Center, they tend to use public assistance rather than protection services. A further point to keep in mind is that although both take in similar types of female client, the standard of resources and equipment at Women's Protection Facilities is lower than for Public Assistance Facilities. Women's Protection Facilities are allocated staff based on maximum client capacity, and are assigned fewer staff per client than Public Assistance Facilities. Consequently, for Women's Protection Facilities to meet the needs of clients with the same issues, it would be necessary to reduce the actual number of clients to less than maximum capacity.

The poor resources at Women's Protection Facilities also mean that the number of users must be reduced to allow multi-user rooms to be used as individual rooms.

For more on the problem of vacancies at Women's Protection Facilities and the background behind it, see Maruyama 2013, "The Spread of Poverty and the Role of Women's Protection Facilities."

8 The Ministry of Health, Labour and Welfare subsequently conducted surveys of the conditions of free or low-rent housing facilities in 2009 and 2011. However, I am using the 2003 Tokyo prefecture survey as the standard of comparison to show the ways in which Facility A was distinct in the context of free or low-rent housing facilities that I surveyed at the time.

9 Violence from family members other than spouses and intimate male partners falls outside the scope of conditions for receiving support under the current Domestic Violence Act. However, in this study, violence from other family members is also categorized as domestic violence. Private facilities like Facility A tend to be used by people who have difficulty accessing support from a public facility because the Domestic Violence Act does not apply to their situation – i.e., victims of violence from their sons and fathers.

10 When public assistance recipients earn income, their aid is reduced in proportion to the income received. However, if the monthly extra income is 8,000 yen or less it is exempted and can be kept along with the public assistance benefit.

Chapter 5

1 Ichimura, a woman rough sleeper, provides extensive accounts of experiencing violence and the fear of violence. (Ichimura 2006; 2008a; and others)

2 A major difference among different local governments in Japan in their policies for helping rough sleepers is whether they allow rough sleepers to receive single-purpose benefits or not; some regions traditionally do not allow this.

Chapter 6

1 "Ticket buyers" place bets on horse races, bicycle races, etc. at illegal gambling houses on behalf of a client.

Chapter 7

1 Men do participate on rare occasions, but only when there is a specific reason for them to do so.

2 At the time, one kilogram of aluminum cans could be sold for about 100 yen (~USD 0.9), although this varied depending on the season and the region. At one period the price of aluminum surged to about 150 yen (~USD 1.4) per kilogram, but since 2008, due to the effects of the recession, this has dropped to as low as 40 yen (~USD 0.4).

3 *The Big Issue* is a magazine sold on the street by rough sleepers. Originally published in London, the Japanese edition was launched in 2003 to provide an income for homeless people. At the time of my survey, sellers were supplied with copies for 90 yen (~USD 0.8) each, which they sold for 200 yen (~USD 1.8), keeping the 110 yen (~USD 1) profit for themselves. The price has gone up and is now 350 yen (~USD 3), of which the seller keeps 180 yen (~USD 1.6). The magazines are sold in predetermined locations by rough sleepers who have registered with *The Big Issue*.

4 When benefits are applied for in this case, the applicant is considered, on paper, to be a resident of an apartment who is no longer a rough sleeper. Bypassing the requirement to enter a facility makes the process smoother, but the initial expenses of moving into an apartment, such as the security deposit and furnishing fees, are not provided by public benefits. They are the individual's responsibility.

5 A simple workers' hostel that has been repurposed to house public assistance recipients. A growing number of welfare apartments have been opened in Kamagasaki in the last fifteen years. There is a range of types, from those that provide only a simple room to those that provide support. The apartment that Yoriko moved into offered living support, with staff available as needed to offer such services as doing casework or managing money.

References

Abe Aya, 2015, "Hinkonritsu no chōkiteki dōkō: Kokumin seikatsu kiso chōsa 1985–2012 o mochiite" (Long-term movements in poverty rates: based on comprehensive survey of living conditions 1985–2012), Kokumin tōkei hōmupēji (Poverty statistics homepage), https://www.hinkonstat.net.

Abramovits, Mimi, 1996, *Regulating the Lives of Women: Social Welfare Policy from Colonial Times to the Present,* Boston: South End Press.

Akagawa Manabu, 2000, "Josei no kaisōteki chii wa dono yō ni kimaru ka?" (What determines the social class of women?), Seiyama Kazuo ed. *Nihon no kaisō shisutemu* 4: *jendā, shijō, kazoku* (The Japanese class system 4: Gender, markets, family), University of Tokyo Press, 47–63.

Althusser, Louis, 1971, Idéologie et appareils idéologiques d'Etat (Ideology and Ideological State Apparatuses), *La Pensée*, 151: 3–38. (Japanese translation 1993, Yanagi Uchitakashi and Yamamoto Tetsuji, "Ideorogii to kokka no ideorogii sōchi," *Aruchusēru no "ideorogii" ron*, Sankōsha.)

Aoki Hideo, 1989, *Yoseba rōdōsha no sei to shi* (The lives and deaths of *yoseba* workers), Akashi shoten.

Aoyama Kaoru, 2007, "*Sekkusu wākā" to wa dare ka: ijū, seirōdō, jinshin torihiki no kōzō to keiken* (Who are sex workers: The structure and experience of migration, sex work, and human trafficking), *Ōtsuki shoten.*

Asakura Mutsuko, Kamiya Masako, and Tsujimura Miyoko eds., 1997, *Gendai no hō 11: jendā to hō* (Contemporary law 11: Gender and law), Iwanami shoten.

Axinn, June, 1990, "Japan: A Special Case," Gertrude Schaffner Gordberg and Eleanor Kremen eds., *The Feminization of Poverty: Only in America?* New York: Praeger Publishers.

Bogue, Donald B., 1963, *Skid Row in American cities*, Chicago: Community and Family Study Center, Chicago: University of Chicago.

Bretherton, J., 2017, "Reconsidering Gender in Homelessness," *European Journal of Homelessness* 11(1): 1–22.

Bridgeman, Rae, 2003, *Safe Haven: The Story of a Shelter for Homeless Women,* Toronto: University of Toronto Press.

Burt, Martha R. and Barbara E. Cohen, 1989, "Differences among Homeless Single Women, Women with Children, and Single Men," *Social Problems*, 36(5): 508–524.

Butler, Judith, 1990, *Gender Trouble: Feminism and the Subversion of Identity,* New York: Routledge. (Japanese translation 1999, Takemura Kazuko, *Jendā toraburu: feminizumu to aidentiti no kakuran*, Seidosha.)

————, 1992, "Contingent Foundations: Feminism and the Question of 'Postmodernism,'" Butler, J. and Scott J. W. eds., *Feminists*

Theorize the Political, New York: Routledge. (Japanese translation 2000, Chūma Shōko, "Gūhatsuteki na kiso tsuke: feminizumu to 'posutomodanizumu' ni yoru toi," *Asoshie* 3: 247–270.)

————, 1997, *Excitable Speech: A Politics of the Performative*, New York: Routledge (Japanese translation 2004, Takemura Kazuko, *Shokuhatsu suru kotoba*, Iwanami shoten.)

Certeau, Michel de, 1980, *Art de Faire*, Paris: Union Générale d'Editions (Japanese translation 1987, Yamada Toyoko, *Nichijōteki jissen no poietiiku*, Kokubunsha).

Chakrabarty, Dipesh, 1995, "Radical Histories and the Question of Enlightenment Rationalism: Some Recent Critiques of Subaltern Studies," *Economic and Political Weekly* (8 April): 751–759. (Japanese translation 1996, Usuda Masayuki, "Kyūshinteki rekishi to keimōteki gōrishugi: saikin no sabarutan kenkyū hihan o megutte," *Shisō* 859: 82–105.)

Christian Women's Reform Society, Osaka Branch, 1929, *Kansha ni afurete: Ōsaka fujin hōmu kakuchō kinen* (Overflowing with thanks: Commemorating the expansion of the Osaka Women's Home).

————, 1937, *Ayumi: Ōsaka fujin hōmu sanjūnen-shi* (History: Thirty years of the Osaka Women's Home).

Chūō hōki, 2012, *Shakai hoshō no tebiki Heisei 24-nenban: shisaku no gaiyō to kiso shiryō* (Introduction to social welfare, 2012 edition: Summary of policies and basic data).

Cornell, Drucilla, 1995, *The Imaginary Domain: Abortion, Pornography & Sexual Harassment*, New York: Routledge (Japanese translation 2006, Nakamasa Masaki supervisor, *Imajinariina ryōiki: chūzetsu, porunogurafi, sekushuaru harasumento*, Ochanomizu shobō).

————, 1998, *At the Heart of Freedom*, Princeton: Princeton University Press (Japanese translation 2001, Ishioka Yoshiharu, Kubota Jun, Gōhara Kai, Minamino Kayo, Satō Tomoko, Sawa Keiko, Nakamasa Masaki, *Jiyū no hāto de*, Jōkyō shuppan).

————, 1999, *Beyond Accommodation: Ethical Feminism, Deconstruction, and the Law*, New York: Rowman & Littlefield Publishers (Japanese translation 2003, Nakamasa Masaki supervisor, Okano Yayo, Mochizuki Sawayo, Fujimoto Kazuisa, Gōhara Kai, Nishiyama Tatsuya, *Datsu kōchiku to hō: tekiō no kanata e*, Ochanomizu shobō).

Delacoste, Frédéric and Priscilla Alexander eds., 1987, *Sex Work*, London: Virago (Japanese translation 1993, Tsunoda Yukiko, Yamanaka Tomiko, Hara Minako, Yamagata Hiroo, *Sekkusu wāku: sei sangyō ni tazusawaru joseitachi no koe*, Gendai shokan).

Deliberative Committee on the National Survey on the Conditions of the Homeless, *see* Hōmuresu no jittai ni kansuru zenkoku chōsa kentōkai.

Edgar, Bill and Joe Doherty eds., 2001, *Women and Homelessness in Europe*, Bristol: The Policy Press.

Ehara Yumiko, ed., 1995, *Sei no shōhinka: feminizumu no shuchō 2* (The commercialization of sex: A feminist critique 2), Keisō shobō.

————, 2000, *Feminizumu no paradokkusu: teichaku ni yoru kakusan* (The paradox of feminism: Gaining hold leading to diffusion), Keisō shobō.

————, 2001, *Jendā chitsujo* (Gender order), Keisō shobō.

————, 2002, *Jiko ketteiken to jendā* (Self-determination and gender), Iwanami shoten.

Fraser, Nancy, 1989, *Unruly Practices: Power, Discourse and Gender in Contemporary Social Theory*, Cambridge: Polity Press.

Fujime Yuki, 1999, *Sei no rekishigaku: kōshō seido, dataizai taisei kara baishun bōshihō, yūseihogohō taisei e* (The history of sex: The change in system from public prostitution and criminalized abortion to a prostitution prevention act and eugenics act), Fuji shuppan.

Fujita Takanori, 2010, "Motomerareru muryō teigaku shukuhakusho no kisei: sherutā kinō e no tokka o" (Regulation needed for free or low-fee housing: Toward specializing in shelter functions), *Toshi mondai* (Municipal problems) 101(7): 78–83.

Gilligan, Carol, 1982, *In A Different Voice: Psychological Theory and Women's Development*, Cambridge: Harvard University Press (Japanese translation 1986, Iwao Sumiko, supervisor, Ikuta Kumiko, Namiki Michiko, trans., *Mō hitotsu no koe: danjo no dōtokukan no chigai to josei no aidentiti*, Kawashima shoten).

Goldberg, Gertrude Schaffner and Eleanor Kremen eds., 1990, *The Feminization of Poverty: Only in America?* New York: Praeger Publishers.

Golden, Stephanie, 1992, *The Women Outside: Meanings and Myths of Homelessness*, Berkeley: University of California Press.

Hasegawa Takahiko, 2005, "OECD shokoku ni okeru hōmuresu no teigi oyobi monitaringu ni kansuru chōsa: OECD shokoku ni okeru hōmuresu seisaku ni kansuru kenkyū (sono 1)" (Survey of the definition and monitoring of homelessness in the OECD countries: Studies on homeless policy in the OECD countries (part 1), *Nihon kenchiku gakkai keikakukei ronbunshū* (Architectural Institute of Japan, Journal of Architecture and Planning) 558: 141–146.

Hashimoto Setsuko, 2003, "'Shakaiteki chii' no poritikusu: kaisō kenkyū ni okeru 'gender inequality' no shatei" (The politics of social status: The range of 'gender inequality' in class studies), *Shakaigaku hyōron* (Japanese Sociological Review) 54(1): 49–63.

Hayashi Chiyo, 1990, "Sei no shōhinka ni tsuite" (The commercialization of sex), Tōkyō-to seikatsu bunka-kyoku (Tokyo metropolitan government life and cultural affairs bureau), *Sei no shōhinka ni kansuru kenkyū* (Research on the commercialization of sex), Tōkyō-to seikatsu bunka-kyoku fujin seishōnen-bu kikaku-ka, 3–24.

————, 2008, "Sōgōtekina josei shiensaku no hitsuyōsei" (The need for a comprehensive policy to support women), Hayashi Chiyo ed., *'Fujin hogo jigyō' 50 nen* (50 years of Women's Protection Services), Domesu shuppan, 188–202.

Hayashi Chiyo ed., 2004, *Josei fukushi to wa nani ka: sono hitsuyōsei to teigen* (What is women's welfare? Why it is needed, and suggestions for implementation), Mineruva shobō.

Hayashi Chiyo ed., 2014, *Kaidai Fujin fukushi iinkai kara fujin hogo iinkai e: zenkoku shakai fukushi kyōgikai no torikumi ni kansuru shiryōshū*, (Bibliographical introduction: From women's welfare committee to women's protection committee: Collected information on efforts by Japan National Council of Social Welfare), Domesu shuppan.

Hōmuresu no jittai ni kansuru zenkoku chōsa kentōkai (Deliberative committee on the *National Survey on the Conditions of the Homeless*), 2007, *Heisei 19-nen Hōmuresu no jittai ni kansuru zenkoku chōsa (seikatsu jittai chōsa) no bunseki kekka* (2007 Discussion of *National Survey on the Conditions of the Homeless* [survey of living conditions]).

Hōmuresu shien zenkoku nettowāku (National homeless support network), 2011, *Kōgi no hōmuresu no kashika to shiensaku ni kansuru chōsa hōkokusho* (Report on survey on awareness of and support policies for homeless persons broadly defined), Hōmuresu shien zenkoku nettowāku kōgi no hōmuresu no kashika to shiensaku ni kansuru chōsa kentō iinkai (Deliberative committee on survey on visualization of and support policies for homeless persons broadly defined).

Huey, Laura and Eric Brendt, 2008, "'You've gotta learn how to play the game': Homeless Women's Use of Gender Performance as a Tool for Preventing Victimization," *The Sociological Review* 56(2): 177–194.

Ichimura Misako, 2006. *Dear Kikuchi-san: burūtento-mura to chokorēto* (Dear Kikuchi: The blue-tent village and chocolate), Kyōtotto shuppan.

————, 2008a, "Korosu shimin: karēraisu de tsunagari ikikaere! (The killing citizen: Unite with curry rice and live again!) *Rosujene* (Lost generation) 2: 58–65.

————, 2008b, "Hōmuresu hōmu" (Homeless home), *Onnatachi no 21-seiki* (The women's 21st century) 54: 37–39.

————, 2009, "Rōdō wa yappari kowai: 'hataraku joseitachi' to no taiwa no ato de" (Working is frightening: After speaking with "working women"), *Onnatachi no 21-seiki* (The women's 21st century) 57: 22–24.

Igarashi Kenji, 1985, *Umeda kōseikan 1: narihibiku ai no kane* (Umeda Kōseikan 1: The ringing bell of love) (no publisher).

————, 1986, *Umeda kōseikan 2: ano kane no oto itsu made mo* (Umeda Kōseikan 2: The sound of that bell, forever) (no publisher).

Ikuta Takeshi, 2007, *Rupo saiteihen: fuantei shūrō to nojuku* (Reporting on the very bottom: Unstable employment and rough sleeping), Chikuma shobō.

Imai Konomi, 2004, "Shakai fukushi to joseishi" (Social welfare and women's history), in Hayashi Chiyo ed., *Josei fukushi to wa nani ka* (What is women's welfare?), Mineruva shobō, 24–42.

Iwata Masami, 1995, *Sengo shakai fukushi no tenkai to daitoshi saiteihen* (The growth of postwar social welfare and the bottom strata of society), Mineruva shobō.

————, 2000, *Hōmuresu/gendai shakai/fukushi kokka: "ikite iku" basho o megutte* (Homelessness/contemporary society/welfare state: On a "place to live"), Akashi shobō.

————, 2005, "Seisaku to hinkon: sengo nihon ni okeru fukushi kategorii to shite no hinkon to sono imi" (Government policy and poverty: The significance of poverty in terms of welfare categories in postwar Japan), in Iwata Masami and Nishizawa Akihiko eds., *Hinkon to shakaiteki haijo fukushi shakai o mushibamu mono* (Poverty and social exclusion: What undermines welfare society), Mineruva shobō, 15–42.

————, 2008, *Shakaiteki haijo: sanka no ketsujo, futashika na kizoku* (Social exclusion: Lack of participation, uncertain position), Yūhukaki.

————, 2009, "'Jūkyo sōshitsu' no tayō na hirogari to hōmuresu mondai no kōzu: nojukusha no ruikei o tegakari ni" (The diverse growth of "home loss" and the composition of the homelessness problem: An approach based on types of rough sleeper), *Kikan shakai hoshō kenkyū* (National Institute of Population and Social Security Research Quarterly) 45 (2): 94–106.

Izuhara Misa, 2005, "Jūtaku kara mita kōrei josei no hinkon: 'mochiie' chūshin no fukushi shakai to josei no haujingu hisutorii" (Poverty in older women in terms of housing: A home ownership-centered welfare society and women's housing history), Iwata Masami and Nishizawa Akihiko ed., *Hinkon to shakaiteki haijo: fukushi shakai o mushibamu mono* (Poverty and social exclusion: What undermines welfare society), Mineruva shobō, 95–117.

Izuo Aijien, 1919, *Izuo Aijien jigyō hōkoku* (Report on activities of Izuo Aijien) (no publisher).

Japan Housing Council, *see* Nihon jūtaku kaigi.

Kaname Yukiko and Mizushima Nozomi, 2005, *Fūzokujō ishiki chōsa: 126-nin no shokugyō ishiki chōsa* (Survey on attitudes of women in the sex industry: Attitudes of 126 women towards their work), Potto shuppan.

Kamiya Masako, 1997, "Jendā to feminisuto hōriron (Gender and feminist legal theory), Tsujimura Miyoko et al. ed., *Iwamani kōza gendai no hō 11: jendā to hō* (Iwanami course in contemporary law 11: Gender and law), Iwanami shoten.

Katada Son Asahi, 2006, "Jendā-ka sareta shutai no ichi: kodomo no jendā e no posuto-kōzō shugiteki na apurōchi no tenkai" (The position of the gendered subject: The development of a post-structuralist approach to children's gender), *Soshioroji* (Sociology) 50 (3): 109–125.

Kawahara Keiko, 2005, "Fukushi seisaku to josei no hinkon: hōmuresu jōtai no hinkon ni taisuru shisetsu hogo" (Welfare policy and women's poverty: Facility custody as a response to homeless poverty), Iwata Masami and Nishizawa Akihiko eds., *Hinkon to shakaiteki haijo* (Poverty and social exclusion), Mineruva shobō, 195–222.

————, 2008, "Hōmuresu mondai e no fukushi taiō to jendā" (Welfare approaches to the homeless problem and gender), Tama Yasuko ed., *Dai 12-ki joseigaku renzoku kōenkai: shakaiteki haijo to jendā* (Season 12 lecture series on women's studies: social exclusion and gender), Ōsaka furitsu daigaku josei kenkyū sentā (Osaka Prefecture University Women's Studies Center), 24–46.

————, 2011, "Fukushi shisetsu riyō ni miru josei no hinkon" (Women's poverty as seen in the use of welfare facilities), *Hinkon kenkyū* (The study of poverty) 6: 67–78.

Kawakita Yoshie, 1999, "Gyakutai sareru joseitachi" (Abused women), Nihon DV bōshi jōhō sentā ed., *Domesutikku baiorensu e no shiten: otto, koibito kara no bōryoku konzetsu no tame ni* (Looking at domestic violence: Eliminating violence from husbands and partners), Toki shobō, 39–59.

Kikuchi Masaharu, Shimizu Kyōe, Tanaka Kazuo, Nagaoka Masami, Murota Yasuo eds., 2003, *Nihon shakai fukushi no rekishi* (The history of social welfare in Japan), Mineruva shobō.

Kimoto, Kimiko and Kumiko Hagiwara, "Feminization of Poverty in Japan: A Special Case?", Gertrude Schaffner Goldberg eds., 2010, *Poor Women in Rich Countries: The Feminization of Poverty Over the Life Course*, New York: Oxford University Press, 202–230.

Kirisuto-kyō fujin kyōfūkai: *see* Christian Women's Reform Society.

Kitagawa Yukihiko, 2001, "Nojukusha no shūdan keisei to iji no katei: Shinjuku-eki shūhenbu o jirei to shite" (The process of group formation and sustenance among rough sleepers: The case of the Shinjuku station area), *Kaihō shakaigaku kenkyū* (The Liberation of Humankind: A Sociological Review) 15: 54–74.

————, 2005, "Tanshin dansei no hinkon to haijo: nojukusha to fukushi gyōsei no kankei ni chūmoku shite" (Poverty and exclusion of single men: Focusing on the relation between rough sleepers and welfare administration), Iwata Masami and Nishizawa Akihiko eds., *Hinkon to shakai haijo: fukushi shakai o mushibamu mono* (Poverty and social exclusion: What undermines welfare society), Mineruva shobō, 223–242.

Kokuritsu shakai hoshō jinkō mondai kenkyūjo. See National Institute of Population and Social Security Research.

Komiya Tomone, 2011, *Jissen no naka no jendā: hō shisutemu no shakaigakuteki kijutsu* (Gender in practice: Sociological accounts of the legal system), Shinyōsha.

Kōsei rōdōshō, *see* Ministry of Health, Labour and Welfare (MHLW).

Kuzunishi Risa and Shiozaki Yoshimitsu, 2004, "Boshi setai to ippan setai no kyojū jōkyō no sōi: jūtaku shoyū kankei, kyojū menseki, jūkyohi, yachin bunseki" (Differences in housing between single-mother and ordinary families: Analysis of home ownership, size [area] of home, housing expenses, and rent), *Nihon kenchiku gakkai keikakukei ronbunshū* (Architectural Institute of Japan, Journal of Architecture and Planning) 581: 119–126.

Kuzunishi Risa, Shiozaki Yoshimitsu, and Horita Yumiko, 2005, "Boshi setai no jūtaku kakuho no jittai to mondai ni kansuru kenkyū" (Research on conditions and problems for single-mother households in obtaining housing), *Nihon kenchiku gakkai keikakukei ronbunshū* (Architectural Institute of Japan, Journal of Architecture and Planning) 588: 147–152.

Liebow, Elliot, 1993, *Tell Them Who I am: The Lives of Homeless Women*, New York: The Free Press (Japanese translation 1999, Kikkawa Tōru, Todoroki Rika, *Hōmuresu ūman: shittemasu ka, watashitachi no koto*, Tōshindō).

MacKinnon, Catharine A., 1987, *Feminism Unmodified: Discourses on Life and Law*, Cambridge: Harvard University Press (Japanese translation 1993, Okuda Akiko, Katō Harueko, Suzuki Midori, Yamazaki Mikako, *Feminizumu to hyōgen no jiyū*, Akashi shoten).

MacNaughton, C., 2009, "Agency, Transgression and the Causation of Homelessness: A Contextualized Rational Action Analysis," *European Journal of Housing Policy*, 9(1), 69–84.

Maruyama Satomi, 2002, "Rojō ni arawareta jendā kakusa" (The gender gap as seen on the streets), *Kyōto shakaigaku nenpō* (Kyoto Journal of Sociology) 10: 239–246.

————, 2004, "Homeless Women in Japan," *Kyōto shakaigaku nenpō* (Kyoto Journal of Sociology) 12: 157–168.

————, 2005, "Kazukazu no dasshutsu o tsunagiawasete: josei hōmuresutachi to no deai kara" (Stringing together one escape after another: What I learned from the homeless women I met), *Gendai shisō* (Contemporary Thought) 33(12): 206–215.

————, 2006a, "Nojukusha no teikō to shutaisei: josei nojukusha no nichijōteki jissen kara" (Resistance and subjectivity in rough sleeping: A view from the daily practices of women rough sleepers), *Shakaigaku hyōron* (Japanese Sociological Review) 56(45): 898–914.

————, 2006b, "Jiyū de mo naku kyōsei de mo naku" (Neither free nor coerced), *Gendai shisō* (Contemporary Thought) 34(9): 211–221.

————, 2006c, "Sabita iro o shita toshi no fūkei: Yokohama merii ni yosete" (View of a rust-colored city: For Yokohama Mary), *Jōkyō* (Situation) 7(5): 213–215.

————, 2006d, "Jiritsu no kage de: hōmuresu no jiritsu shien o megutte" (In the shadow of autonomy: on support for autonomy of homeless persons), *Gendai shisō* (Contemporary Thought) 34(14): 196–203.

————, 2008, "Hinkon seisaku ni okeru josei no ichi: senzen sengo no Ōsaka no jirei kenkyū" (The position of women in poverty policy: A case study of Osaka in the prewar and postwar periods), *Jutsu* (Statement) 2: 152–171, Akashi shoten.

————, 2009, "Sutoriito de ikiru joseitachi: josei nojukusha no jissen" (Women living on the streets: Life practices of women rough sleepers), Sekine Yasumasa ed., *Sutoriito no jinruigaku: Kokuritsu minzokugaku hakubutsukan chōsa hōkoku* (The anthropology of the street: Report on a survey by the National Museum of Ethnology) 80: 185–201.

————, 2010, "Jendā-ka sareta haijo no katei: josei hōmuresu to iu mondai" (The gendered process of exclusion: The problem of homeless women), Aoki Hideo ed., *Hōmuresu sutadīzu: haijo to hōsetsu no riariti* (Homeless studies: The reality of exclusion and inclusion), Mineruva shobō, 202–232.

————, 2013, "Hinkon no hirogari to fujin hogo shisetsu no yakuwari" (The spread of poverty and the role of Women's Protection Facilities), Miyamoto Setsuko and Sudō Yachiyo ed., *Fujin hogo shisetsu to baishun, hinkon, DV mondai: josei shien no hensen to arata na tenkai* (Women's Protection Facilities and the problems of prostitution, poverty, and domestic violence: The evolution of and new developments in women's support), Akashi shoten, 253–286.

————, 2013, *Josei hōmuresu to shite ikiru: hinkon to haijo no shakaigaku* (Living as a homeless woman: the sociology of poverty and exclusion). Sekai shisōsha, 2013.

Matsuda Motoji, 1996, "Shohyō ni kotaete" (Reply to book review), *Soshioroji* (Sociology) 41(2): 115–117.

————, 1999, *Teikō suru toshi* (The resisting city), Iwanami shoten.

Matsuzawa Kureichi and Sutajio potto, 2000, *Baishun kōtei sengen: uru uranai wa watashi ga kimeru* (Affirmation of prostitution: I decide whether or not to sell), Potto shuppan.

May, Jon, Paul Cloke, and Sarah Johnsen, 2007, "Alternative Cartographies of Homelessness: Rendering Visible British Women's Experiences of 'Visible' Homelessness", *Gender, Place and Culture* 14(2): 121–140.

Mayock, M. & Bretherton, J. eds., 2016, *Women's Homelessness in Europe*, Palgrave Macmillan: London.

Ministry of Health, Labour and Welfare (MHLW/Kōsei rōdōshō), 2002, *Danjokan no chingin kakusa ni kansuru kenkyūkai hōkoku* (Report on gender disparities in wages).

————, 2003, *Hōmuresu no jittai ni kansuru zenkoku chōsa hōkokusho* (Report on the *National Survey on the Conditions of the Homeless*).

————, 2007a, *Hōmuresu no jittai ni kansuru zenkoku chōsa hōkokusho* (Report on the *National Survey on the Conditions of the Homeless*).

————, 2007b, *"Heisei 19-nen Hōmuresu no jittai ni kansuru zenkoku chōsa (seikatsu jittai chōsa) no bunseki kekka* (Analysis of 2007 *National Survey on the Conditions of the Homeless* [survey of living conditions]).

————, 2009, *Heisei 20-nen kokumin seikatsu kiso chōsa* (Comprehensive survey of living conditions, 2008)

————, 2011a, *Jūkyo no nai seikatsu hogo jukyūsha ga nyūkyo suru muryō teigaku shukuhaku shisetsu oyobi kore ni junjita hōteki ichizuke no nai shisetsu ni kansuru chōsa kekka ni tsuite* (Results of survey on free or low-rent housing and equivalent facilities lacking legal status used by public assistance recipients lacking a home), Shakai engokyoku hogoka (Social Welfare and War Victims' Relief Bureau).

————, 2011b, *Heisei 22-nenban Hataraku josei no jitsujō* (2010 edition: conditions of working women).

————, 2011c, *Rōdōryoku chōsa* (Survey of the labor force).

————, 2011d, *Heisei 22 nen Shakai fukushi shisetsu tō chōsa kekka no gaikyō* (Summary of results of 2010 survey of social welfare facilities), Daijin kanbō tōkei jōhōbu shakai tōkeika (Minister's Secretariat Statistics and Information Department, Social Statistics Division).

————, 2012, *Hōmuresu no jittai ni kansuru zenkoku chōsa (gaisū chōsa) kekka ni tsuite* (Results of *National Survey on the Conditions of the Homeless* [estimated figures])

————, 2017a, *Hōmuresu no jittai ni kansuru zenkoku chōsa (gaisū chōsa) kekka* (Results of *National Survey on the Conditions of the Homeless* [estimated figures])

————, 2017b, *Hōmuresu no jittai ni kansuru zenkoku chōsa (seikatsu jittai chōsa) no kekka* (Results of *National Survey on the Conditions of the Homeless* [survey of living conditions])

Ministry of Health, Labour and Welfare Employment Stability Bureau (Kōsei rōdōshō shokugyō anteikyoku), 2007, *Jūkyo sōshitsu fuantei shūrōsha tō no jittai ni kansuru chōsa hōkokusho* (Report on survey of conditions of workers lacking a stable home).

Minami Tomoko, Satō Satoshi, Hasurā Akira, Hatano Tomato, Matsuzawa Kureichi, Miyadai Shinji, 2000, "Zadan sei fūzoku to baibaishun" (Discussion of sex entertainment work and prostitution), Matsuzawa Kureichi, Sutajio Potto eds., *Baishun kōtei sengen: uru uranai wa watashi ga kimeru* (Affirmation of prostitution: I decide whether or not to sell), Potto shuppan.

Miyashita Tadako, 2008, *Akai kōto no onna: Tōkyō josei hōmuresu monogatari* (Woman in the red coat: tale of a homeless woman in Tokyo), Akashi shoten.

Mizuuchi Toshio, 2010, "Kyojū hoshō to hōmuresu shien kara mita seikatsu hogo shisetsu" (Public benefits facilities from the perspective of guaranteed housing and homeless support), *Toshi mondai* (Municipal problems) 101(7): 51–63.

Moon Jeong Sil, 2003, "Nojuku to jendā" (Rough sleeping and gender), *Shelter-less* 19: 120–155.

————, 2006, "Josei nojukusha to sutoriito aidentiti: kanojo no "muryokusa" wa teikō de aru" (Women rough sleepers and street identity: Their "powerlessness" is resistance), Kariya Ayumi ed., *Furachi na kibō* (Outrageous hope), Shōraisha, 198–233.

Moss, K., & Singh, O., 2015, *Women Rough Sleepers in Europe: Homelessness and Victims of Domestic Abuse*, Policy Press: Bristol.

Mugikura Tetsu and Furusato no kai, 2006, *Hōmuresu jiritsu shien shisutemu no kenkyū* (Research on support systems for homeless self-reliance), Daiichi shorin.

Nakajima Akiko, Bandō Michiko, Ōsaki Hajime, Sylvia Novac, and Maruyama Satomi, 2005, "Tōkyō ni okeru 'hōmuresu' josei no jiritsu shien to kyojū shien" (Self-reliance and housing support for "homeless" women in Tokyo), *Jūtaku sōgō kenkyū zaidan kenkyū ronbunshū* (Journal of Housing Research Foundation) 31: 229–241.

Nakane Mitsutoshi, 1999, "Haijo to teikō no gendai shakairon: yoseba to "hōmuresu" no shakaigaku ni mukete" (Contemporary sociological theory of exclusion and resistance: Toward a sociology of yoseba and "homelessness"), Aoki Hideo ed., *Basho o akero! Yoseba/hōmuresu no shakaigaku* (Make a place! Sociology of *yoseba* and homelessness), Shōraisha, 75–98.

————, 2001, "Yoseba/nojukusha o kijutsu suru to iu koto" (Describing *yoseba* and rough sleepers), *Kaihō shakaigaku kenkyū* (The Liberation of Humankind: A Sociological Review) 15: 3–25.

Nakanishi Yūko, 2004, "Feminisuto posuto kōzō shugi to wa nanika: keikenteki kenkyū shuhō no kakuritsu ni mukete no ichikōsatsu" (What is feminist post-structuralism? Thoughts on establishing experiential research methods), *Soshiorojisuto: Musashi shakaigaku ronshū* (Sociologist: Musashi sociological studies) 6(1): 185–203.

National Homeless Support Network, *see* Hōmuresu shien zenkoku nettowāku.

National Institute of Population and Social Security Research (Kokuritsu shakai hoshō jinkō mondai kenkyūjo), 2009, *"Seikatsu hogo" ni kansuru kōteki tōkei dētā ichiran* (Overview of public statistical data on public assistance).

National Survey on the Conditions of the Homeless, *see* Ministry of Health, Labour and Welfare (MHLW) and *Hōmuresu no jittai ni kansuru zenkoku chōsa*.

Nihon jūtaku kaigi (Japan Housing Council), 2004, *Hōmuresu to sumai no kenri: jūtaku hakusho 2004–2005* (Homelessness and the right to a home: White paper on housing 2004–2005), Domesu shuppan.

Niji no rengō (Rainbow Coalition), 2007, *Mō hitotsu no zenkoku hōmuresu chōsa: hōmuresu "jiritsu shienhō" chūkannen minaoshi o kikkake ni* (One more national survey of homelessness: On occasion of the interim report).

Nishimura Miharu, 1984, "Fujin hogo jigyō ni okeru "yōhogo joshi" no kitei o megutte" (On the definition of "at-risk women" in Women's Protection Services), *Shakai fukushi* (Social Welfare) 25: 33–44.

⸻, 1994, *Shakai fukushi jissen shisōshi kenkyū* (Research on intellectual history of social welfare practice), Domesu shuppan.

Nishitai Yōko, 1998, "'Jendā to gakkō kyōiku' kenkyū no shikaku tenkan: posuto kōzō shugi teki tenkai e" (Shifting approaches of research on gender and school education: Developing a post-structural approach), *Kyōiku shakaigaku kenkyū* (Journal of Educational Sociology) 62: 5–22.

Nishizawa Akihiko, 1995, *Inpei sareta gaibu: toshi kasō no esunogurafii* (The hidden outside: ethnography of the urban underclass), Sairyūsha.

Noyori Tomoko, 2011, "Hōmuresu mondai no saikōchiku: 'dansei kaseginushi' moderu no shiten kara" (Reconstructing the problem of homelessness: from the perspective of the "male breadwinner" model), *Yuibutsuron kenkyū nenshi* (Studies in Materialism) 16, 102–128.

Okano Yayo, 2000, "Shutai naki feminizumu wa kanō ka" (Is a subject-free feminism possible?), *Gendai shisō* (Contemporary Thought) 28(14): 172–186.

⸻, 2002, *Hō no seijigaku: hō to seigi to feminizumu* (Legal political science: Law, justice, and feminism), Seidosha.

⸻, 2003, *Shitizunshippu no seijigaku: kokumin, kokka shugi hihan* (Political science of citizenship: Critique of nationalism), Hakutakusha.

⸻, 2012, *Feminizumu no seijigaku: kea no rinri o gurōbaru shakai e* (Political science of feminism: Bringing the ethics of care to global society), Misuzu shobō.

Osaka Association for Research on Social Work History, *see* Ōsaka shakai jigyōshi kenkyūkai.

Osaka City Graduate School for Creative Cities *see* Ōsaka shiritsu daigaku sōzō toshi kenkyūka.

Osaka City University Institute on Urban Environmental Problems *see* Ōsaka shiritsu daigaku toshi kankyō kenkyūkai.

Osaka Women's Home, *see* Ōsaka fujin hōmu.

Osaka City, *see* Ōsaka-shi.

Osaka City Office, *see* Ōsaka shiyakusho.

Osaka Prefecture Women's Consultation Center, *see* Ōsaka-fu josei sōdan sentā.

Osaka Prefecture, Social Affairs Section, *see* Ōsaka-fu shakaika.

Ōsaka fujin hōmu (Osaka Women's Home), 1934, *Kirisutokyō kyōfūkai Ōsaka shibu nenpō Shōwa 9-nendo* (Reform society Osaka branch 1934 report).

Ōsaka-fu josei sōdan sentā, 1984–2009, *Jigyō gaiyō*. (Summary of activities; various titles).

Ōsaka-fu shakaika, 1920, *Ōsaka shakai jigyō gairan* (Outline of social work in Osaka).

Ōsaka-shi (Osaka city), 1953, *Shōwa Ōsaka-shi shi, dai-6-kan, shakaihen* (History of Osaka city, Shōwa period, vol. 6).

————, 1966, *Shōwa Ōsaka-shi shi, zokuhen, dai-6-kan, shakaihen* (Sequel History of Osaka city, Shōwa period, vol. 6).

Ōsaka shiritsu daigaku sōzō toshi kenkyūka (Osaka City Graduate School for Creative Cities), Kamagasaki shien kikō, 2008, "*Jakunen fuantei shūrō fuantei jūkyosha kikitori chōsa*" *hōkokusho: "jakunen hōmuresu seikatsusha*" *e no shien no mosaku* (Report on "Interview survey of young people with unstable employment and housing": Exploring ways to support homeless young people).

Ōsaka shiritsu daigaku toshi kankyō mondai kenkyūkai (Osaka City University Institute on Urban Environmental Problems), 2001, *Nojukusha (hōmuresu) ni kansuru sōgōteki chōsa kenkyū hōkokusho* (Report on the general survey of rough sleepers [homeless people]).

Ōsaka shiyakusho shakaibu (Osaka City Office Social Affairs Department), 1923, *Ōsaka shakai jigyō gaiyō* (Summary of social work in Osaka).

Ōsaka shakai jigyōshi kenkyūkai (Osaka Association for Research on Social Work History), 1985, *Yumi wa orezu: Nakamura Mitsunori to Ōsaka no shakai jigyō* (The bow is not broken: Nakamura Mitsunori and social work in Osaka).

"Otto (koibito) kara no bōryoku" chōsa kenkyūkai (Society for survey of abuse by husbands [partners]), 2002, *Domesutikku baiorensu shinpan: jittai, DV hō kaisetsu, bijon* (Domestic violence, new edition: Conditions, explanation of Domestic Violence Act, vision), Yūhikaku.

Parsell, C., & Parsell, M., 2012, "Homelessness as a Choice," *Theory and Society*, 29:4, 420–434.

Passaro, Joanne, 1996, *The Unequal Homeless: Men on the Streets, Women in Their Place*, New York: Routledge.

Plummer, Ken, 1995, *Telling Sexual Stories: Power, Change and Social Worlds*, London and New York: Routledge. (Japanese translation 1998, Sakurai Atsushi, Yoshii Hiroaki, Kobayashi Tazuko, *Sekushuaru stōrii no jidai: katari no poritikusu*), Shinyōsha.

Rainbow Coalition, *see* Niji no rengō.

Ralston, Meredith L., 1996, *Nobody Wants to Hear Our Truth: Homeless Women and Theories of the Welfare State*. Westport: Greenwood Press.

Rossi, Peter H., 1989, *Down and Out in America: The Origins of Homelessness*, Chicago: The University of Chicago Press.

Rowe, Stacy and Jennifer Wolch, 1990, "Social Networks in Time and Space: Homeless Women in Skid Row, Los Angeles," *Annals of the Association of American Geographers* 80(3): 184–204.

Russell, Betty G., 1991, *Silent Sisters: A Study of Homeless Women*, New York: Hemisphere Publishing.

Sakiyama Masaki, 2001, *Sabarutan to rekishi* (The subaltern and history), Seidosha.

Sakurai Atsushi, 2002, *Intabyū no shakaigaku: raifusutōrii no kikikata* (Interviews in sociology: How to ask about life stories), Serika shobō.

Sasanuma Hiroshi, 2008, *Hōmuresu to jiritsu/haijo: rojō ni "kōfuku o yumemiru kenri" wa aru ka* (Homelessness and autonomy/exclusion: Is there a "right to dream of happiness" on the streets?), Ōtsuki shoten.

Scott, Joan Wallach, 1999, *Gender and the Politics of History: Revised Edition*, New York: Columbia University Press (Japanese translation 2004, Ogino Miho, *Jendā to rekishigaku zōho shinpan*, Heibonsha).

Seikatsu hogo mondai taisaku zenkoku kaigi (National conference on measures for solving public assistance problems), supervisor; Bitō Hiroki, Kokubo Tetsurō, Yoshinaga Atsushi, 2011, *Seikatsu hogo "kaikaku" koko ga shōten da!* (Public assistance reform: Here is where to focus!), Akebi shobō.

Seikatsu hogo no dōkō henshū iinkai (Editorial committee on public assistance trends, ed., 2008, *Heisei 20-nendo ban seikatsu hogo no dōkō* (2008 edition public assistance trends), Chūōhōki.

Shakai fukushi hōjin shin'eikai (Social Welfare Corporation Shin'eikai), 2011, *Jigyō hōkokusho* (2010 Report on activities).

Shakai hokenchō (Social Insurance Agency), ed., 2007, *Seifu kanshō kenkō hoken, sen'in hoken, kōsei nenkin hoken, kokumin nenkin, kumiai kanshō kenkō hoken, kokumin kenkō hoken, rōjin hoken: jigyō nenpō sōkatsu hen (Heisei 18-nendo ban)* (Government-run health insurance, mariners' insurance, employees' pension insurance, national pension plan, union-run health insurance, national health insurance, healthcare for the elderly: summary of yearly reports [2006 edition]).

Social Insurance Agency, *see* Shakai hokenchō.

Social Welfare Corporation Shin'eikai, *see* Shakai fukushi hōjin shin'eikai.

Society for survey of abuse by husbands [partners]), *see* "Otto (koibito) kara no bōryoku" chōsa kenkyūkai.

Sōmushō tōkeikyoku (Ministry of Internal Affairs and Communications, Statistics Bureau), 2012, *Sekai no tōkei* (World statistics).

Special Ward Association for Personnel and Welfare, *see* Tokubetsuku jinji kōsei jimu kumiai.

Spivak, G. C., 1988, "Can the Subaltern Speak?" Cary Nelson and Lawrence Grossberg eds., *Marxism and the Interpretation of Culture*, Urbana: University of Illinois Press (Japanese translation 1998, Uemura Tadao, *Sabarutan wa kataru koto ga dekiru ka*, Misuzu shobō).

Sudō Yachiyo, 2000, "Shakai fukushi to joseikan" (Social welfare and view of women), Sugimoto Kiyoe ed., *Jendā eshikkusu to shakai fukushi* (Gender ethics and social welfare), Mineruva shobō, 94–112.

————, 2010, "'Josei fukushi' ron to feminizumu riron: shakai fukushi no taishōron o tegakari ni" ("Women's welfare" theory and feminist theory: An approach through social welfare object theory), *Shakai fukushi kenkyū* (Social Welfare Studies) 12: 25–32.

Sugimoto Kiyoe, 1993, *Shakai fukushi to feminizumu* (Social welfare and feminism), Keisō shobō.

————, 1997, *Joseika suru fukushi shakai* (The feminization of the welfare society), Keisō shobō.

————, 2004, *Fukushi shakai no jendā kōzō* (The gender structure of welfare society), Keisō shobō.

Takahara Sachiko, 2006, *Baikaisha no shisō* (The ideas of the agent), Fukurō shuppan.

Tamai Kingo, 1986, "Nihon shihon shugi to 'toshi' shakai seisaku: Ōsaka-shi shakai jigyō o chūshin ni" (Japanese capitalism and "urban" social policy: A focus on Osaka city social work), Sugihara Kaoru and Tamai Kingo eds., *Taishō/ Ōsaka/suramu: mō hitotsu no Nihon kindaishi* (Taisho/Osaka/slums: Another modern history of Japan), Shinhyōron, 249–295.

Terao Tōru and Okuda Tomoshi, "Taidan: Hinkon bijinesu ron o koete: posuto-hōmuresu shienhō taisei o tenbō suru" (Conversation: going beyond the discourse of "poverty business": Prospects for the social system after the Homeless Self-Reliance Act), *Hōmuresu to shakai* (Homelessness and Society) 2: 8–15.

Tokubetsuku jinji kōsei jimu kumiai (Special Ward Association for Personnel and Welfare), 2010, *Kōsei shisetsu, shukusho teikyō shisetsu, shukuhakusho, rojō seikatsusha taisaku jigyō shisetsu jigyōgaiyō* (Business summary of facility operations for programs to aid rough sleepers: Rehabilitation Facilities and Accommodation Facilities)

Tōkō Gakuen, 1974, *Tōkō gakuen no ayumi: sōritsu rokujisshūnen kinen* (History of Tōkō Gakuen: commemorating the 60th anniversary of the founding).

Tokubetsuku kōsei buchōkai (Special Ward Department of Health and Welfare, meeting of departmental directors), 2009, *Kōsei kankei shisetsu saihen seibi keikaku, kaitōban* (Plan for reorganization of public welfare facilities, revised edition).

Tokyo Metropolitan Government Bureau of Social Welfare, *see* Tōkyō-to fukushikyoku.

Tokyo Metropolitan Government Bureau of Social Welfare and Public Health, *see* Tōkyō-to fukushi hokenkyoku.

Tokyo Metropolitan Government Council for Social Welfare, *see* Tōkyō-to shakai fukushi kyōgikai.

Tōkyō-to fukushikyoku (Tokyo Metropolitan Government Bureau of Social Welfare), 2003, *Shukuhakusho jittai chōsa* (Survey of the state of housing facilities).

Tōkyō-to fukushi hokenkyoku sōmubu (Tokyo Metropolitan Government Bureau of Social Welfare and Public Health, General Affairs Department), ed., 2011, *2011 shakai fukushi no tebiki* (2011 Intro-duction to social welfare).

Tōkyō-to shakai fukushi kyōgikai boshi fukushi bukai (Tokyo Metropolitan Government Council of Social Welfare, Mother-Child Welfare Section), 2011, *Tōkyō-to no boshi seikatsu shien shisetsu no genjō to kadai: Heisei 22-nendo Tōkyō-to no boshi seikatsu shien shisetsu jittai chōsa hōkokusho* (Conditions and challenges of Mother-Child Living Support Facilities in Tokyo prefecture: 2010 report on survey of conditions of Mother-Child Living Support Facilities in Tokyo prefecture), Tōkyō-to shakai fukushi kyōgikai.

Tōkyō-to shakai fukushi kyōgikai fujin hogo bukai chōsa kenkyū iinkai (Tokyo Metropolitan Government Council for Social Welfare, Women's Protection Panel, Survey Assessment Committee), 2010, *Fujin hogo shisetsu jittai chōsa hōkokusho 2008 nendo 2009 nendo* (2008–2009 fact-finding survey on Women's Protection Facilities).

Toshi seikatsu kenkyūkai (Urban Life Institute), 2000, *Heisei 11-nendo rojō seikatsusha jittai chōsa* (Survey on the conditions of the homeless).

Tsumaki Shingo, 2003, "Nojuku seikatsu: 'shakai seikatsu no kyohi' to iu sentaku" (Rough sleeping: The choice to "reject living in society"), *Soshioroji* (Sociology) 48(1): 21–37.

Ueno Chizuko, 1995, "Sai no seijigaku" (The political science of difference), Inoue Shun et al. ed., *Iwanami Kōza gendai shakaigaku 11: jendā no seijigaku* (Iwanami course, contemporary sociology 11: the political science of gender), Iwanami shoten.

Umino Emiko, 1997, "Nihon de no 'hinkon no joseika' ni tsuite no ichikōsatsu: kōrei josei no hinkon no tōkeiteki kentō" (Thoughts on the 'feminization of poverty' in Japan: A statistical assessment of poverty in older women), *Shakai fukushigaku*, Nihon shakai fukushi gakkai (Japanese Journal of Social Welfare, Japanese Society for the Study of Social Welfare), 39(2): 155–171.

Urban Life Institute, *see* Toshi seikatsu kenkyūkai.

Waterston, Alisse, 1999, *Love, Sorrow and Rage: Destitute Women in a Manhattan Residence*, Philadelphia: Temple University Press.

Urban Institute et al. eds., 1999, *Homelessness: Programs and the People They Serve: Findings of the National Survey of Homeless Assistance Providers and Clients*, U.S. Dept. of Housing and Urban Development, Office of Policy Development and Research.

Watson, Sophie, 1999, "A Home is Where the Heart is: Engendering Notions of Homelessness," P. Kennett and A. Marsh eds, *Homeless: Exploring New Terrain*, Bristol: The Policy Press, 81–101.

Watson, Sophie and Helen Austerberry, 1986, *Housing and Homelessness: A Feminist Perspective*, London: Routledge & Kegan Paul.

Williams, Jean Calterone, 2003, *A Roof Over My Head: Homeless Women and the Shelter Industry*, Boulder, Colorado: University Press of Colorado.

Yamaguchi Keiko, 1998, "Shinjuku ni okeru nojukusha no ikinuki senryaku: nojukushakan no shakai kankei o chūshin ni" (Survival strategies for rough sleepers in Shinjuku: Focusing on social relations among rough sleepers), *Nihon toshi shakai gakkai nenpō* (Annals of the Japan Association for Urban Sociology) 16:119–134.

Yamane Sumika, 2007, "Dansei hōmuherupā no seizon senryaku: shakaika sareta kea ni okeru jendā" (Surival strategies of male home helpers: Gender in socialized care), *Soshioroji* (Sociology) 51(3): 91–106.

Yuzawa Naomi, 2000, "Boshi seikatsu shien shisetsu ni okeru josei shien no shiten" (View of women's support in mother-child living support facilities), *Rikkyō daigaku komyuniti fukushi gakubu kiyō* (Bulletin of the College of Community and Human Services, Rikkyō University) 2: 117–129.

Zenkoku kōsei jigyōdan renraku kyōgikai and Zenkoku kyūgo shisetsu kyōgikai (Japan Corporation of Welfare Services Coordinating Committee and Japan National Council of Rehabilitation Facilities, 2003, *Hogo shisetsu ni okeru hōmuresu ukeire ni kansuru kentōkai hōkokusho* (Report on reception of homeless persons in protective facilities).

Name Index

Subject Index

www.ingramcontent.com/pod-product-compliance
Lightning Source LLC
Chambersburg PA
CBHW071847270326
41929CB00013B/2136